CW01657450

The Master As I Saw Him

THE MASTER AS I SAW HIM

BEING PAGES FROM THE LIFE
OF THE SWAMI VIVEKANANDA

BY
HIS DISCIPLE NIVEDITA
OF RAMAKRISHNA-VIVEKANANDA

উদ্বোধন
RAMAKRISHNA MATH
BAGHBAZAR

The Master As I Saw Him
Sister Nivedita

First Edition
February 1910

Twelfth Edition
April 2024

Published by
Swami Nityamuktananda
Ramakrishna Math, Baghbazar
Udbodhan, 1 Udbodhan Lane
Baghbazar, Kolkata-700003

Printed by
D&P Graphics Pvt. Ltd.
143, Old Jessore Road
Kolkata-700132

© The President
Ramakrishna Math, Belur Math

ISBN: 978-81-804045-8-0

SALUTATION TO MOTHER!

In sending out into the world this book—the tribute of her love and gratitude to her Guru—Nivedita has the blessings and good wishes of all his brothers.

Belur Math
Feb. 1, 1910

Saradananda

PREFACE TO THE TWELFTH EDITION

The Master As I Saw Him has undergone a comprehensive revision in this latest edition. Since these books were published over a century, from 1910 to 2023, efforts were made to standardize the editing styles across the editions. This was done to give the book a uniform presentation. When it comes to editing, we usually refer back to the first edition and make corrections accordingly. In this edition, especially, we pursue this as far as possible. Modifications have been made only to those spelling and punctuation, that have evolved, changed, and accepted as correct in present times.

To keep up with the latest developments in printing technology, this edition has been entirely typeset using computers. Let us hope that the present edition will also be warmly embraced by readers.

April 2024 Publisher

PREFACE TO THE ELEVENTH EDITION

While the tenth edition was being exhausted we were getting ready to bring out the next edition after comparing the press copy with the first and second editions. Some minor variations of reading and punctuation were noted and we have corrected them accordingly. Let us hope the present edition will be welcome by the readers of this classical study of the life and mission of a great spiritual personality of our age.

September 1972 Publisher

Contents

CONTENTS

A Word to Western Readers

From the close of the era of the Buddhist Missions, until the day when, as a yellow-clad *Sannyāsin*, the Swami Vivekananda stood on the platform of the Parliament of Religions in the Chicago Exhibition of 1893, Hinduism had not thought of herself as a missionary faith. Her professional teachers, the Brahmins, being citizens and householders, formed a part of Hindu society itself and as such were held to be debarred from crossing the seas. And her wandering *Sādhus*—who are, in the highest cases, as much above the born Brahmin in authority, as saint or incarnation may be above priest or scholar—had simply not thought of putting their freedom to such use. Nor did the Swami Vivekananda appear at the doors of Chicago with any credentials. He had been sent across the Pacific Ocean, as he might have wandered from one Indian village to another, by the eagerness and faith of a few disciples in Madras. And with American hospitality and frankness he was welcomed and accorded an opportunity of speaking. In his case, as in that of the Buddhist missionaries, the impelling force that drove him out to foreign lands was the great personality of One at whose feet he had sat and whose life he had shared for many years. Yet, in the West he spoke of no personal teacher, he gave the message of no limited sect. 'The religious ideas of the Hindus' were his theme at Chicago, and similarly, thereafter, it was those elements which were common to and characteristic of orthodox Hinduism in all its parts, that formed the burden of his teaching. Thus for the first time in history, Hinduism itself formed the subject of the generalisation of a Hindu mind of the highest order.

The Swami remained in America until August of the year 1895, when he came to Europe for the first time. In September he found his way to England, and a month or so later he began teaching in London.

I

The Swami in London—1895

It is strange to remember and yet it was surely my good fortune that though I heard the teachings of my Master, the Swami Vivekananda, on both the occasions of his visits to England in 1895 and 1896, I yet knew little or nothing of him in private life, until I came to India in the early days of 1898. For as the fruit of this want of experience I have it, that at each step of his self-revelation as a personality, my Master stands out in my memory against his proper background of Indian forest, city and highway—an Eastern teacher in an Eastern world. Even in far-away London indeed, the first time I saw him, the occasion must have stirred in his mind, as it does in mine, recalling it now, a host of associations connected with his own sun-steeped land. The time was a cold Sunday afternoon in November and the place, it is true, was a West-end drawing room. But he was seated, facing a half-circle of listeners, with the fire on the hearth behind him, and as he answered question after question, breaking now and then into the chanting of some Sanskrit text in illustration of his reply, the scene must have appeared to him, while twilight passed into darkness, only as a curious variant upon the Indian garden, or on the group of hearers gathered at sundown round the *Sādhu* who sits beside the well, or under the tree outside the village-bounds. Never again in England did I see the Swami, as a teacher, in such a simple fashion. Later, he was always lecturing, or the questions he answered were put with formality by members of larger audiences. Only this first time we were put fifteen or sixteen guests, intimate friends, many of us, and he sat amongst us in his crimson robe and girdle, as one bringing us news from a far land with a curious habit of saying now and again "*Śiva! Śiva!*" and wearing that look of mingled gentleness and loftiness that one sees on the faces of those who live much in meditation, that look, perhaps, that Raphael has painted for us, on the brow of Sistine Child.

That afternoon is now ten years ago and fragments only of the talk come back to me. But never to be forgotten are the Sanskrit verses that he chanted for us in those wonderful Eastern tones, at once so reminiscent of and yet so different from the Gregorian music of our own churches.

He was quite willing to answer a personal question and readily explained in reply to some enquiry that he was in the West, because he believed that the time had come when nations were to exchange their ideals, as they were already exchanging the commodities of the market. From this point onwards, the talk was easy. He was elucidating the idea of the Eastern Pantheism, picturing the various sense-impressions as but so many different modes of the manifestation of One, and he quoted from the Gita and then translated into English : "All these are threaded upon Me, as pearls upon a string."

He told us that love was recognized in Hinduism, as in Christianity, as the highest religious emotion.

And he told us—a thing that struck me very much, leading me during the following winter to quite new lines of observation—that both the mind and the body were regarded by Hindus as moved and dominated by a third, called the Self.

He was describing the difference between Buddhism and Hinduism, and I remember the quiet words, "the Buddhists accepted the report of the senses."

In this respect then, Buddhism must have been in strong contrast with modern agnosticism, whose fundamental suspicion as to the subjective illusion of the senses and therefore of all inference, would surely bring it more into line with Hinduism.

I remember that he objected to the word 'faith,' insisting on 'realisation' instead; and speaking of sects. He quoted an Indian proverb: "It is well to be born in a church, but it is terrible to die there."

I think that the doctrine of Reincarnation was probably touched upon in this talk. I imagine that he spoke of *Karma*, *Bhakti*, and *Jnāna*, as the three paths of the soul. I know he dwelt for a while on the infinite power of man. And he declared the one message of all religions to lie in the call to Renunciation.

There was a word to the effect that priests and temples were not associated in India with the highest kind of religion; and the statement that the desire to reach Heaven was in that country regarded, *by the most religious people*, 'as a little vulgar'.

He must have made some statement of the ideal of the freedom of the soul, which brought it into apparent conflict with our Western conception of the service of humanity, as the goal of the individual. For I remember very clearly that I heard him use the word 'society' for the first time that afternoon, in the sense that I have never been quite sure of having fully understood. He had, as I suppose, stated the ideal and he hastened to anticipate our opposition. "You will say," he said, "that this does not benefit society. But before this objection can be admitted you will first have to prove that the maintenance of society is an object in itself."

At the time, I understood him to mean 'humanity' by 'society' and to be preaching the ultimate futility of the world and therefore of the work done to aid it. Was this his meaning? In that case, how is one to reconcile it with the fact that the service of humanity was always his whole hope? Or was he merely stating an idea and standing aside to give it its full value? Or was his word 'society' again only a faulty translation of the curious Eastern word *Samaj*, coloured as that is, with theocratic associations and meaning something which includes amongst other things, our idea of the church?

He touched on the question of his own position as a wandering teacher and expressed the Indian diffidence with regard to religious organisation, or, as someone expresses it, "with regard to a faith that ends in a church." "We believe," he said, "that organisation always breeds new evils."

He prophesied that certain religious developments, then much in vogue in the West, would speedily die owing to the love of money.

And he declared that "Man proceeds from truth to truth and not from error to truth."

This was indeed, the master thought which he continually approached from different points of view, the equal truth of all religions and the impossibility for us of criticising any of the Divine Incarnations, since all were equally forth-shinings of the One. And here he quoted that greatest of all verses of the Gita : "Whenever religion decays and irreligion prevails, *then I manifest Myself.* For the protection of the good, for the destruction of the evil, for the firm establishment of the truth, I AM BORN AGAIN AND AGAIN."

We were not very orthodox or open to belief, who had come to meet the Hindu Yogi, as he was called in London at that time. The white-haired lady, with the historic name, who sat on the Swami's left and took the lead in questioning him with such exquisiteness of courtesy, was perhaps the least unconventional of the group in matters of belief, and she had been a friend and disciple of Frederick Denison Maurice. Our hostess and one or two others were interested in those modern movements which have made extended psychology the centre of a faith. But most of us had, I incline to think, been singled out for the afternoon's hospitality on the very score of our unwillingness to believe, for the difficulty of convincing us of the credibility of religious propaganda in general.

Only this habit, born of the constant need of protecting the judgment against ill-considered enthusiasm, can, as I now think, furnish any excuse for the coldness and pride with which we all gave our private verdicts on the speaker at the end of our visit. "It was not new," was our accusation, as one by one we spoke with our host and hostess before leaving. All these things had been said before.

For my own part, however, as I went about the tasks of that week, it dawned on me slowly that it was not only ungenerous, it was also unjust to dismiss in such fashion the message of a new mind and a strange culture. It occurred to me that though each separate *dictum* might find its echo or its fellow amongst things already heard or already thought, yet it had never before fallen to my lot to meet with a thinker who in one short hour had been able to express all that I had hitherto regarded as highest and best. I therefore took the only two opportunities that remained to me, of hearing the Swami lecture, while he was still in London.

The feeling that great music wakes in us, grows and deepens with its repetition. And similarly, as I read over the notes of those two lectures now, they seem to me much more wonderful than they did then. For there was a quality of blindness in the attitude I presented to my Master, that I can never sufficiently regret. When he said, "The universe is like a cobweb and minds are the spiders; for the mind is one as well as many" : he was simply talking beyond my comprehension. I noted what he said, and was interested in it, but could pass no judgment upon it, much less accept it. And that statement describes more or less accurately the whole of my relation to his system of teaching, even in the following year, when I had listened to a season's lectures—even perhaps on the day when I landed in India.

There were many points in the Swami's teachings of which one could see the truth at once. The doctrine that while no religion was true in the way commonly claimed, yet all were equally true in a very real way, was one that commanded the immediate assent of some of us. When he said that God, really Impersonal, seen through the mists of sense became Personal, one was awed and touched by the beauty of the thought. When he said that the spirit behind an act was more powerful than the act itself, or when he commended vegetarianism, it was possible to experiment. But his system as a whole, I, for one, viewed with suspicion, as forming only another of those theologies which if a man should begin by accepting, he would surely end by transcending and rejecting. And one shrinks from the pain and humiliation of spirit that such experiences involve.

It is difficult at this point to be sufficiently explicit. The time came, before the Swami left England, when I addressed him as 'Master'. I had recognized the heroic fibre of the man and desired to make myself the servant of his love for his own people. But it was his *character* to which I had thus done obeisance. As a religious teacher I saw that although he had a system of thought to offer, nothing in that system would claim him for a moment, if he found that truth led elsewhere. And to the extent that this recognition implies, I became his disciple. For the rest, I studied his teaching sufficiently to become convinced of its coherence, but never, till I had had experiences that authenticated them, did I inwardly cast in my lot with the final justification of the things he came to say. Nor did I at that time, though deeply attracted by his personality, dream of the immense distance which I was afterwards to see, as between his development and that of any other thinker or man of genius whom I could name.

Referring to this scepticism of mine, which was well known at the time to the rest of the class, a more fortunate disciple, long afterwards, was teasing me, in the Swami's presence, and claiming that she had been able to accept every statement she had ever heard him make. The Swami paid little or no attention to the conversation at the time, but afterwards, he took a quiet moment to say, "Let none regret that they were difficult to convince! I fought my Master for six long years, with the result that I know every inch of the way! Every inch of the way!"

One or two impressions, however, stand out from those first discourses. Christianity had once meant to me that realisation of God as the Father. But I had long mourned over my own loss of faith in this symbolism and had desired to study its value as an idea, apart from its objective truth or untruth. For I suspected that such a conception would have its own effect on the character and perhaps on the civilisation of those who held it.

The Personification of God

This question, however, I had been unable to follow up for want of material of comparison. And here was one who told us of no less than five systems of worship, founded on similar personifications of the divine idea! He preached a religion which began with the classification of religious ideas!

I was very much struck further by the strangeness, as well as the dignity, of some of the Indian conceptions which I now heard of for the first time. The very newness of those metaphors and of the turn of thought made them an acquisition. There was the tale, for instance, of the saint who ran after a thief, with the vessels he had dropped in his terror at being discovered and cast them all at his feet, crying, "O Lord, I knew not that Thou wast there! Take them, they are Thine! Pardon me Thy child!" And again, of the same saint, we heard how he described the bite of a cobra, when at nightfall he recovered by saying, "A messenger came to me from the Beloved." There was the inference again that the Swami himself had drawn from the mirage in the desert. Fifteen days he had seen it and taken it always to be water. But now that he had been thirsty and found it to be unreal, he might see it again for fifteen days, but always henceforth he would know it to be false. The experience to which such achievements had been possible, the philosophy that could draw some parallel between this journey in the desert and life, were such as it seemed an education to understand.

Indian Religious Concepts

But there was a third element in the Swami's teaching whose unexpectedness occasioned me some surprise. It was easy to see that he was no mere lecturer, like some other propounders of advanced ideas whom I had heard even from the pulpit. It was by no means his intention to set forth dainty dishes of poetry and intellectuality for the enjoyment of the rich and idle classes. He was, to his own thinking at least, as clearly an apostle, making an appeal to men, as any poor evangelical preacher, or Salvation Army officer, calling on the world to enter into the kingdom of God. And yet he took his stand on what was noblest and best in us. I was not thinking of his announcement that sin was only an evil dream. I knew that such a theory might merely be part of a cumbrous system of theology, and no more a reality to its elucidator than the doctrine that when a man steals our coat we should give to him our cloak also, was to ourselves. The thing that I found astonishing was a certain illustration urged by him. His audience was composed for the most part of fashionable young mothers and he spoke of their terror and their flight, if a tiger should suddenly appear before them in the street. "But suppose," he said with a sudden change of tone, "suppose there were a baby in the path of the tiger! Where would your place be then? At his mouth— any one of you— I am sure of it."

These, then, were the things I remembered and pondered over, concerning the Swami, when he had left England that winter for America— first, the breadth of his religious culture; second, the great intellectual newness and interest of the thought he had brought to us; and thirdly, the fact that his call was sounded in the name of that which was strongest and finest, and was not in any way dependent on the meaner elements in man.

II

The Swami in London—1896

The Swami returned to London in April of the year following and taught continuously at the house where he was living with his good friend, Mr. E.T. Sturdy in S. George's Road, and again after the summer holidays in a large class-room near Victoria Street. During July, August and September he travelled in France, Germany and Switzerland with his friends, Mr. and Mrs. Sevier and Miss H. F. Muller. In December, he left for India with some of his disciples by way of Rome and arrived at Colombo in Ceylon on January the 15th, 1897.

Many of the lectures which he gave during the year 1896, have since been published and in them, all the world may read his message and the interpretation by which he sought to make it clear. He had come to us as a missionary of the Hindu belief in the Immanent God and he called upon us to realize the truth of his gospel for ourselves.

Neither then, nor at any aftertime, did I ever hear him advocate to his audience any specialized form of religion. He would refer freely enough to the Indian sects, or as I would like to call them 'churches,' by way of illustration of what he had to say. But he never preached anything but that philosophy which, Indian thinking, underlies all creeds. He never quoted anything but the Vedas, the Upanishads and the Bhagavad Gita. And he never in public mentioned his own Master, nor spoke in specific terms of any part of Hindu mythology.

He was deeply convinced of the need for Indian thought, in order to enable the religious consciousness of the West to welcome and assimilate the discoveries of modern science and to enable it also to survive that destruction of local mythologies which is an inevitable result of all world-consolidations. He felt that what was wanted was a formulation of faith which could hold its adherents fearless of truth. "The salvation of Europe depends on a rationalistic religion," he exclaims in the course of one of his lectures; and again, many times repeated, "The materialist is right! There is but One. Only he calls that One matter and I call it God!" In another and longer passage, he describes the growth of the religious idea and the relation of its various forms to one another. "At first," he says, "the goal is far off, outside Nature and far beyond it, attracting us all towards it. This has to be brought near, yet without being degraded or degenerated, until when it has come closer and closer, the God of Heaven becomes the God in Nature, till the God in Nature becomes the God who is Nature, and the God who is Nature becomes the God within this temple of the body, and the God dwelling in the temple of the body becomes the temple itself, becomes the soul of man. Thus it reaches the last words it can teach. He whom the sages have sought in all these places, is in our own hearts. Thou art He, O Man! Thou art He!"

Lectures on *Māyā*

He always considered, for his own part, that his greatest intellectual achievement during this period had consisted in his lectures on *Māyā*, and it is only by reading these carefully that an idea can be formed of the difficulty of the task he undertook, in trying to render the conception in modern English. Throughout the chapters in question, we feel that we are in the presence of a *struggle* to express an idea which is clearly apprehended, in a language which is not a fit vehicle for it. The word is wrongly understood, says the Swami, to mean 'delusion'. Originally it meant something like 'magic,' as "Indra through his *Māyā* assumed various forms." But this meaning was subsequently dropped and the word went through many transformations. A milestone in the series of conceptions that finally determined its meaning is found in the text : "Because we talk in vain and because we are satisfied with the things of the senses and because we are running after desires, therefore we, as it were, *cover this reality with a mist.*" Finally, the word is seen to have assumed its ultimate meaning in the quotation from the Svetasvatara Upanishad : "Know nature to be *Māyā*. And the mind, the ruler of this *Māyā*, as the Lord Himself." "The *Māyā* of the Vedanta," says the speaker, "in its latest development, is a simple statement of facts— what we are and what we see around us."

But that these words are not intended, as a definition will be seen by anyone who reads the whole of the lectures on *Māyā* for himself. It is there evident that the word does not simply refer to the Universe as known through the senses, but also describes the tortuous, erroneous and self-contradictory character of this knowledge. "This is a statement of fact, not a theory," says the Swami, "that this world is a Tantalus' hell, that we do not know anything about this Universe; yet at the same time we cannot say that we do not know. To walk in the midst of a dream, half-sleeping, half-waling, passing all our lives in a haze, this is the fate of every one of us. This is the fate of all sense-knowledge. This is the Universe." We see here, as in many other of his interpretations, that an Indian word is incapable of exact rendering into English, and that the only way of arriving at an understanding of it is to try to catch the conception which the speaker is striving to express, rather than to fasten the attention on a sentence or two here or there. By *Māyā* is thus meant that shimmering, elusive, half-real, half-unreal complexity, in which there is no rest, no satisfaction, no ultimate certainty, of which we become aware through the senses and through the mind as dependent on the senses. At the same time—"And *That* by which all this is pervaded, know *That* to be the Lord Himself!" In these two conceptions, placed side by side, we have the whole theology of Hinduism, as presented by the Swami Vivekananda in the West. All other teachings and ideas are subordinated to these two. Religion was a matter of the growth of the individual, "a question always of being and becoming". But such growth must presuppose the two fundamental facts, and the gradual transference of the centre of gravity as it were, out of the one into the other—out of *Māyā* into the Self. The condition of absorption in *Māyā* was 'bondage' in the Eastern sense. To have broken that bondage was 'freedom' or Mukti, or even Nirvana. The path for the would-be breaker of bondage must always be by seeking for renunciation, not by seeking for enjoyment. In this matter, the Swami was, as he said himself, only echoing what had been the burden of all religions. For all religions, Indian and other, have called a halt in the quest for pleasure. All have sought to turn life into a battlefield rather than a ballroom. All have striven to make man strong for death rather than for life. Where I think that the Swami perhaps differed somewhat from other teachers was in his acceptance of every kind of mastery as a form of renunciation. Towards the end of his life, I told him that 'renunciation'

Renunciation or Conquest

was the only word I had ever heard from his lips. And yet in truth, I think that 'conquer!' was much more characteristic of him. For he pointed out that it was by renunciation, that is to say, by sustained and determined effort, by absorption in hard problems through lonely hours, by choosing toil and refusing ease, that Stephenson, for instance, invented the steam engine. He pointed out that the science of medicine represented as strong, a concentration of man's mind upon healing as would be required for a cure by prayer or by thought. He made us feel that all study was an austerity directed to a given end of knowledge. And above all, he preached that character, and character alone, was the power that determined the permanence of a religious wave. Resistance was to his mind the duty of the citizen, non-resistance of the monk. And this is because, for all, the supreme achievement was strength. "Forgive," he said, "when you also can bring legions of angels to an easy victory." While victory was still doubtful, however, only a coward, to his thinking, would turn the other cheek.

One reads the same lesson in his Master's story of the boy who for twenty years, worked to acquire the power to walk on water. "And so," said a saint, "you have given twenty years of effort to doing that for which others give the ferryman a penny"

The Real and the Unreal

The lad might have answered that no ferryman could give his passengers what he had acquired by twenty years of patient striving. But the fact remains that to these teachers, supremely sane, the world's art of navigation had its own full value and its proper place. Years afterwards, in Paris, someone approached him with a question as to the general history of the development of Indian ideas on these subjects. "Did Buddha teach that the many was real and the ego unreal, while Orthodox Hinduism regards the One as the Real, and the many as unreal?" he was asked. "Yes", answered the Swami. "And what Ramakrishna Paramahamsa and I have added to this is that the Many and the One are the same Reality, perceived by the same mind at different times and in different attitudes."

Gifted to an extraordinary degree with a living utterance of metaphysics, drawing always upon a classical literature of wonderful depth and profundity, he stood in our midst as, before all, the apostle of the inner life, the prophet of the subordination of the objective to the subjective, "Remember!" he said once to a disciple, "Remember! The message of India is always *'Not the soul for Nature, but Nature for the soul!'* " And this was indeed the organ note, as it were, the deep fundamental vibration, that began gradually to make itself heard through all the intellectual interest of the things he discussed and the point of view he revealed. Like the sound of the flute, heard far away on the banks of some river in the hour of dawn, and regarded as but one amongst many sweet songs of the world; and like the same strain when the listener has drawn nearer and nearer and at last with his whole mind on the music, has become himself the player—may have

The Life of the Soul

seemed to some who heard him long, the difference between the life of the soul in Western thinking and in Eastern. And with this came the exaltation of renunciation. It was not, perhaps, that the word occurred in his teachings any oftener than it had done before. It was rather that the reality of that life, free, undimensioned, sovereign in its mastery, was making itself directly felt. A temptation that had to be fought against was the impulse to go away and bind upon oneself intellectual shackles not to be borne, in order to be able to enter in its fullness upon the life of poverty and silence.

An occasion came, when this call was uttered with great force. Some dispute occurred in the course of a question-class. "What the world wants today," said the Swami—"the determination to throw a bomb," as he called it, evidently taking sudden possession of him—"What the world wants today, is twenty men and women who can dare to stand in the street yonder and say that they possess nothing but God. Who will go?" He had risen to his feet by this time and stood looking round his audience as if begging some of them to join him. "Why should one fear?" And then! In tones of which, even now, I can hear again the thunderous conviction, *"If this is true, what else could matter? If it is not true, what do our lives matter?"*

"What the world wants is character," he says, in a letter written at this time to a member of his class. "The world is in need of those whose life is one burning love—selfless. The love will make every word tell like a thunderbolt. Awake, awake, great souls! The world is burning in misery. Can you sleep?"

I remember how new to myself at that time was this Indian idea that it was character that made a truth tell, the love expressed that made aid successful, the degree of concentration behind a saying that gave it force and constituted its power. "Thus the text 'Consider the lilies, how they grow,' holds us," said the Swami, "not by the spell of its beauty but by the depth of renunciation that speaks in it."

The Spirit behind the word

Was this true? I felt that the question might be tested by experience, and after some time I came to the conclusion that it was. A quiet word from a mind that put thought behind language carried immediate weight, when the same utterance from the careless would pass by unheeded. I do not know a stronger instance of this fact than a certain saying that is recorded of the Caliph Ali. Many have heard, and none surely without emotion, the words of the Lion of Islam, "Thy place in life is seeking after thee. Therefore be thou at rest from seeking after it!" But never until we relate them to the speaker, four times passed over in the succession to the Caliphate, never until we know how the man's whole life throbs through them, are we able to explain the extraordinary power of these simple sentences.

I found also that an utterance consciously directed to the mind, instead of merely to the hearing of the listener, evoked more response than the opposite. And having begun to make these psychological discoveries, I was led gradually to the perception that if indeed one's reason could, as one had long thought, make no final line of demarcation as between mind and matter, yet at least that aspect of the One-substance which we called Matter was rather the result of that called Mind or Spirit, than the reverse. The body, not the will, must be regarded as a byproduct of the individuality. This, in turn, led to the conception of a consciousness held above the body, a life-governing matter, and free of it, so that it might conceivably disrobe and find new garments, or cast off the form known to us, as that form itself casts off a wounded skin. Till at last, I found my own mind echoing the Swami's great pronouncement on immortality, "The body comes and goes." But this ripening of thought came gradually and did not complete itself for many months.

Realisations

In the meantime, as I look back upon that time, I feel that what we all really entered upon in the Swami's classes was not so much an intellectual exposition, as a life of new and lofty emotions, or, as they would be called in India, 'realisations'.

We heard the exclamation, in describing the worship of God as a child, "do we *want* anything from Him?" We bowed to the teaching that "love is always a manifestation of bliss" and that any pang of pain or regret was therefore a mark of selfishness and physicality. We accepted the austere ruling that any, even the slightest, impulse of differentiation, as between ourselves and others was 'hatred', and that only the opposite of this was 'love'. Many who have ceased to believe in the creed of their childhood have felt that at least the good of others was still an end in itself, and that the possibility of service remained to give a motive to life. It is strange, now that ten years have passed, to remember the sense of surprise with which, holding this opinion, we listened to the decorous Eastern teaching, that the highest of all gifts was spirituality, a degree lower, intellectual knowledge, and that all kinds of physical and material help came last. All our welling pity for sickness and poverty is classified in this fashion! It has taken me years to find out, but I now know that in train of the higher giving the lower must needs follow.

Physical refinement in India

Similarly, to our Western fanaticism about pure air and hygienic surroundings, as if these were marks of saintliness, was opposed to the stern teaching of indifference to the world. Here, indeed, we came up against a closed door and had no key. When the Swami said, in bold consciousness of paradox that the saints had lived on mountain-tops 'to enjoy the scenery,' and when he advised his hearers to keep flowers and incense in their worship-rooms, and to care much for the purity and cleansing of food and person, we did not understand enough to connect the two extremes. But in fact, he was preaching our own doctrine of physical refinement, as it would be formulated in

India. And is it not true that until we in the West have succeeded in cleansing the slums of our great cities, our fastidiousness is very like the self-worship of the privileged?

A like fate awaited our admiration for such saints as knew how to order their worldly affairs with conspicuous success and prudence. True spirituality was indifferent to, nay contemptuous and intolerant of, the things of this world. This message the Swami never mitigated. In giving it, he never faltered. The highest spirituality cannot tolerate the world.

Spirituality, East and West

We understood clearly enough that these were the ideals of sainthood only. We were learning chapter after chapter of a great language which was to make it easy for us to hold communion with the ends of the earth. We gathered no confusion as to those questions which concern the life of citizenship and domestic virtue and form what may be regarded as the kindergarten of the soul. The idea that one country might best advance itself by learning to appreciate those ideals of order and responsibility which formed the glory of another was in no wise discredited. At the same time, we were given, as the eternal watchword of the Indian ideals, "Spirituality cannot tolerate the world." Did we, in contradiction, point to monastic orders, well-governed, highly organised, devoted to the public good, and contrast our long roll of abbots, bishops and saintly lady-abbesses, with a few ragged and God-intoxicated beggars of the East? Yet we had to admit that even in the West, when the flame of spirituality had blazed suddenly to its brightest, it had taken their form. For those who know the land of Meera Bae and Chaitanya, of Tukaram and Ramanuja, can hardly resist the impulse to clothe with the yellow garb the memory of St. Francis of Assisi also.

In one of the volumes of the English translation of the 'Jataka— Birth-Tales,' there occur over and over again the words, *"when a man has come to that place where he dreads heaven as much as hell"*—and I do not know how the realisation that the Swami's presence brought could be better described. Most of those who listened to him in London, in the year 1896, caught some glimpse, by which they were led to understand a little of the meaning of the Eastern longing to escape from incarnation.

But master of all these moods and dominating them, was one that had barely been hinted at, in the words, "If this is true, what other thing could matter? If it is not true, what do our lives matter?" For there was a power in this teacher, to sum up all the truth he himself had come to teach, together with his own highest hope, and to treat the whole as a mean bribe, to be flung away fearlessly, if need were, for the good of others. Years after, this spoke more clearly in the indignant reply with which he turned on some remark of my own, "Of course I would commit a crime and go to hell forever, if by that I could really help a human being!" It was the same impulse that spoke also, in his constant

The Crown of Freedom

repetition to some few of us, as if it had a special bearing on the present age, of the tale of that Bodhisattva, who had held himself back from Nirvana till the last grain of dust in the universe should have gone in before him to salvation. Does it mean that the final mark of freedom lies in ceasing from the quest of freedom? I have found the same thing since, in many of the Indian stories; in Ramanuja, for instance, breaking his vow, and proclaiming the sacred *mantram* to all the pariahs; in Buddha, keeping no secret, but spending his whole life in work; in Sishupal, choosing to be the enemy of God, that he might the sooner return to him; and in innumerable legends of the saints fighting against the deities.

But the Swami was not always entirely impersonal. Once after a lecture, he came up to a small group of us and said, *apropos* of some subject that had been opened up, "I have a superstition—it is nothing, you know, but a personal superstition!—that the same soul who came once as Buddha came afterwards as Christ." And then, lingering on the point of departure, he drifted into talk of his 'old Master,' of whom we then heard for the first time, and of the girl who, wedded and forgotten, gave her husband his freedom with tears. His voice had sunk lower, as he talked, till the tones had become dream-like. But finally, almost in soliloquy, he shook off the mood that had stolen upon him, saying with a long breath, "Yes, yes! These things have been, and they will again be. Go in peace, my daughter, thy faith hath made thee whole!"

It was in the course of a conversation much more casual than this, that he turned to me and said, "I have plans for the women of my own country in which you, I think, could be of great help to me", and I knew that I had heard a call which would change my life. What these plans were, I did not know, and the effort of abandoning the accustomed perspective was for the moment so great that I did not care to ask. But I had already gathered that there was much to learn, if one's conception of the world were to be made inclusive of the viewpoint of foreign peoples. "And you have *blasted* other cities!" had once been the startling reply, when I had spoken of the necessity of making London fair. For to me the mystery and tragedy of London had long been the microcosm of the human problem, standing as the symbol of the whole world's call. "And you have *blasted* other cities, to make this city of yours beautiful!" I could elicit no more, but the words echoed in my ears for many days. In my eyes, our city was not beautiful. My question had been misunderstood. But through this misunderstanding, I had discovered that *there was another point of view.* "The English are born on an island, and they are always trying to live on it," said the Master once to me, and certainly the remark seems true of myself, as I look back on this period of my life, and see how determinately insular even my ideals had hitherto been. I learnt

Personal Glimpses

no more of the Indian point of view, during my life in England. The friend who afterwards called me to her side in India, chose a certain evening in London, when both the Swami and myself were her guests for an hour, to tell him of my willingness to help his work. He was evidently surprised, but said quietly, "For my own part, I will be incarnated two hundred times, if that is necessary to do this work amongst my people, that I have undertaken."And the words stand in my own mind beside those which he afterwards wrote to me on the eve of my departure, *"I will stand by you unto death,* whether you work for India or not, whether you give up Vedanta, or remain in it. The tusks of the elephant come out, but they never go back. Even so are the words of a man."

The Message of the Guru

But these references to the Swami's own people were merely personal, and as such were strictly subordinate. In his classes, in his teachings, his one longing seemed to be for the salvation of men from ignorance. Such love, such pity, those who heard him never saw elsewhere. To him, his disciples were his disciples. There was neither Indian nor European there. And yet he was profoundly conscious of the historic significance of his own preaching. On the occasion of his last appearance in London, (at the Royal Society of Painters in Watercolours, on Sunday afternoon, December the 15th, 1896) he pointed out the fact that history repeats itself, and that Christianity had been rendered possible only by the Roman Peace.

Historic Religions

And it may well have been that the Buddha-like dignity and calm of bearing which so impressed us, were but the expression of his far outlook and serene conviction that there would yet be seen a great army of Indian preachers in the West, reaping the harvest that he had sown so well, and making ready in their turn new harvest, for the more distant reaping of the future.

III

The Conflict of Ideals

"He knew nothing of Vedanta, nothing of theories! He was contented to live that great life and to leave it to others to explain." So said the Swami Vivekananda once, referring to his Master, Ramakrishna Paramahamsa. And, as an expression of the idea that there may in a great life be elements which he who lives it may not himself understand, the words have often come back to me, in reference to his own career.

The Duality of Life

In the West, the Swami had revealed himself to us as a religious teacher only. Even now, it needs but a moment's thought and again one sees him in the old lecture room, on the seat slightly raised above his class, and so enthroned, in Buddha-like calm, once more in a modern world is heard through his lips, the voice of the far past. But renunciation, the thirst after freedom, the breaking of bondage, the fire of purity, the joy of the witness, the mergence of the personal in the impersonal—

these, and these alone, had been the themes of that discourse. It is true that in a flash of two one had seen a great patriot. Yet the secret signal is sufficient where destiny calls, and moments that to one form the turning point of a life, may pass before the eyes of a hundred spectators, unperceived. It was as the apostle of Hinduism, not as a worker for India, that we saw the Swami in the West. "Oh, how calm," he exclaimed, "would be the work of one, who really understood the divinity of man! For such, there is nothing to do, save to open men's eyes. All the rest does itself." And out of some such fathomless peace had come all that we had seen and heard of him.

From the moment of my landing in India, however, I found something quite unexpected underlying all this. It was not Ramakrishna Paramahamsa, nor even the ideas which were connected with him, that formed so strange a revelation here. It was the personality of my Master himself, in all the fruitless torture and struggle of a lion caught in a net. For, from the day that he met me at the ship's side, till that last serene moment, when, at the hour of cow-dust, he passed out of the village of this world, leaving the body behind him, like a folded garment, I was always conscious of this element inwoven with the other, in his life.

But wherein lay the struggle? Whence came the frequent sense of being baffled and thwarted? Was it a growing consciousness of bodily weakness, conflicting with the growing clearness of a great purpose? Amongst the echoes that had reached his English friends of his triumphal reception in India, that had been the note carried by man-friend to my own ear. Banished to the Himalayas with shattered health, at the very moment when his power had reached its height, he had written a letter to his friend which was a cry of despair. And some of us became eager to take any step that might make it possible to induce him to return to the West, and leave his Indian undertakings on other shoulders. In making such arrangements, how little must we have realized of the nature of those undertakings, or of the difficulty and complexity of the education that they demanded!

The Religion of Work

To what was the struggle actually due? Was it the terrible effort of translating what he had called the 'super-conscious' into the common life? Undoubtedly he had been born to a task which was in this respect of heroic difficulty. Nothing in this world is so terrible as to abandon the safe paths of accepted ideals, in order to work out some new realisation, by methods apparently in conflict with the old. Once in his boyhood, Sri Ramakrishna had asked 'Noren', as he was then called, what was his highest ambition in life, and he had promptly answered, "to remain always in *Samadhi*." His Master, it is said, received this with a smile. "I thought you had been born for something greater, my boy!" was all his reply, We may take it, I think, that the moment marked an epoch in the disciple's career. Certainly in years to come, in these last five and a half years, particularly, which were his crowning gift to his own people, he stood for work without attachment, or work for impersonal ends, as one of the highest expressions of the religious life. And for the first time in the history of India, an order of monks found themselves banded together, with their faces set primarily towards the evolution of new forms of civic duty. In Europe, where the attainment of the direct religious sense is so much rarer, and so much less understood than in the East, such labour ranks as devotional in the common acceptance. But in India, the head and front of the demand made on a monastic order is that it produces saints. And the value of the monk who, instead of devoting himself to maintaining the great tradition of the super-conscious life, turns back to help society upwards, has not in the past been clearly understood.

In the Swami's scheme of things, however, it would almost seem as if such tasks were to

Service as Worship

The Public Good

take that place in the spiritual education which had previously been occupied by systems of devotion. To the *Adwaitin*, or strict believer in the Indian philosophy of Vedanta, the goal lies in the attainment of that mood in which all is One and there is no second. To one who has reached this, worship becomes impossible, for there is none to worship, none to be worshipper; and, all acts being equally the expression of the Immanent Unity, none can be distinguished as in any special sense constituting adoration. Worship, worshipper and worshipped are one. Yet it is admitted, even by the Adwaitin, that systems of praise and prayer have the power to 'purify the heart' of him who uses them. For clearly, the thought of self is more quickly restrained in relation to that of God, than to any other. Worship is thus regarded as the school or preparation, for higher stages of spiritual development. But the self-same sequence would seem to have held good in the eyes of the Swami, with regard to work, or the service of man. The 'purifying of the heart' connoted the burning out of selfishness. Worship is the very antithesis of use. But service or giving, is also its antithesis. Thus he hallowed the act of aid, and hallowed, too, the name of man. Till I know of one disciple, who, in the early days of the Order, was so filled with the impulse of this reverence that he sucked the sores of the lepers to bring them ease. The nursing of the sick and the feeding of the poor had indeed from the first been natural activities of the Children of Ramakrishna. But when the Swami Vivekananda returned from the West, these things took on a larger aspect. They were considered from a national point of view. Men would be sent out from the Monastery to give relief in famine-stricken areas, to direct the sanitation of a town, or to nurse the sick and dying at a pilgrim centre. One man started an orphanage and industrial school at Murshidabad. Another established a teaching nucleus in the South. These were, said the Swami, the 'sappers and miners' of the army of religion. His schemes however went much further. He was consumed with a desire for the education of Indian women, and for the scientific and technical education of the country. How the impersonal motive multiplies the power to suffer, only those who have seen can judge. Was his life indeed a failure, as he was sometimes tempted to feel it, since there never came to his hands that 'twenty million pounds' with which, as he used to say, he could have set India on her feet? Or were there higher laws at work, that would eventually make a far greater success than any that could have been gathered within a single lifetime?

The Pain of the Pioneer

His view was penetrative as well as comprehensive. He had analysed the elements of the development to be brought about. India must learn a new ideal of obedience. The Math was placed, therefore, on a basis of organisation which was contrary to all the current ideas of religious freedom. A thousand new articles of use must be assimilated. Therefore, though his own habits were of the simplest, two or three rooms were provided with furniture. Digging, gardening, rowing, gymnastic exercises, the keeping of animals, all these were by degrees made a part of the life of the young *Brahmachārins* and himself. And he would throw a world of enthusiasm into a long course of experiments on such problems as the sinking of a well or the making of brown bread. On the last Charok Puja day of his life, a gymnastic society came to the Math for sports and prizes, and he spoke of his desire that the Hindu Lent should be celebrated henceforth by special courses of athletic exercises. The energy which had hitherto gone into the mortification of the body, might rightly, in his opinion, under modern conditions, be directed to the training of the muscles.

To a Western mind, it might well seem that nothing in the Swami's life had been more admirable than this. Long ago, he had defined the mission of the Order of Ramakrishna as that of realizing and exchanging the highest ideals of the East and of the West. And assuredly he here proved his own power to engage in such an undertaking as much by his gift of learning as by that of teaching. But it was inevitable that he himself should from time to time go through the anguish of revolt. The Hindu ideal of the religious life, as a reflection on earth of that of the Great God in the Divine Empyrean—the Unmoving, the Untouched, 'pure, free, ever the Witness'—is so clear and so deeply established that only at great cost to himself could a man carry it into a fresh channel. Has anyone realized the pain endured by the sculptor of a new ideal? The very sensitiveness and delicacy of perception that are necessary to his task, that very moral exaltation which is as the chisel in his hand, are turned on himself in passive moments, to become doubt, and terror of responsibility. What a heaven of ease seems then, to such a soul, even the hardest and sternest of those lives that are understood and authenticated by the imitative moral sense of the crowd! I have noticed in most experiences this consciousness of being woven out of two threads, one that is chosen and another endured. But in this case, the common duality took the form of a play upon two different ideals, of which either was highest in its own world, and yet each, to those who believed in its fellow, almost as a crime.

His Doubt of the Present

Occasionally, to one who was much with him, a word, let fall unconsciously, would betray the inner conflict. He was riding on one occasion, with the Rajah of Khetri, when he saw that his arm was bleeding profusely, and found that the wound had been caused by a thorny branch which he had held aside for himself to pass. When the Swami expostulated, the Rajput laughed the matter aside, "Are we not always the Defenders of the Faith, Swamiji?" he said. "And then, " said the Swami, telling the story, "I was just going to tell him that they ought not to show such honour to the *Sannyāsin*, when suddenly I thought that perhaps they were right after all. Who knows? Maybe I too am caught in the glare of this flashlight of your modern civilisation, which is only for a moment." "—I have become entangled," he said simply, to one who protested that to his mind the wandering *Sādhu* of earlier years, who had scattered his knowledge and changed his name as he went, had been greater than the Abbot of Belur, burdened with much work and many cares, "I have become entangled," And I remember the story told by an American woman, who said she could not bear to remember his face, at that moment when her husband explained to this strange guest that he must make his way from their home to Chicago with money which would be paid gladly to hear him speak of religion, "It was," she said, "as if something had just broken within him, that could never again be made whole." One day he was talking, in the West, of Meera Bae—that saint who once upon a time was Queen of Chitore—and of the freedom her husband had offered her, if only she would remain within the royal seclusion. But she could not be bound. "But why should she not?" someone asked, in astonishment. "Why should she?" he retorted. "Was she living down here *in this mire?*" And suddenly the listener caught his thought, of the whole nexus of the personal life, with its inter-relations and reaction upon reactions, as intolerable bondage and living anguish.

And so, side by side with that sunlit serenity and childlike peace which enwrapped the Swami as a religious teacher, I found in his own country another point of view, from which he was very, very human. And here, though the results of his efforts may have been choicer, or more enduring than those of most of us, yet they were wrought at the selfsame cost of having to toil on in darkness and uncertainty, and only now and then emerging into light. Often dogged by the sense of failure, often overtaken by a loathing of the limitations imposed alike by the instrument and the material, he dared less and less, as years went on, to make determinate plans, or to dogmatize about the unknown. "After all, what do you know?" he said once, "Mother used it all. But we are only fumbling about."

This has not perhaps been an element in the lives of the great teachers on which their narrators have cared to dwell much. Yet one catches a hint of it in the case of Sri Ramakrishna, when we are told how he turned on God with the reproach, "Oh Mother! what is this You have brought me to? All my heart is centred in these lads!" And in the eleventh chapter of the Dhammapada one can see still, though twenty-four centuries have passed since then, the wave marks of similar storms on the shores of the consciousness of another Teacher.*

India the Mother

There was one thing, however, deep in the Master's nature, that he himself never knew how to adjust. This was his love of his country and his resentment of her suffering. Throughout those years in which I saw him almost daily, the thought of India was to him like the air he breathed. True, he was a worker at foundations. He neither used the word 'nationality,' nor proclaimed an era of "nation-making". 'Man-making,' he said, was his own task. But he was

* Seeking for the maker of this tabernacle and not finding, I must run through a course of many births; and painful is birth again and again. But not, maker of the tabernacle, thou hast been seen! Thou shalt not again build up this tabernacle. All thy rafters are fallen. Thy ridge pole is broken. The mind, approaching the Eternal, has attained to the extinction of all desires.

born a lover, and the queen of his adoration was his Motherland. Like some delicately-poised bell, thrilled and vibrated by every sound that falls upon it, was his heart to all that concerned her. Not a sob was heard within her shores that did not find in him a responsive echo. There was no cry of fear, no tremor of weakness, no shrinking from mortification, that he had not known and understood. He was hard on her sins, unsparing of her want of worldly wisdom, but only because he felt these faults to be his own. And none, on the contrary, was ever so possessed by the vision of her greatness. To him, she appeared as the giver of English civilisation. For what, he would ask, had been the England of Elizabeth in comparison with the India of Akbar? Nay, what would the England of Victoria have been, without the wealth of India, behind her? Where would have been her refinement? Where would have been her experience? His country's religion, history, geography, and ethnology poured from his lips in an inexhaustible stream. With equal delight be treated of details and of the whole, or so it would often seem to those who listened. Indeed there would sometimes come a point where none who wished to remember what had been said already, could afford to listen any longer. And still, with mind detached, one might note the unwearied stream of analysis of

Response to India

the laws regarding female inheritance, or the details of caste customs in different provinces, or some abstruse system of metaphysics or theology, proceeding on and on for a couple of hours longer.

The Epic of India

In these talks of his, the heroism of the Rajput, the faith of the Sikh, the courage of the Mahrata, the devotion of the saints and the purity and steadfastness of noble women, all lived again. Nor would he permit that the Mohammedan should be passed over. Humayoon, Sher Shah, Akbar, Shah Jehan, each of these and a hundred more found a day and a place in his bead-roll of glistening names. Now it was that coronation song of Akbar which is still sung about the streets of Delhi, that he would give us in the very tone and rhythm of Thanasena. Again, he would explain how the widows of the Mogul House never re-married, but lived like Hindu women, absorbed in worship or in study, through the lonely years. At another time he would talk of the great national genius that decreed the birth of Indian sovereigns to be of a Moslem father and of a Hindu mother. And yet again he would hold us breathless, as we lived through with him the bright, but ill-starred reign of Sirajud-Daulah; as we heard the exclamation at Plassy of the Hindu general, listening to an order sent in treachery, "Then is the day lost!" and saw him plunge with his horse into the Ganges; as finally, we lingered with the faithful wife, clad in the white sari of the widow amongst her own people, through long years tending the lamp above the grave of her dead lord.

Sometimes the talk would be more playful. It would arise out of some commonplace incident. The offering of a sweetmeat, or the finding of a rare commodity like musk or saffron, or events simpler still, would be enough to start it. He told us how he had longed, when in the West, to stand once more at dusk some little way outside an Indian village and hear again the evening calls—the noise of children growing sleepy at their play, the evensong bells, the cries of the herdsmen and the half-veiled sound of voices through the quickly-passing twilight. How homesick he had been for the sound of the July rains, as he had known them in his childhood in Bengal! How wonderful was the sound of water in the rain, or waterfall, or sea! The most beautiful sight he could remember was a mother whom he had seen, passing from stepping-stone to stepping-stone across a mountain brook and turning as she went, to play with and caress the baby on her back. The ideal death would be to lie on a ledge of rock in the midst of Himalayan forests and hear the torrent beneath, as one

The Love of India

passed out of the body, chanting eternally 'Hara! Hara! The Free! The Free!'

Like some great spiral of emotion, its lowest circles held fast in love of soil and love of nature; its next embracing every possible association of race, experience, history, and thought; and the whole converging and centring upon a single definite point, was thus the Swami's worship of his own land. And the point in which it was focused was the conviction that India was not old and effete, as her critics had supposed, but young, ripe with potentiality and standing, at the beginning of the twentieth century, on the threshold of even greater developments than she had known in the past. Only once, however, do I remember him to have given specific utterance to this thought. "I feel myself" he said in a moment of great quiet, "to be the man born after many centuries. *I see that India is young.*" But in truth this vision was implied in every word he ever spoke. It throbbed in every story he told. And when he would lose himself, in splendid scorn of apology for anything Indian, in fiery repudiation of false charge or contemptuous criticism or in laying down for others the elements of a faith and love that could never be more than a pale reflection of his own, how often did the habit of the monk seem to slip away from him and the armour of the warrior stand revealed!

But it is not to be supposed that he was unaware of the temptations of which all this implied. His Master had said of him, in the years of his first discipleship, "It is true that there is a film of ignorance upon his mind. My Mother has placed it there, so that Her work may be done. And it is thin, as thin as a sheet of tissue paper. It might be rent at any moment!" And so, as one who has forsworn them will struggle against thoughts of home and family, he would endeavour time and again to restrain and suppress these thoughts of country and history, and to make of himself only that poor religious wanderer, to whom all countries and all races should be alike. He came back, in Kashmir from one of the great experiences of his life, saying with the simplicity of a child, "There must be no more of this anger. Mother said, 'What even if the unbeliever should enter My temples and defile My images, what is that to you? DO YOU PROTECT ME? OR DO I PROTECT YOU?' "

His personal ideal was that *Sannyāsin* of the Mutiny, who was stabbed by an English soldier, and broke the silence of fifteen years to say to his murderer— "And thou also art He!"

He was always striving to be faithful to the banner of Ramakrishna, and the utterance of a message of his own seemed often to strike him as a lapse. Besides, he believed that force

Instinct not Theory

spent in mere emotion was dissipated, only force restrained being conserved for expression in work. Yet again the impulse to give all he had would overtake him and before he knew it, he would once more be scattering those thoughts of hope and love for his race and for his country, which apparently without his knowledge, fell in so many cases like seen upon soil prepared for it, and have sprung up already, in widely distant parts of India, into hearts and lives of devotion to the Motherland. Just as Sri Ramakrishna, in fact, without knowing any books, had been a living epitome of the Vedanta, so was Vivekananda of the national life. But of the theory of his, he was unconscious. In his own words, applied to his own Master, "He was contented simply to live that great life and to leave it to others to find the explanation!"

IV

The Swami Vivekananda and the Order of Ramakrishna

It was amongst the lawns and trees of Ganges side that I came to know, in a personal sense, that leader to whose work my life was already given. At the time of my landing in India (January 28th, 1898), the ground and building had just been purchased at Belur, which were afterwards to be transformed into the Calcutta Monastery of the Order of Ramakrishna. A few weeks later still, a party of friends arrived from America, and with characteristic intrepidity took possession of the half-ruined cottage to make it simply but pleasantly habitable. It was as the guest of these friends, here at Belur, and later travelling in Kumaon and in Kashmir, that I began with them the study of India, and something also of the home aspects and relationships of the Swami's own life.

Our cottage stood on a low terrace, built on the western bank of the river, a few miles above Calcutta. At flood-tide, the little gondola-like boat—which to those who live beside the Ganges serves the purpose of a carriage—could come up to the very foot of the steps, and the river between us and the opposite village, was from half to three-quarters of a mile broad. A mile or so further up the eastern bank, could be seen the towers and trees of Dakshineswar, that temple-garden in which the Swami and his brothers had once been boys at the feet of Ramakrishna Paramahamsa. The house which was in actual use at that time as the Monastery, lay some half mile or so to the south of our cottage, and between us and it were several other garden-houses and at least one ravine, crossed by a doubtful-looking plank made out of half of the stem of a palm tree. To our cottage here, then came the Swami daily, at sunrise, alone or accompanied by some of his brothers. And here under the trees, long after our early breakfast was ended, we might still be found seated, listening to that inexhaustible flow of interpretation, broken but rarely by question and answer, in which he would reveal to us some of the deepest secrets of the Indian world. I am struck afresh whenever I turn back upon this memory, by the wonder as to how such a harvest of thought and experience could possibly have been garnered, or how, when once ingathered, could have come

Morning Talks

such energy of impulse for its giving-forth. Amongst brilliant conversationalists, the Swami was peculiar in one respect. He was never known to show the slightest impatience at interruption. He was by no means indifferent as to the minds he was addressing. His deepest utterances were heard only in the presence of such listeners as brought a subtle sympathy and reverence into the circle about him. But I do not think he was himself aware of this, and certainly no external circumstance seemed to have the power to ruffle him. Moods of storm and strength there were in plenty; but they sprang, like those of sweetness, from hidden sources; they were entirely general and impersonal in their occasion.

Eastern Ideals

It was here that we learnt the great outstanding watchwords and ideals of the Indian striving. For the talks were, above all, an exposition of ideals. Facts and illustrations were gathered, it is true, from history, from literature and a thousand other sources. But the purpose was always the same, to render some Indian ideal of perfection clearer. Nor were these ideals always so comprehensible as might have been supposed. This was a world in which concentration of mind was the object of more deliberate cultivation than even the instincts of benevolence could require, but the time was not yet come in which this was to be argued as for or against India. The attainment of the impersonal standpoint was boldly proposed, in matters personal. "Be the Witness!" was a command heard oftener than that which bids us pray for our enemies. The idea of recognizing an enemy would have seemed to this mind a proof of hatred. Love was not love, it was insisted, unless it was 'without a reason,' or without a 'motive,' as a western speaker might have attempted, though perhaps with less force, to express the same idea. Purity and renunciation were analysed untiringly. The great God, tempted by nothing— not kingship nor fatherhood; not wealth nor pleasure;— in all the worlds He had created, proving on the contrary, in matters worldly, 'a very simple fellow,' incurious, easily deceived and begging His daily handful of rice from door to door, shone through all our dreams. *Titiksha* or non-correction of evil was a mark of the religious life, and of this we might find a western example in that monk who was a leper, and who, when the maggots fell from his finger-joints, stooped and replaced them, saying, "Eat brother!" The vision of Raghunath was one of the perfections of the soul, and that saint had had it, who fainted, when the bullocks were beaten in his presence, while on his back were found the weals made by the lash. We were even called upon to understand a thought immeasurably foreign to all our past conceptions of religion, in which sainthood finds expression in an unconsciousness of the body, so profound that the saint is unaware that he goes naked. For that delicate discrimination of a higher significance in certain cases of nudity, which in Europe, finds its expression in art, in India finds it in religion. As we, in the presence of the Greek statue, experience only reverence for the ideal of beauty, so the Hindu sees in the naked saint only a glorified and childlike purity.

The Struggle for Freedom

There was one aspiration, however, which was held in this new thought world, to be of the same sovereign and universal application in the religious life as that of the concentration of the mind. This was the freedom of the individual soul, including all the minor rights of thought, opinion, and action. Here lay the one possession that the monk was jealously to guard as his own, the one property on which he must brook the foot of no intruder; and as I watched the working out of this in daily life, I saw that it amounted to a form of renunciation. To accept nothing, however pleasant, if it concealed a fetter; at a word to stand ready to sever any connection that gave a hint of bondage, how clear must be the mind that would do this, how pure the will! And yet this ideal, too, was eloquent of many things. One could not help seeing that it accounted for the comparative non-development of monasticism in India, for the fact that the highest types of the religious life in the past had been solitary, whether as hermits or wanderers. In the monastery beside us there were men, as we were told, who did not approve of their leader's talking with women; there were others who objected to all rites and ceremonies; the religion of one might be described as atheism tempered by hero-worship; that of another led him to a round of practices which to most of us would constitute an intolerable burden; some lived in a world of saints, visions and miracles; others again could not away with such nonsense, but must need to guide themselves by the coldest logic. The fact that all these could be bound together in a close confraternity, bore silent witness to their conception of the right of the soul to choose its own path. It also, as I could not help thinking, both then and after, accounted for the failure, in certain respects, of the old Indian forms of authority. For, in order that the highest and most disinterested characters may throw themselves into the work of the city and the state, it is surely necessary that they should sincerely hold the task of such organisation to be the highest and most honourable which they could aspire to carry out. In the India of the past, however, the best men had been too conscious of the more remote spiritual ideals, and amongst them, of this conception of freedom, to be capable of such an enthusiasm for the assertion of the civic and national discipline. And we cannot wonder that in spite of the existence of ability and character, certain advantages of the modern system have thus been left for the moderns to demonstrate. That Hinduism, nevertheless, is capable enough of adding to her development that of the inspiration and sustenance of such activities, is shown, as I believe, in the very fact of the rise of Ramakrishna and his disciple Vivekananda, with their characteristic contribution to the national thought.

The Exchange of Ideals

It was perhaps as an instance of that 'exchange of ideals' which he had ever in mind, that the Swami gravely warned us again and again, as the great fault of the Western character, against making any attempt to force upon others that which we had merely found to be good for ourselves. And yet at the same time, when asked by some of his own people what he considered, after seeing them in their own country, to be the greatest achievement of the English, he answered, 'that they had known how to combine obedience with self-respect.'

But it was not the Swami alone whom we saw at Belur. We were accounted by the monastery as a whole, as its guests. So back and forth would toil the hospitable monks, on errands of kindness and service for us. They milked the cow that gave us our supply, and when the servant whose duty it was at nightfall to carry the milk, was frightened by the sight of a cobra in the path and refused to go again, it was one of the monks themselves who took his place in this humble office. Some novice would be deputed daily, to deal with the strange problems of our Indian house-keeping. Another was appointed to give Bengali lessons. Visits of ceremony and of kindness were frequently paid us by the older members of the community. And finally, when the Swami Vivekananda himself was absent for some weeks on a journey, his place was always duly taken at the morning tea-table by someone or another who felt responsible for the happiness and entertainment of his guests. In these and a thousand similar ways, we came in touch with those who could reveal to us the shining memory that formed the warp, on which, as woof, were woven all these lives of renunciation.

Monastic Hospitality

For they had only one theme, these monastic visitants of ours, and that was their Master Sri Ramakrishna and his great disciple. The Swami had now been back with them for thirteen or fourteen months only, and scarcely yet had they recovered from their first pleasure and surprise.

Before that, he had been practically lost to them for some six years. It was true that of late he had corresponded with them freely and that for no time had they been long, altogether off his track. And yet, when his first success in America had been heard of, most of his brethren had had only their confidence in the great mission foretold by his Master, to tell them that it was he.

Those who have witnessed here or there some great life of asceticism, will recognise a mood of passionate longing to lose one's own identity, to be united with the lowliest and most hidden things, to go forth from amongst men and be no more remembered by them, as an element in the impulse of renunciation. This is which explains, as I think, the long silence and seclusion in caves; the garb of mud and ashes, so often worn as a man wanders from forest to forest, and village to village; and a thousand other features of this type of religion, which to the Western onlooker might seem inexplicable. This mood would seem to have been much with the Swami in the early years after the passing of his Master. And again and again, he must have left the little band of brethren, in the hope never to be heard of more. Once he was brought back from such an expedition by the community itself, who heard that he was lying ill at a place called Hathras, and sent to take him home. For such was the love that bound them all to each other, and especially to him, that they could not rest without nursing him themselves. A few months later he was followed to the monastery by a disciple whom he had called to himself during his wanderings. This man's name, in religion, was Sadananda, and from his account, with its strong broken English, I glean the record of the life that was lived at this period in the monastery. When he arrived—it had taken him some two or three months, by means of railway service, to earn his way to Calcutta from his old home—he found the Swami on the point of setting out once more. But for his sake, this journey was abandoned, and the departure that was to have taken place that evening did not occur till twelve months later, "The Swami's mission began with me," says this first disciple proudly, referring to this time.

A First Recruit

During this year, he the Master, "would work twenty-four hours at a time. He was lunatic-like, he was so busy!" Early in the morning, while it was still dark, he would rise and call the others, signing "Awake! Awake! All ye who would drink of the divine nectar!" Then all would proceed to meditation, afterwards drifting almost unconsciously into singing and talking, which would last till noon or even later. From hymns and chanting they would pass into history. Sometimes it would be the story of Ignatius Loyola; again Joan of Arc, or the Rani of Jhansi; and yet again the Swami would recite long passages from Carlyle's French Revolution, and they would all sway themselves backwards and forwards dreamily, repeating together *"Vive Ia Rèpublique! Vive Ia Rèpublique!"* Or the subject of their reveries might be St. Francis of Assisi, and with the same unconscious instinct of the dramatist, they would lose themselves in an endless identification with his "Welcome, sister Death!" It might perhaps be one or two o'clock when Ramakrishnananda—the cook, housekeeper and retualist of the community—would drive them all with threats to bathe and eat. But after this, they would 'again group'—again would go on the song and talk, till at last evening had come bringing with it the time for the two hours of *Arati* to Sri Ramakrishna. As often as not, even this would scarcely break the absorption, again would come the trances of meditation. Or on the roof, till long after midnight it might be, they would sit and chant "Hail Sita-Rama!" The special festivals of all religions brought each their special forms of celebration. At Christmas time, for instance, they would recline, with long shepherds' crooks, around a lighted log, and talk in low tones of the coming of the angels to the lonely watchers by

The First Love

their flocks, and the singing of the world's first Gloria. Very curious is the story of how they kept Good Friday. Hour after hour had gone by and they had risen gradually to that terrible exaltation of spirit which comes to those who give themselves to that day. Food was not to be thought of, but they had contrived to have by them a few grapes, and the juice was squeezed out and mixed with water, to be drunk out of a single cup by all. In the midst of such scenes, the voice of a European was heard at the door, calling on them in the name of Christ. With inexpressible delight they swarmed down on him, twelve or fifteen men of them, eager to hear of the day from the lips of a Christian."— But he said he belonged to the Salvation Army and knew nothing about Good Friday. They only kept General Booth's birthday and something else, I forget what," said Sadananda, and in the cloud that overcast the face and voice of the teller, one could realize the sudden depression that fell, at this discovery, upon the monks, It seems that in their first disappointment, they snatched his Bible from the unfortunate missionary, saying he was not worthy to possess it, and drove him forth. It is said however that one of their number stole round by another door and brought him back to eat and have his property secretly restored to him.

"Those were hot days," says the teller of the tale with his face aglow, "there was no minute of rest. Outsiders came and went, pundits argued and discussed. But, he, the Swami, was never for one moment idle, never dull. Sometimes he was left alone for a while and he would walk up and down, saying, 'Hari bol! bol! bol! Call on the Lord! Call! Call!' or 'Oh Mother!' in all these ways preparing himself for his great work. And I watched all the time from a distance and in some interval said, 'Sir, will you not eat?—always to be answered playfully." Sometimes the talk took place while cooking was going on or during the service of the altar, offices in which all shared without distinction. For in spite of the poverty of those days, many came to the monks to be fed. Their own resources were scanty. They had only one piece of cloth amongst them that was good enough to be worn across the shoulders, outside the monastery. So this was kept on a line and used by anyone who went out. And they could afford no more. Yet food was found somehow for the poor and for guests, and many came for help or teaching. They begged funds enough also, to buy and distribute some hundreds of copies of the *Bhagavad Gita* and the *Imitation of Christ*, the two favourite books of the Order at that time. "Silence, all ye teachers! And silence, ye prophets! Speak Thou alone, O Lord, unto my soul!" was,

The Great Preparation

Glimpses of Early Days

years after, a sentence that the Swami quoted at a venture as all that he then remembered of Thomas à Kempis. For it is perhaps needless to say that while this book took its place by degrees amongst experiences remembered, the *Gita* grew every day in fullness of power and beauty in the minds of these Hindu children of Ramakrishna.

So passed some twelve months. Then the Swami went away to Ghazipur to visit Pavhari Baba,* that saint whom he always held second only to Ramakrishna. He came back in a couple of months to share the treasure he had gained with others. Suddenly news came that one of the brothers by name Yogananda, was lying ill with smallpox at Allahabad and a party followed by the Swami, started to nurse him.

At Allahabad, to take up once more Sadananda's account, many days were passed in religious education. It was as if Yogananda's sickness had been a mere incident, a call given through him and the whole town came and went in a great stirring. Small groups would enter and leave, in a constant succession for days and nights together, the swami being always in his highest and greatest mood. On one occasion he saw a Mohammedan saint, a Paramahamsa, "whose every line and curve told that he was a Paramahamsa," and this was the occasion of a great hour.

* Pavhari Baba was a saint who lived near Ghazipur. He died by burning in 1898.

"Sometimes naked, sometimes mad,
Now as a scholar, again as a fool,
Here a rebel, there a saint,
Thus they appear on the earth, the
Paramahamsas."

—So repeating 'The Marks of the Paramahamsas' from the *Vivekachudamani* of Sankaracharya, there passed, as the disciple would put it, 'a whole night fermenting'. Such experiences lasted perhaps for two weeks, and then the party left Allahabad, and by twos and threes returned to the monastery in the village of Baranagore on the banks of the Ganges. But now there came a time in the year 1890, when the Swami left his brothers, not to return till the great triumph of the year 1897.

The Wandering Friar

This time he set out with a monk known as Akhandananda, who took him to Almora and left him there, enjoying the hospitality of a family who had formerly befriended himself on a journey to Tibet. It is said that on the way up the mountains, the Swami one day fainted with hunger, when a poor Mohammedan found him, and prepared and gave him a cucumber which practically saved his life. How long the brothers had been without food I do not know. It may have been that at this time, as certainly later, he was under the vow to ask for nothing, waiting always for food and drink till they were offered.

He told someone who knew him during that period and questioned him, that the longest time he had ever gone without food, under this austerity, was five days.

After this, the thread of his wanderings was lost. He wrote occasionally, but the monks themselves were scattered. 'It has been so dull after they lost him!' says the narrator. And even the first home had to be abandoned, for the landlord talked of rebuilding. There was one monk, however, Ramakrishnananda by name, who would not leave the ashes of their Master, but vowed with rock-like determination to keep a roof overhead, come storm, come shine, so to speak, for them and for his brothers, till they should all foregather in their worship-room once more. He, then, with Nirmalananda, the occasional resident, one Premananda and the new member of the fold as 'dish-washer', removed to a house some distance away, but still in the immediate neighbourhood of Dakshineswar, and the monastery which had previously been at Baranagore was now known as the Alumbazar Math.

The Leader Lost

Akhandananda at this time, was always 'chasing', always in pursuit of the absent leader. Every now and then he would hear of him in some town and would arrive there, only in time to hear that he was gone, leaving no trace.

Once the Swami Trigunatita found himself in trouble in a Guzerati state, when someone said that a Bengali *Sādhu* was staying with the Prime Minister, and if he appealed to him, would surely give him aid. He made his appeal, and found that the unknown *Sādhu* was the Swami himself. But he, after rendering the assistance that was needed, sent his brother onwards, and himself proceeded alone. The great words of Buddha, constantly quoted by him, "Even as the lion, not trembling at noises, even as the wind, not caught in a net, even as the lotus leaf untouched by the water, so do thou wander alone, like the rhinoceros!" were the guiding principle of his life at this time.

It had been at Almora, as we now know, that news reached him, of the death in pitiful extremity, of the favourite sister of his childhood and he had fled into the wilder mountains, leaving no clue. To one who, years after, saw deep into his personal experience, it seemed that this death had inflicted on the Swami's heart a wound, whose quivering pain had never for one moment ceased. And we may, perhaps, venture to trace some part at least of his burning desire for the education and development of Indian women to this sorrow.

At this time he passed some months in a cave overhanging a mountain village. Only twice have I known him to allude to his experience. Once he said, "Nothing in my whole life ever so filled me with the sense of work to be done. It was as if I were *thrown out* from that life in caves to wander to and fro in the plains below." And again he said to someone, "It is not the form of his life that makes a *Sadhu*. For it is possible to sit in a cave and have one's whole mind filled with the question of how many pieces of bread will be brought to one for supper!"

A Vow of Pilgrimage

It was perhaps at the end of this period, and in expression of that propulsive energy of which he spoke, that he made a vow to worship the Mother at Cape Comorin. In carrying this out, he was lavish of time, yet it must have taken him only about two years to accomplish the vow. In the course of his wanderings towards this end, he seems to have touched upon and studied every phase of Indian life. The stories of this period are never ended. The list of the friends he made is never full. He received the initiation of the Sikhs; studied the Mimansa Philosophy with Mahratta pundits; and the Jain Scriptures with Jains; was accepted as their *Guru* by Rajput princes; lived for weeks with a family of sweepers in Central India; was able to observe at first-hand such obscure questions as the caste-customs of Malabar; saw many of the historic sights and natural beauties of his mother-land, and finally reached Cape Comorin too poor to pay for a seat in a ferry-boat to the shrine of Kanya Kumari, and swam across the strait to the Island, in spite of sharks, to offer the worship he had vowed.* It was on his return northwards through Madras, that he formed the strong group of disciples who became the means of sending him to America, for which country he sailed finally from Bombay about the beginning of June 1893.

The Call of Destiny

Even this however he was not eager to do. His disciples in Madras still tell how the first five hundred rupees collected for the object were immediately spent by him in worship and charity, as if he would *force* on his own destiny, as it were, the task of driving him forth. Even when he reached Bombay, he was still waiting for the feeling of certainty. Struggling to refuse the undertaking, he felt as if the form of his own Master appeared to him constantly, and urged him to go. At last, he wrote secretly to Sarada Devi, the widow of Sri Ramakrishna, begging her, if she could, to advise and bless him, and charging her to tell no one of this new departure, till she could hear from him again. It was only

* The author herself did not visit this pilgrimage. So a slight mistake has crept into the narration. The fact is, there is a small rocky island on the South of the Shrine, separated by a short strait; Swamiji in his desire to go outside India swam across the strait to the island. —Ed.

after receiving, in answer to this letter, her warm encouragement and the assurance of her prayers, that he actually left India for the West. Now, at last, there was no escaping fate. That quest of forgottenness that had first borne him out of the doors of the monastery, had led him also to change his name in each Indian village that he reached. And in later years someone heard from him how, after his first great speech at Chicago, the mingling of the bitterness of this defeat with the cup of his triumphant achievement, racked his consciousness all night long. He stood now in the glare of publicity. The unknown beggar could remain unknown no more!

In this wanderings through India, I find the third and final element, in my Master's realisation of that great body of truth, which was to find in him at once its witness and its demonstration.

There can be no doubt, I think, that the formative influences in his life were three-fold; first, his education in English and Sanskrit literature; second, the great personality of his Guru, illustrating and authenticating that life which formed the theme of all the sacred writings; and thirdly, as I would maintain his personal knowledge of India and the Indians peoples, as an immense religious organism, of which his Master himself, with all his greatness, had been only, as it were, the personification and utterance. And these three sources can, as I think, be distinctly traced in his various utterances. When he preaches Vedanta and upholds before the world the philosophy of his people, he is for the most part drawing upon the Sanskrit books of past ages, though, it is true, with a clearness and certainty of touch that could only be the result of having seen them summed up in a single wonderful life. When he talks of *Bhakti* as "a devotion beginning, continuing and ending in love," or when he analyzes Karma Yoga, 'the secret of work,' we see before us the very personality of the Master himself, we realize that the disciple is but struggling to tell of that glorified atmosphere in which he himself has dwelt at the feet of another. But when we read his speech before the Chicago Conference, or his equally remarkable 'Reply to the Madras Address,' or the lectures in which at Lahore in 1897, he portrayed the lineaments of a generalized and essential Hinduism, we find ourselves in presence of something gathered by his own labours, out of his own experience. The power behind all these utterances lay in those Indian wanderings of which the tale can probably never be complete. It was of this first-hand knowledge, then, and not of vague sentiment or willful blindness, that his reverence for his own people and their land was born. It was a robust

Formative Influences

and cumulative induction, moreover, be it said, ever hungry for new facts, and dauntless in the face of hostile criticism. "'The common bases of Hinduism had,' as he once said, 'been the study of his whole life.' And more than this, it was the same thorough and first-hand knowledge that made the older and simpler elements in Hindu civilisation loom so large in all his conceptions of his race and country. Possessed of a modern education that ranked with the most advanced in his own country, he yet could not, like some moderns, ignore the *Sannyāsin* or the peasant, the idolater or the caste-ridden, as elements in the great whole called India. And this determined inclusiveness was due to that life in which he had for years together been united with them.

It must be remembered, however, that we have not entirely analyzed a great career when we have traced, to their origin in the personal experience, those ideas which form its dominant notes. There is still the original impulse, the endowment of perennial energy that makes the world-spectacle so much more full of meaning to one soul than to another, to be accounted for. And

His love of the People

I have gathered that from his cradle Vivekananda had a secret instinct that told him he was born to help his country. He was proud afterwards to remember that amidst the temporal vicissitudes of his early days in America, when sometimes he did not know where to turn for the next meal, his letters to his disciples in India showed that this innate faith of his had never wavered. Such an indomitable hope resides assuredly in all souls who are born to carry out any special mission. It is a deep unspoken consciousness of greatness, of which life itself is to be the sole expression. To Hindu thinking, there is a difference as of the poles, between such consciousness of greatness and vanity, and this is seen, as I think, in the Swami himself at the moment of his first meeting with Sri Ramakrishna, when he was decidedly repelled, rather than attracted, by what he regarded as the old man's exaggerated estimate of his powers and of himself.

The Master's Recognition

He had come, a lad of eighteen, as a member of a party visiting Dakshineshwar, and someone, probably knowing the unusual quality of his voice and his knowledge of music, suggested that he should sing. He responded with a song of Ram Mohan Roy's,* ending with the words, "And for support keep the treasure in secret—purity."

This seems to have acted like a signal—"My boy! My boy!" cried Sri Ramakrishna, "I have been looking for you these three years, and you have come at last!" From that day the older man may be said to have devoted himself to welding

* The song in question was composed by Sj. Ajodhyanath Pakrasi.

the lads about him into a brotherhood whose devotion to 'Noren', as the Swami was then called, would be unswerving. He was never tired of foretelling his great fame, nor of pointing out the superiority of his genius. If most men had two, or three, or even ten or twelve gifts, he said, he could only say of Noren that his numbered a thousand. He was in fact "the thousand-petalled lotus", Even amongst the great, while he would allow that with one might be found some "two of those gifts which are the marks of *Śiva*," Noren had at least eighteen of such.

He was sensitive to the point of physical pain himself, in his discrimination of hypocrisy and on one occasion refused to accept a man whose piety of life was regarded by those about him as unimpugnable. The man, he said, with all his decorum, was a whited sepulchre*. In spite of constant purification, his presence was contamination, while Noren, on the other hand, if he were to eat beef in an English hotel, would nevertheless be holy, so holy that his very touch would convey holiness to others. By such sayings, he sought constantly to build up an enduring relation, based firmly on essentials, between those who were to be his supporters, and this disciple who was to lead.

---

* An evil person who feigns goodness; hypocrite. Bible, Matthew 23:27.

Vivekananda's Past

It was his habit, when a new disciple came to him, to examine him mentally and physically in all possible ways. For the human body was to his trained eye, as significant in all its parts, as any model of a machine to a skilled scientific observer. These examinations moreover would include the throwing of the newcomer into a sleep, in which he had access to the subconscious mind. The privileged, as I have been told, were permitted in this condition to relate their own story; while from the less honoured it was evoked by means of questions. It was after such an examination of 'Noren' that the Master told all about him, that when the day should come for this boy to realize who and what he was, he would refuse for a moment longer to endure the bondage of bodily existence, going out from life, with its limitations. And by this was always understood by the disciples, the remembering by the lad of what he had already attained even in this world, in lives anterior to his present consciousness. No menial service to himself was permitted by Sri Ramakrishna from this particular follower. Fanning, the preparation of tobacco, and the thousand and one little attentions commonly rendered to the Guru, all these had to be offered to the Master by others.

Amongst the many quaint-seeming customs of the East, none is more deep-rooted than the

The Roaring Fire

prejudice against eating food cooked by one who is not respected. And on this point, the Swami's Master was as sensitive as a woman. But what he would not eat himself he would give freely to his favourite disciple, for Noren, he said, was the "roaring fire", burning up all impurity. The core of divinity again, in this boy's nature was masculine in its quality, as compared to his own merely feminine. Thus, by an attitude of admiration, not unmixed with actual reverence, he created a belief in the destiny of this particular lad, which, when he himself had passed away, was to stand him in good stead, in furnishing authenticity and support to his work. For the Swami was nothing, if not a breaker of bondage. And it was essential that there should be those about him who understood the polar difference between his breaches of custom and those of the idly self-indulgent. Nothing in the early days of my life in India struck me so forcibly or so repeatedly as the steadiness with which the other members of the Order fulfilled this part of the mission laid upon them. Men whose own lives were cast in the strictest mould of Hindu orthodoxy, or even of asceticism, were willing to eat with the Europeans whom their leader had accepted. Was the Swami seen dining in Madras with an Englishman and his wife? Was it said that while in the West he had touched beef or wine? Not a quiver was seen on the faces of his brethren. It was not for them to question, not for them to explain, not even for them to ask for final justification and excuse. Whatever he did, wherever he might lead, it was their place to be found unflinching at his side. And surely none can pass this spectacle in review, without its being borne in upon him, that meaningless as would have been the Order of Ramakrishna without Vivekananda, even so futile would have been the life and labours of Vivekananda, without, behind him, his brothers of the Order of Ramakrishna. It was said to me lately by one of the older generation that "Ramakrishna had lived for the making of Vivekananda". Is it indeed so? Or is it not rather impossible to distinguish with such fixity between one part and another, in a single mighty utterance of the Divine Mother-heart? Often it appears to me, in studying all these lives, that there has been with us a soul named Ramakrishna-Vivekananda, and that, in the penumbra of his being, appear many forms, some of which are with us still, and of none of whom it could be said with entire truth that there ends, in relation to him, the sphere of those others, or that there begins his own.

V

Wanderings in Northern India

The summer of 1898 stands out in my memory as a series of pictures, painted like old altar pieces, against a golden background of religious ardour and simplicity, and all alike glorified by the presence of one who, to us in his immediate circle, formed their central point. We were a party of four Western women, one of whom was Mrs. Ole Bull of Cambridge, Massachusetts, and another a member of the higher official world of Anglo-Indian Calcutta. Side by side with us travelled the Swami, surrounded by his brethren (or *gurubhāīs*) and disciples. Once arrived at Almora, he and his party became the guests of Mr. and Mrs. Sevier, who were then residing there, and we occupied a bungalow some distance away. Thus pleasantly grouped, it was possible to combine a high degree of freedom and intercourse. But when, after a month or so, we left Almora for Kashmir, the Swami went with us, as the guest of Mrs. Ole Bull, and left behind him all his attendants.

The Peasant's Welcome

What scenes were those through which we journeyed from the beginning of May until the end of October! And with what passionate enthusiasm were we introduced one by one to each point of interest, as we reached it! The ignorance of educated Western people about India—excepting of course those who have in some measure specialized on the subject—might almost be described as illiteracy, and our object-lessons began, I have no doubt, with Patna, the ancient Pataliputra, itself. The river-front of Benares, as one approaches it by railway from the East, is amongst the sights of the world, and could not fail of our leader's eager praise. The industries and luxuries of Lucknow must need to be dwelt upon and enumerated. But it was not only the great cities of admitted beauty and historic importance, that the Swami, in his eagerness, would strive to impress on our memory. Perhaps nowhere did his love seem more ardent, or his absorption more intense, than as we passed across the long stretched of the Plains covered with fields and farms and villages. Here his thought was free to brood over the land as a whole and he would spend hours explaining the communal system of agriculture, or describing the daily life of the farm housewife, with such details as that of the *pot-āu-feu* of mixed grains left boiling all night, for the morning porridge. It was the memory, doubtless, of his own days as a wanderer, that so brightened his eyes and thrilled in his voice, as he told us these things. For I had heard it said by *sadhus* that there is no hospitality in India like that of the humble peasant home. True, the mistress had no better bedding to offer than straw, no better shelter than an outhouse built of mud. But it is she who steals in at the last moment, before she goes to rest herself amongst her sleeping household, to place a tooth-brush twig and a bowl of milk where the guest will find them, on waking in the morning, that he may go forth from beneath her roof comforted and refreshed.

It would seem sometimes as if the Swami lived and moved and had his very being in the sense of his country's past. His historic consciousness was extraordinarily developed. Thus, as we journeyed across the Terai, in the hot hours of an afternoon near the beginning of the rains, we were made to feel that this was the very earth on which had passed the youth and renunciation of Buddha. The wild peacocks spoke to us of Rajputana and her ballad lore. An Occasional elephant was the text for tales of ancient battles, and the story of an India that was never defeated, so long as she could oppose to the tide of conquest the military walls of these living artillery.

A Righteous Ruler

As we had crossed the boundary from Bengal into the North-west Provinces, the Swami had stopped to tell us of the wisdom and methods of the great and merciful English ruler who was at that time at the head of their administration. "Unlike others," he said, in words that impressed my memory at the time, "he understands the need of personal government in Oriental countries, where a strong public opinion is not yet developed, so no hospital, no college, no office knows the day when he will pay it a visit of inspection. And even the poorest believes that if only he can reach him personally, he will receive justice at his hands." This idea of the importance of personality in Eastern governments often came uppermost in his talk. He constantly spoke of a democracy as theoretically the worst form for an imperial government to take. And one of his favourite speculations was that it had been a perception of this truth that had urged Julius Caesar on, to aspire to the imperial authority. We realized sometimes, as we listened to him, how hard it had been for the Indian poor, to understand the transition from the personal rule of sovereigns, always accessible to appeal, always open to the impulse of mercy, and able to exercise a supreme discretion, to the cold bureaucratic methods of a series of departments. For we heard from him the personal histories of innumerable simple folk, who, in the early years of British rule, had spent their all in the vain hope of reaching the Queen, and gaining her ear, at Windsor. Heart-broken pilgrims for the most part, who died, of want and disillusionment, far from the homes and villages that they would never see again!

Love of the Punjab

It was as we passed into the Punjab, however, that we caught our deepest glimpse of the Master's love of his own land. Anyone who had seen him here, would have supposed him to have been born in the province, so intensely had he identified himself with it. It would seem that he had been deeply bound to the people there by many ties of love and reverence; had received much and given much; for there were some amongst them who urged that they found in him a rare mixture of 'Guru Nanak and Guru Govind,' their first teacher and their last. Even the most suspicious amongst them trusted him. And if they refused to credit his judgment, or endorse his outflowing sympathy, in regard to those Europeans whom he had made his own, he, it may have been, loved the wayward hearts all the more for their inflexible condemnation and incorruptible sternness. His American disciples were already familiar with his picture—

that called to his own face a dreamy delight—of the Punjabi maiden at her spinning wheel, listening to its "Shivoham! Shivoham! I am He! I am He!" Yet at the same time, I must not forget to tell that it was here, on entering the Punjab, even as, near the end of his life, he is said to have done again at Benares, that he called to him a Mussalman vendor of sweetmeats, and bought and ate from his hand Mohammedan food.

As we went through some village, he would point out to us those strings of marigolds above the door, that distinguished the Hindu homes. Again he would show us the pure golden tint of skin, so different from the pink and white of the European ideal, that constitutes the 'fairness' admitted by the Indian races. Or as one drove beside him in a tonga, he would forget all, in that tale of which he never wearied, of *Śiva*, the Great God, silent, remote upon the mountains, asking nothing of men but solitude, and 'lost in one eternal meditation.'

We drove from Rawalpindi to Murree, where we spent a few days. And then, partly by tonga, partly by boat, we proceeded to Srinagar in Kashmir, and made it our centre and headquarters, during the wanderings of the following months.

It would be easy to lose oneself here in the beauty of our journeys, in descriptions of

Beauty of Kashmir

mountain forests on the road to Almora, or of cathedral rocks and corn-embosomed villages in the Jhelum Pass. For, as one returns upon that time, its record is found in a constant succession of scenes of loveliness. Not least of these pictures is the memory of the handsome old woman, wearing the crimson coronet and white veil of Kashmiri peasants, who sat at her spinning wheel under a great chennar tree* in a farm-yard, surrounded by her daughters-in-law, when we passed that way, and stopped to visit her. It was the Swami's second call on her. He had received some small kindness at her hands the year before, and had never tired of telling how after this, when he had asked, before saying farewell, "—And, mother, of what religion are you?" her whole face had lighted up with pride and joy, and her old voice had rung out in triumph as she answered loudly and clearly, "I thank our God, by the mercy of the Lord, I am a Mussalman!"

Or I might tell of the avenue of lofty Lombardy poplars outside Srinagar, so like the well-known picture by Hobbema, where we listened to discourse after discourse on India and the Faith.

Or I might linger over the harvest merriment of the villagers, playing in reaped fields on moonlit evenings; or talk of the red bronze of

---

* The Chennar tree is the Oriental Palm

amaranth crops, or the green of young rice under tall poplars at Islamabad. Forget-me-nots of a brilliant blue form the commonest wildflower of the Kashmiri fields in summer; but in autumn and spring, fields and river banks are violet-tinged with small purple irises, and one walks amongst their spearlike leaves as if they were grass. How infinitely tender are the suggestions of those little iris-covered hillocks, rounding off the rise of some roadside against the sky, that mark the burial places of the Mussalman dead!

Apple-tree and Irises

Here and there, too, amidst grass and irises, one comes on groups of gnarled apple trees, or pear, or plum, the remains of the village orchards which the State, once upon a time, supplied to all its subjects free of cost. Walking here once at twilight along the high banks of the river, I watched a party of Mussalman herdsmen, crooks in hand, driving a small flock of long-haired goats before them to their village. And then, as they came to a knot of apple trees, they stopped a while, and spreading a blanket for praying carpet, they proceeded to offer their evening worship in the deepening dusk. Verily, says my heart, there is no end of beauty. There is no end.

But in good sooth it is not of these things that I am attempting, in the course of the present pages, to speak. Mine is the broken and faltering witness of one who is fain to tell—not of geography nor of polities, nor yet of the ways and customs of interesting peoples and unknown races, but rather of the glimpses vouchsafed to her of a great religious life of the ancient order, living itself out, amidst the full and torturing consciousness of all the anomalies and perplexities of the Modern Transition. Sri Ramakrishna had been, as the Swami himself said once of him, "like a flower," living apart in the garden of a temple, simple, half-naked, orthodox, the ideal of the old time in India, suddenly burst into bloom in a world that had thought to dismiss its very memory. It was at once the greatness and the tragedy of my own Master's life that he was not of this type. His was the modern mind in its completeness. In his consciousness, the ancient light of the mood in which man comes face to face with God might shine, but it shone on all those questions and all those puzzles which are present to the thinkers and workers of the modern world. His hope could not pass by unheeded—it might include or it might reject—the hope of men of the nineteenth century. That sudden revelation of the misery and struggle of humanity as a whole, which has been the first result of the limelight irradiation of facts by the organisation of knowledge, had been made to him also, as

The Modern Despair

to the European mind. We know the verdict that Europe has passed on it all. Our art, our science, our poetry, for the last sixty years or more, are filled with the voices of our despair. A world summed up in the growing satisfaction and vulgarity of privilege and the growing sadness and pain of the dispossessed; and a will of man too noble and high to condone the evil, yet too feeble to avert or arrest it, this is the spectacle of which our greatest minds are aware. Reluctant, wringing her hands, it is true, yet seeing no other way, the culture of the West can but stand and cry, "To him that hath shall be given, and from him that hath not shall be taken away even that which he hath. *Vae Victis!* Woe to the Vanquished!"

Is this also the verdict of the Eastern wisdom? If so, what hope is there for humanity? I find in my Master's life an answer to this question. I see in him the heir to the spiritual discoveries and religious struggles of innumerable teachers and saints in the past of India and the world, and at the same time the pioneer and prophet of a new and future order of development. In the place which a problem took in his mind, I find evidence regarding its final solution which—short of my own definite arrival at an opposite conclusion, as he himself would have been the first to point out—is of the highest value to

The Answer of the East

myself. And thinking thus, I believe that each trace of those higher and uncommon modes of thought and consciousness to which he held the key, has its significance for the modern age. I believe that much which has passed myself by, uncomprehending, will fall on its proper soil in other lives. And I pray only to give always true witness, without added interpolation, or falsifying colour.

VI

The Awakener of Souls

I had heard of 'the spiritual life' in Calcutta, as of a thing definite and accessible, to be chosen deliberately, and attained by following certain well-known paths. I found it, on reaching the mountains, to have its roots deep in a yearning love of God, in an anguished pursuit of the Infinite, of which I cannot hope to give any description. For this was characteristic of our Master. Where others would talk of ways and means, he knew how to light a fire. Where others gave directions, he would show the thing itself.

I wish here to be exceedingly explicit. My own part, throughout the years of my discipleship, appears to me to have been something like that of a thought-reader. The only claim that I can make is that I was able to enter sufficiently into the circuit of my Master's energy to be able to give evidence regarding it from direct perception. And since I believe that such an experience is subject to laws as definite as those of any physical force, I must endeavour to describe accurately the conditions under which this happened to me.

Personal Reserve

The Swami himself was, on personal subjects, intensely reserved. He had received confessions, of course, in many parts of the world, yet no one ever lived who more anxiously sought to escape the office of spiritual director. A hot flush and an accession of delicate *hauteur* were his immediate response, even to such merely theoretical questions as appeared to him to demand too intimate a revelation of the personal experience. I have sometimes heard enquiries forced upon him in his London classes—as to such matters as the feeling which accompanies *Samadhi*, for instance—when it was clear to all listeners that he would rather have endured a careless touch upon an exposed nerve.

He had himself suggested my joining his travelling party, for the purpose of receiving his personal training for the work he wished me to do in India. But the method of this training proved entirely general. We would sit all together in the garden or verandah, and listen, all together, to the discourse of the hour, each appropriating as much as she chose, and studying afterwards as she liked.

In all that year of 1898, I can remember only one occasion when the Swami invited me to walk alone with him for half an hour, and then our conversation—for it was towards the end of the summer, when I had begun to understand my own position a little—was rather of the policy and aims of the future, than of anything more subjective.

Undoubtedly, in the circle that gathers round a distinguished thinker, there are hidden emotional relationships which form the channels, as it were, along which his ideas circulate and are received. Even a mathematician will succeed in impressing himself on his generation, only in proportion to the radiance of feeling on which his thought is carried, But these expressions are wholly impersonal, and are appreciated by different receivers in very different ways. One holds himself as servant; another, as brother, friends, or comrade; a third may even regard the master-personality as that of a beloved child. These things have been made into a perfect science in India, and it is there boldly understood and accepted that without some such dramatisation of their own relation to it, ordinary minds cannot be made susceptible of a great religious impulse. In my own case the position ultimately taken proved that most happy one of a spiritual daughter, and as such I was regarded by all the Indian people and communities, whom I met during my Master's life.

The Drama of Thought

But at the beginning of these journeys, before this and other things became clear to me, my mind was wholly in bewilderment, and it was my great good fortune that I was given at this time, as my daily teacher in Bengali and in Hindu religious literature, the young monk known as the Swami Swarupananda. For I have always thought that it was to the fact that I found myself on the line of communication between his mind and that of our Master—as on the pathway of interaction between some major and minor heliograph—that I owed my ability thereafter to read and understand a little of those feelings and ideals with which the air about us was charged.

The Swami Swarupananda

The Swami Swarupananda had been received at the Monastery within a few days of my own admission, in the chapel there, to the vows of a novice. But he, after some few weeks of probation, had received the yellow cloth, and taken the rank of a *Sannyāsin*, at the hands of the Swami. The story of his mental development was of extraordinary interest to me. For this man had been brought up in his childhood in the Vaishnava faith, that is to say, in an idea of God as the kind and loving Lord and Preserver of men, and of Krishna as the Saviour and Divine Incarnation, which is practically tantamount to the Christianity of the West. The usual revulsion, familiar to all of us, had been encountered. In the early and most chivalrous years of manhood, he had witnessed a few instances of the injustice of life, had seen bitter proof that the battle in this world was to the strong, and found himself unable to believe longer in the sweet myth of his childhood, of an all-kind Providence. One of these stories I remember. Passing through a crowded street one day, he found a poor woman kneeling and crying softly, as, grain by grain, she picked up from the dust a handful of rice, that had been jostled out of the bowl in her hand, by a passer-by. And then the man found himself in his passionate pity, crying indignantly, "What the devil would God be doing, if He existed, to let such things happen?"

Two or three such experiences precipitated him upon a year of mental suffering so keen that he never again knew perfect health. But he emerged from it in the peace that comes of a settled attitude towards life. *He would break the dream.* In other words, he had reached the conclusion that thousands of Indian students had arrived at, both before and since the time of Buddha. It was henceforth impossible to him to imagine that the solution of the problem might ultimately be found in any picture of God seated on a throne, and the soul of man, in any attitude or relation, kneeling before Him. Rather, he saw

The Dream of Duality

in the ignorance and selfishness of the mind itself, the source of all such dreams as this, and of those further dreams, of pain and pleasure, of justice and injustice, of which the world, as we know it, is made up. And he determined to conquer this illusion, to reach the point of utmost insight and certainty, to gain deliverance from the perception of opposites, and to attain to that permanent realisation of Oneness which is known, in the Hindu conception of life, as *Mukti*.

From this time on, his schooling of himself to reach the highest would appear to have become a passion. One came to understand, in many ways, that the remaining years of his life in his father's house had been almost more severe than those spent in most monasteries. And I, reading the Bhagavad Gita under his guidance, long afterwards at Almora, was made able to conceive of what we call the love of God as burning thirst.

Under the influence of the Swami Swarupananda, I began seriously the attempt at meditation. And if it had not been for this help of his, one of the greatest hours of my life would have passed me by. My relation to our Master at this time can only be described as one of clash and conflict. I can see now how much there was to learn, and how short was the time for learning to be, and the first of lessons doubtless is the destroying of self-sufficiency in the mind of the taught. But I had been little prepared for that constant rebuke and attack upon all my most cherished prepossessions which was now my lot. Suffering is often illogical and I cannot attempt to justify by reason the degree of unhappiness which I experienced at this time, as I saw the dream of a friendly and beloved leader falling away from me, and the picture of one who would be at least indifferent, and possibly, silently hostile, substituting itself instead.

The Birth of Peace

Fortunately, it never occurred to me to retract my own proffered service, but I was made to realise, as the days went by, that in this there would be no personal sweetness. And then a time came when one of the older ladies of our party, thinking perhaps that such intensity of pain inflicted might easily go too far, interceded kindly and gravely with the Swami. He listened silently and went away. At evening however, he returned and finding us together in the verandah, he turned to her and said with the simplicity of a child, "You were right. There must be a change. I am going away into the forests to be alone, and when I come back I shall bring peace." Then he turned and saw that above us the moon was new, and a sudden exaltation came into his voice as he said, "See! The Mohammedans think much of the new moon. Let us also with the new moon begin a new life!" As the words ended, he lifted his hands and blessed, with silent depths of blessing, his most rebellious disciple, by this time kneeling before him... It was assuredly a moment of wonderful sweetness of reconciliation. But such a moment may heal a wound. It cannot restore an illusion that has been broken into fragments. And I have told its story, only that I may touch upon its sequel. Long, long ago, Sri Ramakrishna had told his disciples that the day would come when his beloved 'Noren' would manifest his own great gift of bestowing knowledge with a touch. That evening at Almora, I proved the truth of his prophecy. For alone, in meditation, I found myself gazing deep into an Infinite Good, to the recognition of which no egoistic reasoning had led me. I learnt, too, on the physical plane, the simple everyday reality of the experience related in the Hindu books on religious psychology. And I understood for the first time, that the greatest teachers may destroy in us a personal relation only in order to bestow the Impersonal Vision in its place.

VII

Flashes From the Beacon-Fire

This was not perhaps the only experience of its kind, but it was certainly the only one to which I need to refer in detail, and the whole incident of which it formed a part gave me the clue to the attitude which the Eastern teacher demands of a disciple. Before all things, this attitude must be one of passivity. I have also heard it urged, that it must be one of personal service. Under these conditions, it is said, the thoughts of the master become seeds, and germinate in the mind of the pupil. I cannot tell. My own offerings in this kind were limited to very brief and very occasional requisitions of the needle or the pen. A daughter must not at any time act, said the Swami, as if in her father's house were too few servants! Yet I do believe—for in some cases I have known its truth—that by the loving performance of humble offices for those above us, we may enter into spiritual and intellectual communion with them, which may bear strange and beautiful fruit in our own lives.

The Worship of Guru

The feeling which people of certain schools in the West devote to the Church, that mixture of perfect faith and adoring love, the Eastern disciple is called upon to render to his *Guru*, or spiritual master. It is he and his achievement, which are the power behind his follower. And the unpardonable sacrilege is a failure to acknowledge, or a repudiation of, this debt. Each will express his devotion in his own way. Greatest of all Gurus is he who realizes most deeply the freedom of the disciple. But devotion to the uttermost there must be. And dry-rot, it is believed, invades that spiritual life which seeks to base its message on itself.

We had at this time, it will be remembered, become part of a society in which solitude was regarded as the greatest medium of self-development. Nothing, said the Swami, better illustrated to his own mind, the difference between Eastern and Western methods of thought, than the European idea that a man could not live alone for twenty years, and remain quite sane, taken side by side with the Indian notion that till a man had been alone for twenty years, he could not be regarded as perfectly himself. And the contrast, though necessarily expressed with some exaggeration, is nevertheless essentially

Hindu Virtues

correct. To Hindu thinking it is only in silence and aloneness that we can drink so deep of the Impersonal Self that all the facets and angles of our personal littleness are rounded out, as by growth from within. Thus, the faces of the Buddhas, in the hour of Nirvana, are always *calm*. The world, in all its aspects and relations, is but a childish interruption of the flow of thought. Behind everything is felt to be that unutterable fullness, of which the thing seen is so paltry and distorted and expression. Human relations are too poor to tempt those who have bathed in the well-spring of all such relations at the Ultimate Source. And this Ultimate Source is not thought of here, it must be remembered, as love or compassion or heroism, though all these may be roads by which to reach it, but as the perception of Oneness, and that alone. I have always thought that this is the reason why steadiness, quiet and self-effacement are virtues so much more central, in the Hindu conception, than the more active and aggressive characteristics prized in the West. Every respect in which we, being persons, can yet be consistently indifferent to our own personalities, is so much gained.

Under the domination of these ideas, then, it appeared self-evident to all of us, in that wonderful summer of 1898, that far beyond any of the Saviours-made-visible, were those greater souls who had entered into the Impersonal and the Unmanifested, never to return. "It is a sin even to *think* of the body," the Swami would say, now and again; or, "It is wrong to *manifest* power!" And even in the compassion of a Buddha, there was memory of persons! Even in the purity of Jesus, there was manifestation!

This last thought seems to form a common motive with Indian *Sadhus*, for on one occasion when our tents had been pitched indiscreetly near a pilgrims' camp, and the Swami was half-minded to insist, against hundreds of obstreperous complainants, on leaving them where they were, a strange monk came up to him, and said in a low voice, "You *have* this power, Swamiji, but you ought not to manifest it!" And he at once had them removed.

Contempt of the Unreal

As to the power of silence and retirement to make illumination visible, we had many opportunities of judging. For over and over again the Swami would break away, to return unexpectedly. It sometimes seemed as if life in society were an agony to him. He grew nervous under the gaze of numbers of admirers who had heard of his great fame, and would enter his boat and sit watching him, leaving him no privacy. The life of the silent ashen-clad wanderer, or the hidden hermit, he thought of, it would now and then seem, as the lover might think of the beloved. At no time would it have surprised us, had someone told us that today or tomorrow he would be gone forever; that we were now listening to his voice for the last time. He, and necessarily we, in all that depended on him, were as straws carried on the Ganges of the Eternal Will. At any moment It might reveal Itself to him as silence. At any moment, life in the world might end for him.

This planlessness was not an accident. Never can I forget the disgust with which he turned on myself once, a couple of years later, when I had offered him some piece of worldly wisdom regarding his own answer to a letter which he had brought for me to see. "Plans! Plans!"; he exclaimed in indignation. "That is why you Western people can never create a religion! If any of you ever did, it was only a few Catholic saints, who had no plans. Religion was never never preached by planners!"

As it was, in the course of that pleasant summer journey, we were always liable to hear from the servants that the Swami's boat had left its moorings an hour ago, and would not return today. He might be away, in fact, either one or many days. We never knew. But always he returned from these lonely retreats with the shining of radiance and peace, and ever-deepening utterance of knowledge. To all the disciples of Ramakrishna, religious customs consecrated by the faith of others, have great significance.

One of them speaks of the Scala Santa in Rome as moving him deeply. The ideal of the Order moreover, is to participate in the worship of the accustomed devotees in every detail. Thus I have seen my own Master, when visiting holy places, make the same offerings of milk and rice, or tell his beads in the same manner, as the humblest of the women about him. The minutest rules of conduct, both secular and religious, would be scrupulously observed by him on these occasions. Thus he one-d himself with the people, before rising to his own greatest heights.

Holy Places

Two places in Kashmir are regarded as extremely sacred, one is Kshir Bhowani, a spring at which the Divine Motherhood is worshipped, and the other is Amarnath, a mountain cave in which there is an ice-emblem of *Śiva*. And the most notable events of our summer were his pilgrimages to these two shrines. But we also were ambitious. We desired to be taught to meditate, in systematic fashion, and begged to be allowed to make a retreat in some lonely place, where we might keep hours of silence, and make our attempts under definite direction. For this reason, tents were brought, and we camped for a week on the edge of a forest, at a place called Achhabal, in the beginning of September. The pilgrimage to Amarnath had been made at the beginning of August, and the Swami left us for

Kshir Bhowani on the thirtieth of September. Finally, we parted from him, and our journey was over, at Baramulla, on October the twelfth.

Even apart from the greater revelations and experiences, flashes from the beacon fire of that life in whose shadow we dwelt, fell constantly upon us. Once he had just returned from an absence, and as he sat talking of *Bhakti*, a servant came to say his meal was ready. But we could see how intolerable was the thought of food, to one who was still living on the heights of the love of God. Again it was evening, and we women-folk were seated in the boat of *Sthir Mata*, as we called our hostess, chatting in low tones, in the falling dusk, when suddenly he came in to spend a few minutes with us. The talk turned on the approaching departure for Europe, but it soon ended; and then one, who expected to be left alone in India, spoke of how the others would be missed. The Swami turned on her with a wonderful gentleness. "But why so serious about it?" he said. "Why not touch hands and part with a smile? You are so morbid, you Westerns! You worship sorrow! All through your country, I found that. Social life in the West is like a peal of laughter, but underneath, it is a wail. It ends in a sob. The fund and frivolity are all on the surface: really, it is full of tragic intensity. Now here, it is

Life and the Idea

sad and gloomy on the outside, but underneath are carelessness and merriment.

The Cosmos as play

"You know, we have a theory that the Universe is God's manifestation of Himself, just for fun, that the Incarnations came and lived here, 'just for fun.' Play, it was all play. Why was Christ crucified? It was mere play. And so of life. Just play with the Lord. Say, 'It is all play. It is all play.' Do you do anything?" And then, without another word, he turned and went out into the starlight, and passed into his own boat. And we also, in the hush of the river, said goodnight and parted.

One evening, in our week of retreat, we sat under the great trees beside the stream, and it was of leadership that he talked. He began by comparing certain notable movements of the hour, of which one had grown daily during the lifetime of its founder, both in numbers and complexity, while the other had been seen breaking up into its component parts. Finally he said, "I am persuaded that a leader is not made in one life. He has to be born for it. For the difficulty is not in organisation, and making plans; the test, the real test of a leader, lies in holding widely different people together, along the line of their common sympathies. And this can only be done unconsciously, never by trying."

From this, the talk somehow strayed to Plato, and someone asked for an explanation of the doctrine of Ideas. He gave this, and as he ended, he said, addressing one of the groups in particular, "And so you see, all this is but a feeble manifestation of the great ideas which alone are real and perfect. Somewhere is an ideal you, and there is an attempt to manifest it! The attempt falls short still in many ways. Still—go on! You will interpret the ideal some day."

"I cannot feel the longing to get out of life that Hindus feel," said one on another occasion, in response to something he had said about breaking the bonds of life. "I think I would a great deal rather come back and help the causes that interest me, than achieve personal salvation." "That's because you cannot overcome the idea of progress," he retorted quickly. "But things do not grow better. They remain as they were, and *we* grow better, by the changes we make in them."

Life and the Idea

This last sentence has to myself the ring of a *Veda*. "We grow better, by the changes we make in them." Similarly, when we were at Almora, I remember a certain elderly man with a face full of amiable weakness, who came to put to him a question about *karma*. What were they to do, he asked, whose *karma* it was, to see the strong oppress the weak? The Swami turned on him in surprised indignation : "Why thrash the strong, of course!" he said. "You forget your own part in this *karma*—Yours is always the right to rebel!"

VIII

Amarnath

It was in the course of an open-air meal in the Mogul Gardens at Achhabal, that the Swami suddenly announced that he would go to Amarnath with the pilgrims, and take his daughter with him. Within our little party, there was too much feeling of delighted congratulation, for any obstacle to be put in the way of the fortunate member. And aided thus, as well as by the State officer, in charge of the journey, preparations went forward for this unique experience.

Kashmir seemed, in those weeks, to be full of pilgrims. We left Achhbal, and returned to our boats at Islamabad, for final arrangements, and everywhere we saw the march of gathering hosts. It was all very quiet, orderly and picturesque. Two or three thousand people would encamp in a field, and leave it before dawn, with no trace of their occupation, save the ashes of their cooking fires. They carried a bazaar with them, and at each halting place, the pitching of tents, and opening of shops, took place with incredible rapidity. Organisation appeared to be instinctive. A broad street would run through the middle of one part of the camp, and here one could buy dried fruits, milk, dahls and rice. The tent of the Tehsilder—with that of the Swami on one side, and my own on the other—was generally placed near some advantageous spot for the lighting of the evening fire, and thus his neighbourhood tended to form a social centre.

The Talk of Sadhus

There were hundreds of monks, of all the orders, with their *gerrua* tents, some no larger than a good-sized umbrella, and amongst these, the Swami's influence appeared to be magnetic. The more learned of them swarmed about him at every halting place, filling his tent, and remaining absorbed in conversation, throughout the hours of daylight. The talk on their side, he told us afterwards, had been all of *Śiva*, and they had remonstrated with him seriously, when he had insisted, occasionally, on drawing their attention to the world about them. Even foreigners, they urged, were men. Why make such distinctions between *Swadesh* and *Bidesh*? Nor could many of them understand the warmth of his love and sympathy for Mohammedanism. The same other-worldliness that made *Swadesh* and *Bidesh* indistinguishable, also prevented these simple souls from formally conceiving of a unity, in which Hindu and Mohammedan were but rival elements. The soil of the Punjab, they argued, was drenched with the blood of those who had died for the faith. Here, at least, let him practice a narrow orthodoxy! In answer to this, as became one who was, in fact 'an anachronism of the future,' the Swami made those practical concessions of the moment that were expressive of this love for the brethren, and drove his principles home to their minds with the greater force and vehemence. But, as he told the tale of his warm discussions, the foreign mind could not help, with some amusement, noting the paradox that the Tehsildar himself and many officers and servants of the pilgrimage, had been Mussalmans, and that no one had dreamt of objecting to their entering the Cave with the Hindu worshippers, on the ultimate arrival at the shrine. The Tehsildar came afterwards, indeed, with a group of friends, begging formal acceptance by the Swami as disciples; and in this, no one seemed to find anything incongruous or surprising.

Leaving Islamabad, we caught up somewhere with the pilgrimage, and camped with it, for that night, at Pawan, a place famous for its holy springs. I can remember yet the brilliance of the light reflected in the clear black waters of the tank that evening, and throngs of pilgrims proceeding in little groups from shrine to shrine.

At Pahlgam—the village of the shepherds—the camp halted for a day, to keep *ekadasi.* It was a beautiful little ravine floored, for the most part with sandy islands, in the peddle-worn bed of a mountain stream. The slopes about it were dark with pine trees, and over the mountain at its head was seen, at sunset, the moon, not yet full. It was the scenery of Switzerland or Norway, at their gentlest and loveliest. Here we saw the last of human dwellings, a bridge, a farmhouse with its ploughed fields, and a few saeter-huts. And here, on a grassy knoll, when the final march began, we left the rest of our party encamped.

Mountain Villages

Through scenes of indescribable beauty, three thousand of us ascended the valleys that opened before us as we went. The first day we camped in a pine wood; the next, we had passed the snow-line, and pitched our tents beside a frozen river. That night, the great camp-dire was made of juniper, and the next evening, at still greater heights the servants had to wander many miles, in search of this scanty fuel. At last the regular pathway came to an end, and we had to scramble up and down, along goat-paths, on the face of steep declivities, till we reached the boulder-strewn gorge, in which the Cave of Amarnath was situated. As we ascended this, we had before us the snow peaks covered with a white veil, newly fallen; and in the Cave itself, in a niche never reached by sunlight, shone the great ice-lingam, that must have seemed, to the awe-struck peasants who first came upon it, like the waiting Presence of God.

The Swami had observed every rite of the pilgrimage, as he came along. He had told his beads, kept fasts and bathed in the ice-cold waters of five streams in succession, crossing the river gravels on our second day. And now, as he entered the Cave, it seemed to him, as if he saw *Śiva* made visible before him. Amidst the buzzing, swarming noise of the pilgrim-crowd, and the overhead fluttering of the pigeons, he knelt and prostrated two or three times, unnoticed; and then, afraid lest emotion might overcome him, he rose and silently withdrew. He said afterwards that in these brief moments he had received from *Śiva* the gift of *Amar*—not to die, until he himself had willed it. In this way, possibly, was defeated or fulfilled that presentiment which had haunted him from childhood, that he would meet with death, in a *Śiva* temple amongst the mountains.

The Shrine

Outside the Cave, there was no Brahminic exploitation of the helpless people. Amarnath is remarkable for its simplicity and closeness to nature. But the pilgrimage culminates on the great day of *Rakhibandhan**, and our wrists were tied with the red and yellow threads of that sacrament. Afterwards, we rested and had a meal, on some high boulders beside the stream, before returning to our tents.

The Swami was full of the place. He felt that he had never been to anything so beautiful. He sat long silent. Then he said dreamily, "I can well imagine how this Cave was first discovered. A party of shepherds, one summer day, must have lost their flocks, and wandered in here in search of them. Then, when they came home to the valleys, they told how they had suddenly come upon Mahadev!"

Of my Master himself, in any case, a life story was true. The purity and whiteness of the ice-pillar had startled and enwrapt him. The cavern had revealed itself to him as the secret of Kailas. And for the rest of his life, he cherished the memory of how he had entered a mountain-cave, and come face to face there with the Lord Himself.

---

* It means 'the bond of protection'; a universal Indian festival celebrating the relationship between brothers,cousins and sisters;It involves tying of a Rakhi (the sacred thread) by a sister on her brother's wrist.

IX

Kshir Bhowani

Everything in our life up to the time of the pilgrimage to Amarnath had been associated with the thought of *Śiva*. Each step had seemed to draw us closer to the great snow-mountains that were at once His image and His home. The young moon, resting at nightfall above the glacier-cleft and the tossing pines, had suggested irresistibly the brow of the Great God. Above all, that world of meditation on whose outskirts we dwelt, had Him as its heart and centre, rapt and silent, "above all qualities and beyond the reach of thought." Undoubtedly this Hindu idea of *Śiva* is the highest conception of God as approached by the spiritual intuition of man. He is the Divine accessible *within*, and purified of all externals.

It may possibly be, that in the pursuit of uttermost knowledge, this personification of the unmanifesting, is necessarily succeeded by the opposite conception of God—as the power behind all manifestation. It is clear at least that he who has sounded the depths of both these, will be capable of understanding the significance of every possible human symbol of the divine, since all must be included in one or other of the two. If the Supreme is thought of by man at all, it must be either as Infinite Being or as Infinite Power. Whether there is any such law of nature behind the fact or not, must remain a speculation. In some imperceptible way, at all events, the Swami's attention appeared to shift, during the month of August, from *Śiva* to the Mother. He was always singing the songs of Ramprasad, as if he would saturate his own mind with the conception of himself as a child. He told some of us once, that wherever he turned he was conscious of the presence of the Mother, as if She were a person in the room. It was always his habit of speak simply and naturally of 'Mother,' and some of the older members of the party caught this, so that such phrases as "Well, well! Mother knows best!" were a constant mode of thought and speech amongst us, when, for instance, some cherished intention had to be abandoned.

Gradually, however, his absorption became more intense. He complained bitterly of the malady of thought, which would consume a man, leaving him no time for sleep or rest, and would often become as insistent as a human voice. He had constantly striven to make clear to us the ideal of rising beyond the pairs of opposites, beyond pain and pleasure, good and evil alike—that conception which forms the Hindu solution of the problem of sin—but now he seemed to fasten his whole attention on the dark, the painful and the inscrutable, in the world, with the determination to reach by this particular road the One Behind Phenomena. Baffled as he found himself in the object of his visit to Kashmir,* "the worship of the Terrible" now became his whole cry. Illness or pain would always draw forth the reminder that "She is the organ. She is the pain. And She is the Giver of pain, Kali! Kali! Kali!"

The pairs of opposites

His brain was teeming with thoughts, he said one day, and his fingers would not rest till they were written down. It was that same evening that we came back to our houseboat from some expedition, and found waiting for us, where he had called and left them, his manuscript lines on "Kali the Mother". Writing in a fever of inspiration, he had fallen on the floor, when he had finished—as we learn afterwards—exhausted with his own intensity.

Kali the Mother

* He had come, at the express invitation of the Maharajah, to choose a piece of land, for the establishment of a Math and Sanskrit College. But his choice was twice vetoed, on the list of agenda for Council by Sir Adalbert Talbot, then acting as Resident. Thus it could not even be discussed.

Kali the Mother

The stars are blotted out
The clouds are covering clouds,
It is darkness vibrant, sonant.
In the roaring, whirling wind,
Are the souls of a million lunatics,
Just loosed from the prison house,
Wrenching trees by the roots
Sweeping all from the path.
The sea has joined the fray
And swirls up mountain waves,
To reach the pitchy sky.
The flash of lurid light
Reveals on every side
A thousand, thousand shades
Of death, begrimed and black.
Scattering plagues and sorrows,
Dancing mad with joy,
Come, Mother, come!
For Terror is Thy name.
Death is in Thy breath.
And every shaking step
Destroys a world for e'er.
Thou "Time" the All-Destroyer!
Come, O Mother, come!
Who dares misery love,
Dance in destruction's dance,
And hug the form of death—
To him the Mother comes.

About this time, he had taken his boat away from our vicinity, and only a young Brahmo doctor, who was also living in Kashmir that summer—and whose kindness and devotion to him were beyond all praise—was allowed to know where he was, and to enquire about his daily needs. The next evening the doctor went, as usual, but finding him lost in thought, retired without speaking, and the following day, September the thirtieth, he had gone, leaving word that he was not to be followed, to Kshir Bhowani, the coloured springs. He was away, from that day till October the sixth.

* * * *

The Return

In the afternoon of that day we saw him coming back to us, up the river. He stood in front of the *dunga*, grasping with one hand the bamboo roof-pole, and with the other holding yellow flowers. He entered our houseboat—a transfigured presence, and silently passed from one to another blessing us, and putting the marigolds on our heads. "I offered them to Mother," he said at last, as he ended by handing the garland to one of us. Then he sat down. "No more 'Hari Om!' It is all 'Mother', now!" he said with a smile. We all sat silent. Had we tried to speak, we should have failed, so tense was the spot with something that stilled thought. He opened his lips again. "All my patriotism is gone. Everything is gone. Now it's only 'Mother Mother!'"

"I have been very wrong," he said simply, after another pause. "Mother said to me, 'What, even if unbelievers should enter My temples, and defile My images! What is that to you? Do you protect Me? Or do I protect you?' So there is no more patriotism. I am only a little child!"

Then he spoke on indifferent matters, about the departure for Calcutta, which he desired to make at once, with a word or two as to the experience of physical ill into which his perplexities of mind had translated themselves, throughout the past week. "I may not tell you more now; it is not in order," he said gently, adding, before he left us—"But spiritually, *spiritually*, I was not bound down!"

We saw very little of the Swami during the next few days. Before breakfast the next morning, indeed, two of us were with him on the riverbank for a moment, when, seeing the barber, he said "All this must go!" and left us, to come out again half an hour later, without a hair. Somehow, in ways and words that could scarcely be recounted, came to us now and then a detail of that austerity, by which, in the past week, such illumination had come. We could picture the fasting; the offering of milk and rice and almonds daily, in the spring; and the morning worship of a Brahmin pundit's little daughter, as Uma Kumari—the Divine Virgin;—the whole meanwhile, in such a passion of self-renunciation, that not one wave of reaction could be found in his consciousness for any injury, however great.

Householder versus *Sannyāsin*

A man came one day to ask a question, and the Swami, in monastic dress and with a shaven head, happened to enter. "Ought one to seek an opportunity of death, in defence of right, or ought one to take the lesson of the Gita* and learn never to react?" was the problem put to him. "I am for no reaction," said the Swami, speaking slowly, and with a long pause. Then he added "—for *Sannyāsins*. Self-defence for the householder!"

The mood seemed to grow upon him, and deepen. He spoke of this time once, as 'a crisis in his life'. Again, he called himself a child, seated on the lap of the Mother, and being caressed. And the thought came to us, unspoken, that these Her kisses might make themselves known to mind and nerves as anguish, yet be welcomed with rapture of recognition. Did he not say, "There could be bliss in torture?"

* It is perhaps worthwhile to say that for my own part I could never understand how this enquirer gathered this particular lesson from the Gita!

The Farewell

As soon as it could be arranged, we left for Baramulla, which we reached on Tuesday evening, October the eleventh. It had been settled that he would go on to Lahore the following afternoon, while we waited some days longer. On the way down the river, we saw very little of him. He was almost entirely silent, and took long walks by the riverside alone, rarely even entering our houseboat for a moment. His health had been completely broken, by the labours of his return to India; and the physical ebb of the great experience through which he had just passed—for even suffering becomes impossible, when a given point of weariness is reached; and similarly, the body refuses to harbour a certain intensity of the spiritual life for an indefinite period!—was leaving him, doubtless, more exhausted than he himself suspected. All this contributed, one imagines, to a feeling that none of us knew for how long a time we might now be parting, and it was this thought perhaps, that brought him to say goodbye on Wednesday morning, as we finished breakfast, and made him stay to talk.

Hour after hour went by, that morning, and it is easier to tell of the general impression created, than to build it up again detail by detail. We who listened, seemed to be carried into an innermost sanctuary. Sometimes he would sing and translate some snatch or other of devotional poetry, always to the Mother. And it was always Kali, with her foot on the heart of Her worshipper, Who grew clearer to our minds; though he dwelt much, and over and over again, on the thought of the Mother, seated in the market-place of this world, playing amongst the players; flying Her own kite, and in hundred thousand cutting the strings of only one or two.

"Scattering plagues and sorrows," he quoted from his own verses,

"Dancing mad with joy
Come, O Mother, come!
For Terror is Thy name!
Death—is in Thy breath.
And every shaking step
Destroys a world for e'er."

"It all came true, every word of it," he interrupted himself to say.

"Who dares misery love,
Dance in Destruction's dance,
And hug the form of death—

To *him* the Mother does indeed come. I have proved it. For I have hugged the form of Death!"

He spoke of the future. There was nothing to

Illusion

be desired, but the life of the wanderer, in silence and nudity, on the banks of the Ganges. He would have nothing. 'Swamiji' was dead and gone.

Who was he, that he should feel responsible for teaching the world? It was all fuss and vanity. The Mother had no need of him, but only he of Her. Even work, when one had seen this, was nothing but an illusion.

There was no way but love. If people sinned against us, we must love them till it is impossible for them to resist it. That was all. Yet, as I write the words, I know well that I can give no idea of the *vastness* of which all this was utterance—as if no blow, to any in the world, could pass and leave our Master's heart untouched; as if no pain, even to that of death, could elicit anything but love and blessing.

He told us the story of Vasishta and Viswamitra; of Vasishta's hundred descendants slain; and the King left alone, landless and crownless, to live out his life. Then he pictured the hut standing in the moonlight, amongst the trees, and Vasishta and his wife within. He is poring intently over some precious page, written by his great rival, when she draws near and hangs over him for a moment, saying, "Look, how bright is the moon tonight!" and he, without looking up—"But ten thousand times brighter, my love, is the intellect of Viswamitra!"

All forgotten! the deaths of his hundred children, his own wrongs, and his sufferings, and his heart lost in admiration of the genius of his foe! Such, said the Swami, should be our love also, like that of Vasishta for Viswamitra, without the slightest tinge of personal memory.

Altar-Blossoms

At this moment a peasant brought sprays of pear blossom, and laid them down on the table at which we sat. And one of us lifted them, saying, "Swami! These were made for worship, for they will bear no fruits!" But he looked at her, smiling, and she could not break the spell, to offer them.

And so he went. We all, servants and boat-people, friends and disciples, parents and children, accompanied him to the *tonga* on the roadside, to say goodbye. One sturdy little figure, the four-year-old daughter of his chief boatman, whose devotion to him we had long noted, trotted determinedly at his side, with a tray of fruit for his journey on her black head, and stood, smiling farewell, as he drove away. And we, not less deeply touched than this little child, but infinitely less unselfish, in our grown-up complexity of thought and emotion, knew not when we should look upon his face again, yet failed not to realize that we had that day lived through hours, within whose radiance all our future would be passed.

X

Calcutta and the Holy Women

The Swami had one remarkable characteristic. He made all who were near him appear great. In his presence, one saw and loved, at its highest, their unspoken purpose; and even their faults and failings, if one realized them, would seem to be justified and accounted for. We surely stand at many different grades of perception! Some of us see and recognize only the form and the acts of a man. Others will refer his features to a central type, and note on his external aspects the tide-marks of the will, in all its mixedness and complexity of ebb and flow. But still others are aware of a vast magazine of cause behind, against which a life stands out as a single fragmentary effect. We ourselves cannot gauge the knowledge that prompts our own words and deeds.

Something after this fashion was the vision that grew upon me, of the world into which I had entered, as the Swami's disciple, on my arrival in Calcutta, early in November 1898. During the months between that date and the following July, I saw him always in the midst of his own people, without even the friendly intervention of a European home. I became myself one of the people, living with them in surroundings which his genius had created. And thus enveloped by his interpretation, thus dominated by his passionate love of his own race, it was like walking in some twilight of the gods, where the forms of men and women loomed larger than their wont.

A Girls' School

It had been taken for granted from the first, that at the earliest opportunity I would open a girls' school in Calcutta. And it was characteristic of the Swami's methods, that I had not been hurried in the initiation of this work, but had been given leisure and travel and mental preparation. To myself it was clear that this school, when opened, must at first be only tentative and experimental. I had to learn what was wanted, to determine where I myself stood, to explore the very world of which my efforts were to become a part. The one thing that I knew was, that an education effort must begin at the standpoint of the learner, and help him to development in his one way. But I had no definite plans or expectations, save to make some educational discovery which would be qualitatively true and universally applicable to the work of the modern education of Indian women.*

Others, however, had probably thought more largely of the matter, and I had heard much as to the desirability of holding myself above all sects. But all these questions were solved once for all, on a certain evening in camp, in the forest of Vernag, in Kashmir, when the Swami turned to me, as we all sat in a circle about the log-fire, and asked me what were now my plans for the school. I replied eagerly, begging to be freed from collaborators, to be allowed to begin in a small way, spelling out my method; and urging, above all, the necessity of a definite religious colour, and the usefulness of sects.

The Swami listened and accepted, and as far as his loyalty went to every wish of mine, in this matter, thenceforth, he might have been the disciple and I the teacher. Only in one respect was he inflexible. The work for the education of Indian women to which he would give his name, might be as sectarian as I chose to made it. "You wish through a sect to rise beyond all sects," had

* It must here be pointed out that the school in question proved even more tentative than I had imagined. In the autumn of 1903,the whole work for Indian women was taken up and organised by an American disciple, Sister Christine, and to her, and her faithfulness and initiative alone, it owes all its success up to the present. From the experiment which I made in 1898 to 1899, was gathered only my own education.—*Nivedita.*

been his sole reply to this part of my statement. He withdrew, at the first sign of hesitation on my side, the name of an Indian lady whose help had been proffered. But he would not, on the other hand, countenance my own seeking of assistance amongst the few acquaintances I had already made. For the ocean of Indian character I had as yet no plummet, and it was safer to go long unaided than to commit an error at the start.

A Guest Self-invited

It was to carry out this plan, then, that I arrived in Calcutta alone, in the beginning of November. I was able to find my way at once, from the station to the north end of the town. But once there, with insular rigidity, insisted on being made the guest of the women. The Swami was himself staying, as it happened, at a sort of parish-room of the Order, in Calcutta. Through him, therefore, the negotiations were carried on. The widow of Sri Ramakrishna—Sarada Devi, or 'the Holy Mother,' as she is called amongst us—was living close by, with her community of ladies, and in the course of the day, I was accorded possession of an empty room in her house.

This is one the occasions on which people look back, feeling that their courage was providentially determined by their ignorance. It is difficult to see how else a necessary solution could have been found. Yet had I deeply understood at the time, the degree of social embarrassment which my rashness might have brought, not only upon my innocent hostess but also on her kindred in their distant village, I could not have acted as I did. At any cost, I must in that case have withdrawn. As it was, however, I imagined caste to be only a foolish personal prejudice—which must yield to knowledge—against some supposed uncleanness of foreign habits, and thus cheerfully assuming all the ignorance to be on her side, confidently forced myself upon this Indian lady's hospitality.

In the event, fortunately the Swami's influence proved all-powerful, and I was accepted by society. Within a week or ten days, a house in the close neighbourhood was found for me. But even then, I spent all my afternoons in the Mother's room. And when the hot weather came, it was by her express command that I returned to her better-arranged house, for sleeping-quarters. And then I occupied no room apart, but shared the cool and simple dormitory of the others, with its row of mats, pillows, and nets, against the polished red earthenware of the floor.

The Mother's Home

It was a strange household, of which I now found myself a part. Downstairs, in one of the guard-rooms beside the front-door, lived a monk, whose severe austerities, from his youth up, had brought him to the threshold of death, from consumption, in the prime of manhood. To his room I used to go for Bengali lessons. In the kitchen behind, worked a disciple of his and a Brahmin cook, while to us women-fold belonged all above-stairs, with roofs and terraces, and the sight of the Ganges hard by.

Of the head of our little community, it seems almost presumptuous to speak. Her history is well known. How she was wedded at five, and forgotten by her husband till she was eighteen; how she then, with her mother's permission made her way on foot from her village-home to the temple of Dakshineswar on the Ganges-side, and appeared before him; how he remembered the bond, but spoke of the ideals of the life he had adopted; and how she responded by bidding him Godspeed in that life, and asking only to be taught by him as the Guru—all these things have been told of her many times over. From that time she lived faithfully by his side for many years, in a building in the same garden, at once nun and wife, and always chief of his disciples. She was young when her tutelage began and in hours of quiet talk, she will tell sometimes in how many directions his training extended. He was a great lover of order, and taught her even such trifles as where to keep her lamp and its appurtenances, during the day. He could not endure squalor, and notwithstanding severe asceticism, he loved grace and beauty and gentle dignity of bearing. One story that is told of this period of her life, is of her bringing to him a basket of fruit and vegetables one day, with all the eagerness and pride of a happy child. He looked at it gravely, and said, "But why so extravagant?"

—"At least it was not for myself!" said the young wife, all her sunshine gone, in sudden disappointment, and she turned and went away, crying quietly. But this Sri Ramakrishna could not bear to see. "Go, one of you," he said, turning to the boys beside him, "and bring her back. My very devotion to God will take wings, if I see her weep!"

Sri Ramakrishna's Love

So dear she was to him. Yet one of her most striking traits is the absolute detachment with which she speaks of the husband she worships. She stands like a rock, through cloud and shine, as those about her tell, for the fulfilment of every word of his. But '*Guru Deb*!', 'Divine Master' is the name she calls him by, and not one word of her uttering ever conveys the slightest trace of self-assertion with regard to him. One who did not know who she was, would never suspect, from speech of hers, that her right was stronger, or her place closer, than that of any other of those about her. It would seem as if the wife had been long ago forgotten, save for her faithfulness, in the disciple. Yet so deeply is she reverenced by all about her, that there is not one of them who would, for instance, occupy a railway berth above her, when travelling with her. Her very presence is to them a consecration.

The Ideal Woman

To me, it has always appeared that she is Sri Ramakrishna's final word as to the ideal of Indian womanhood. But is she the last of an old order, or the beginning of a new? In her, one sees realized that wisdom and sweetness to which the simplest of women may attain. And yet, to myself, the stateliness of her courtesy and her great open mind are almost as wonderful as her sainthood. I have never known her hesitate, in giving utterance to large and generous judgment, however new or complex might be the question put before her. Her life is one long stillness of prayer. Her whole experience is of theocratic civilisation. Yet she rises to the height of every situation. Is she tortured by the perversity of any about her? The only sign is a strange quietness and intensity that comes upon her. Does one carry to her some perplexity or mortification born of social developments beyond her ken? With unerring intuition, she goes straight to the heart of the matter, and sets the questioner in the true attitude to the difficulty. Or is there a need for severity? No foolish sentimentality causes her to waver. The novice whom she may condemn, for so many years to beg his bread, will leave the place within the hour. He who has transgressed her code of delicacy and honour, will never enter her presence again. "Can't you see," said Sri Ramakrishna, to one who had erred in some such way, "can't you see that *the woman* in her is wounded? And that is dangerous!"

And yet is she, as one of her spiritual children said of her, speaking literally of her gift of song, "full of music," all gentleness, all playfulness. And the room wherein she worships, withal, is filled with sweetness.

Sarada Devi's Culture

The Mother can read, and much of her time is passed with her *Rāmāyana*. But she does not write. Yet it is not to be supposed that she is an uneducated woman. Not only has she had long and arduous experience in administration, secular and religious; but she has also travelled over a great part of India, visiting most of the chief places of pilgrimage. And it must be remembered that as the wife of Sri Ramakrishna, she had had the highest opportunity of personal development that it is possible to enjoy. At every moment, she bears unconscious witness to this association with the great. But in nothing perhaps does it speak more loudly than in her instant power to penetrate a new religious feeling or idea.

I first realised that gift in the Holy Mother, on the occasion of a visit that she paid us in recent years, on the afternoon of a certain

Easter Day. Before that, probably, I had always been too much absorbed, when with her, in striving to learn what she represented, to think of observing her in the contrary position. On this particular occasion, however, after going over our whole house, the Mother and her party expressed a desire to rest in the chapel, and hear something of the meaning of the Christian festival. This was followed by Easter music, and singing, with our small French organ. And in the swiftness of her comprehension, and the depth of her sympathy with these resurrection hymns, unimpeded by any foreignness or unfamiliarity in them, we saw revealed for the first time, one of the most impressive aspects of the great religious culture of Sarada Devi. The same power is seen to a certain extent, in all the women about her, who were touched by the hand of Sri Ramakrishna. But in her, it has all the strength and certainty of some high and arduous form of scholarship.

The same trait came out again, one evening, when, in the midst of her little circle, the Holy Mother asked my *Gurubhagini* and myself, to describe to her a European wedding. With much fun and laughter, personating now the "Christian Brahmin," and again the bride and bridegroom, we complied. But we were neither of us prepared for the effect of the marriage vow.

"For better for worse, for richer for poorer, in sickness and in health—till death us do part," were words that drew exclamations of delight from all about us. But none appreciated them as did the Mother. Again and again, she had them repeated to her "Oh, the *Dharmmi* words! The righteous words!" she said.

The Marriage Vow

Amongst the ladies who lived more or less continuously in the household of Sarada Devi at this time were Gopal's Mother, Jogin-Mother, Rose-Mother (Golap-Mother), Sister Lucky, and a number of others. These were all widows—the first and the last child widows—and they had all been personal disciples of Sri Ramakrishna when he lived in the temple garden at Dakshineshwar. Sister Lucky, or Lakshmididi as is the Indian form of her name, was indeed a niece of his, and is still a comparatively young woman. She is widely sought after as a religious teacher and director, and is a most gifted and delightful companion. Sometimes she will repeat page after page of some sacred dialogue, out of one of the *Jatras*, or religious operas, or again she will make the quiet room ring with gentle merriment, as she poses the different members of the party in groups for religious *tableaux*. Now it is Kali, and again Saraswati, another time it will be Jagadhattri, or yet again, perhaps, Krishna under his Kadamba tree, that she will arrange, with picturesque effect and scant dramatic material.

Amusements like these were much approved of, it is said, by Sri Ramakrishna, who would sometimes himself, according to the ladies, spend hours in reciting religious plays, taking the part of each player in turns, and making all around him realise the utmost meaning of the prayers and worship uttered in the poetry.

Gopal's Mother (*Gopaler-Mā*) was an old woman. She had already been old, fifteen or twenty years before, when she had first walked over, one day at noon, from her cell at Kamarhatty, by the Ganges-side, to see the

Gopaler-Mā

Master in the garden at Dakshineshwar. He received her, so they say, standing at his door, as if he expected her. And she, whose chosen worship had been for many years Gopala, the Babe Krishna, the Christ Child of Hinduism saw Him revealed to her, as in a vision, as she drew near. How true she always was to this! Never once through all the years that followed, did she offer salutation to Sri Ramakrishna, who took her thenceforth as his mother. And never have I known her to speak of our Holy Mother, save as "my daughter-in-law".

In the months which I spent with the Mother and her ladies, *Gopaler-Mā* would sometimes be in Calcutta, and sometimes for weeks together, away at Kamarhatty. There, a few of us went one full moon night, to visit her. How beautiful was the Ganges, as the little boat crept on and on! And how beautiful seemed the long flight of steps rising out of the water, and leading up, through its lofty bathing ghat, past the terraced lawn, to the cloister-like verandah on the right, where, in a little room—built probably in the first place for some servant of the great house at its side—*Gopaler-Mā* had lived and told her beads, for many a year. The great house was empty now. And her own little room was absolutely without comforts. Her bed was of stone, and her floor of stone, and the piece of matting she offered her guests to sit on, had to be taken down from a shelf and unrolled. The handful of parched rice and sugar candy that formed her only store, and were all that she could give in hospitality, were taken from an earthen pot that hung from the roof by a few cords. But the place was spotlessly clean, washed constantly by Ganges-water of her own sturdy carrying. And in a niche near her hand lay an old copy of the *Rāmāyana*, her great horn spectacles, and the little white bag containing her beads. On those beads, *Gopaler-Mā* had become a saint! Hour after hour, day and night, absorbed in them!

The radiant white moonlight made the trees and flowers outside seem like black shadows, moving and whispering in a dream world of white marble. But nothing could seem so dream-like, as, in the midst of our busy hurrying world, the thought of spots like this little cell of *Gopaler-Mā*, enshrining her silent intensity of peace. "Ah!" said the Swami, when he heard of the visit, "this is the *old* India that you have seen, the India of prayers and tears, of vigils and fasts, that is passing away, never to return!"

In Calcutta, *Gopaler-Mā* felt, perhaps a little more than others, the natural shock to habits of eighty years' standing at having a European in the house. But once overruled, she was generosity itself. Conservative she always was: stubbornly prejudiced, never. As far as the daily life went, there can have been little difference, to her consciousness, between her own hermitage on the Ganges-bank, and the conventual round of the Mother's household. The days were full of peace and sweetness. Long before dawn, one and another rose quietly and sat on the sleeping mat, from which sheets and pillows were now removed, beads in hand, and face turned to the wall. Then came the cleansing of the rooms and personal bathing. On great days, the Mother and one other would be carried down to the river in a palkee, and till this arrived, the time was spent in reading the *Rāmāyana*.

The Mothers's Worship

Then came the Mother's worship in her own room, with all the younger women busy over lights and incense, Ganges-water and flowers and offerings. Even *Gopaler-Mā* would aid, as this hour came round, in the preparation of fruits and vegetables. The noonday meal and the restful afternoon would pass, and again as evening drew on, the servant going by the door with the lighted lamp would break in upon our chat. Groups would break up. Each of us would prostrate before image or picture, and touch the feet of *Gopaler-Mā* and the Mother, or accompany the latter to where the light was placed, near the basil plant on the terrace; and fortunate indeed was she who from this was permitted to go, like a daughter, and sit beside the Mother at her evening-meditation, there to learn those salutations to the Guru which formed, with her, the beginning and end of all worship.

The Indian home thinks of itself as perpetually chanting the beautiful psalm of custom. To it, every little act and detail of household method and personal habit is something inexpressibly precious and sacred, an eternal treasure of the nation, handed down from the past, to be kept unflawed, and passed on to the future. This mode of thought is interwoven with the passionate quest of ideal purity, and with the worship of motherhood, to make the guiding and restraining force of the whole Indian character. The East worships simplicity, and herein lies one of the main reasons why vulgarity is impossible to any Eastern people.

But no one can point out such a secret as this, at the moment when one needs it, for the simple reason that no one can place himself sufficiently outside his own consciousness to find out that others were born, not only with a different equipment of associations, but also with a different instinct as to their value. Fortunately, however, by watching the Swami, and puzzling over the contrasts he unconsciously presented, I was able to discover it, and many things were made easier thereby. No one was ever more clearly aware that character was everything, or, as he phrased it, that "custom was nothing," yet none could be more carried away than he by the perfection and significance of all with which he was familiar. To the customs of his own people, he brought the eye of a poet, and the imagination of a prophet. He had learnt that "custom was nothing" when he had met with ideal womanhood and faith amongst polyandrous peoples, or delicacy and modesty adorned in the evening costumes of the West. But these things had not shaken his reverence for the conventionalities of his own country. The plain white veil of the widow was to

The Swami and Custom

him the symbol of holiness as well as sorrow. The Gerrua rags of the *Sannyāsin*, the mat on the floor for a bed, the green leaf instead of a plate, eating with the fingers, the use of the national costume, all these things he appeared to regard as a veritable consecration. Each of them whispered to him some secret of spiritual power or human tenderness. And he answered with a passion of loyalty that would achieve for them, if it could, the very conquest of the world; but failing, would think all heaven lay in sharing their defeat.

Thus he taught me also to sing the melodious song, in feeble and faltering fashion, it is true, but yet in some sort of unison with its own great choir, inasmuch as, with them. I learnt to *listen* through the music, even while following, for the revelation it could bring of a nation's ideals and a nation's heart.

Those months between November 1898 and June 1899, were full of happy glimpses. My little school was begun on the day of Kali Puja, and the Mother herself came and performed the opening ceremony of worship. At the end, she gave a whispered blessing spoken aloud by Rose-Mother. She 'prayed that the blessing of the great Mother might be upon the school, and the girls it should train be ideal girls'. And somehow to know that an undertaking is remembered and fraught with prayer in the lofty mind and heart of our Mother, is to me a benediction that makes content. I cannot imagine a grander omen than her blessing, spoken over the educated Hindu womanhood of the future.

The Daily Round

The Swami lived commonly at the monastery, five or six miles out of Calcutta, and on the opposite bank of the river. But, on his frequent visits to town, he would almost always send for me to join him, either at the noon or evening meal, and to those who showed me kindness, he would always make a special effort to offer hospitality at Belur.

Even his smallest actions often had a meaning that was not evident to a new eye. I did not dream, when he came to me one day and asked me to cook for him a certain invalid dish, that there was any special intention in the request. And when I heard afterwards that on receiving it, he had himself eaten very little, preferring to share it with those about him, I was only disappointed, being at that time unaware of the almost sacramental nature of this act. It was many months before I learnt to understand the deep forethought and kindness with which he—and also the Holy Mother on his behalf—was constantly working to make a place for me, as a foreigner, in Hindu society. The aim of his whole life was, as he had said to me, in Kashmir, "to make Hinduism aggressive, like Christianity and Islam," and this was one of the ways in which he sought to realize that ideal.

Hinduism Progressive

The same purpose spoke again in his definition of the aims of the Order of Ramakrishna—"to effect an exchange of the highest ideals of the East and the West, and to realize these in practice"—a definition whose perfection and special appropriateness to the present circumstances of India, grows on one with time. To his mind, Hinduism was not to remain a stationary system, but to prove herself capable of embracing and welcoming the whole modern development. She was no congeries of divided sects, but a single living Mother-Church, recognizing all that had been born of her, fearless of the new, eager for the love of her children, wherever they might be found, wise, merciful, self-directing, pardoning and reconciling. Above all, she was the holder of a definite vision, the preacher of a distinct message amongst the nations. To prove her this, however, he relied on no force but that of character. The building of the temple of his faith was all-important, it was true; but for it, there was infinite time, and with it worked the tendency and drift of things. For himself, the responsibility was to choose sound bricks. And he chose, not with an eye to the intellect, or power of attraction, or volume of force, of those who were chosen, but always for a certain quality of simple sincerity, and, as it seemed, for that alone. Once accepted, the ideal put before them all was the same: not Mukti but renunciation, not self-realisation, but self-abandonment. And this rather, again, on behalf of man, than as an offering to God. It was the *human motive* that he asserted to his disciples. May one of them never forget a certain day of consecration, in the chapel at the monastery, when, as the opening step in a lifetime, so to speak, he first taught her to perform the worship of *Śiva*, and then made the whole culminate in an offering of flowers at the feet of the Buddha! "Go thou," he said, as if addressing in one person each separate soul that would ever come to him for guidance, "and follow Him, who was born and gave His life for others FIVE HUNDRED TIMES, before He attained the vision of the Buddha!"

XI

The Swami and Mother-Worship

The story of the glimpses which I caught of this part of the Swami's life would be singularly incomplete, if it contained no mention of his worship of the Mother. Spiritually speaking, I have always felt that there were two elements in his consciousness. Undoubtedly he was born a *Brahmajnāni*, as Ramakrishna Paramahamsa so frequently insisted. When he was only eight years old, sitting at his play, he had developed the power of entering *Samādhi*. The religious ideas towards which he naturally gravitated, were highly abstract and philosophical, the very reverse of those which are commonly referred to as 'idolatrous'. In his youth, and presumably when he had already been sometime under the influence of Sri Ramakrishna, he became a formal member of the Sadharan Brahmo Samaj. In England and America, he was never known to preach anything that depended on a special form. The realisation of Brahman was his only imperative, the Advaita philosophy his only system of doctrine, the Vedas and Upanishads his sole scriptural authority.

And yet, side by side with this, it is also true that in India the word 'Mother' was forever on his lips. He spoke of Her, as we of one deeply familiar in the household life. He was constantly preoccupied with Her. Like other children, he was not always good. Sometimes he would be naughty and rebellious. But always to Her. Never did he attribute to any other, the good or evil that befell. On a certain solemn occasion, he entrusted to a disciple a prayer to Her that in his own life had acted as a veritable charm. "And mind!" he added suddenly, turning with what was almost fierceness upon the receiver, "*make* Her listen to you, when you say it! *None of that cringing* to Mother! Remember!" Every now and then he would break out with some new fragment of description. The right hand raised in blessing!" would be the sudden exclamation that ended a long reverie. Or becoming half-lyric in the intensity of his feeling, "Deep in the heart of hearts of Her own, flashes the blood-red knife of Kali. Worshippers of the Mother are they from their birth, in Her incarnation of the sword!" From him was gathered, in such moments as these, almost every line and syllable of a certain short psalm, called the "Voice of the Mother," which I wrote and published about this time. "I worship the Terrible!" he was continually saying—and once, "It is a mistake to hold that with all men pleasure is the motive. Quite as many are born to seek after pain. Let us worship the Terror for Its own sake."

The Terrible

He had a whole-hearted contempt for what he had regarded as squeamishness or mawkishness. He wasted few words on me, when I came to him with my difficulties about animal sacrifice in the temple. He made no reference, as he might have done, to the fact that most of us, loudly as we may attack this, have no hesitation in offering animal sacrifice to ourselves. He offered no argument, as he easily might have done, regarding the degradation of the butcher and the slaughter house, under the modern system. "Why not a little blood, to complete the picture?" was his only direct reply to my objections. And it was with considerable difficulty that I elicited from him, and from another disciple of Sri Ramakrishna, sitting near, the actual facts of the more austere side of Kali-worship, that side which has transcended the sacrifice of others. He told me however that he had never tolerated the blood-offering commonly made to the "demons who attend on Kali". This was simple devil worship, and he had no place for it. His own effort being constantly to banish fear and weakness from his own consciousness and to

No Devil-Worship

learn to recognize THE MOTHER as instinctively in evil, terror, sorrow and annihilation, as in that which makes for sweetness and joy, it followed that the one thing he could not away with was any sort of watering-down of the great conception. "Fools!" he exclaimed once—as he dwelt in quiet talk on "the worship of the Terrible," on "becoming one with the Terrible"—"Fools! They put a garland of skulls round Thy neck, and then start back in terror, and call Thee 'the Merciful'!" And as he spoke, the underlying egoism of worship that is devoted to the *kind* God, to Providence, the consoling Divinity, without a heart for God in the earthquake, or God in the volcano, overwhelmed the listener. One saw that such worship was at the bottom, as the Hindu calls it, merely 'shop-keeping,' and one realized the infinitely greater boldness and truth of the teaching that God manifests through evil *as well as* through good. One saw that the true attitude for the mind and will that are not to be baffled by the personal self, was, in fact, the determination, in the stern words of the Swami Vivekananda, 'to seek death, not life; to hurl oneself upon the sword's point, to become one with the Terrible for evermore!'

It would have been altogether inconsistent with the Swami's idea of freedom, to have sought to impose his own conceptions on a disciple.

But everything in my past life as an educationist had contributed to impress on me now the necessity of taking on the Indian consciousness, and the personal perplexity associated with the memory of the pilgrimage to Amarnath was a witness not to be forgotten to the strong place which Indian systems of worship held in that consciousness. I set myself therefore to enter into Kali-worship, as one would set oneself to learn a new language, or take birth deliberately, perhaps, in a new race. To this fact, I owe it that I was able to understand as much as I did of our Master's life and thought. Step by step, glimpse after glimpse, I began to comprehend a little. And in matters religious, he was, without knowing it, a born educator. He never checked a struggling thought. Being with him one day when an image of Kali was brought in, and noticing some passing expression, I suddenly said "Perhaps, Swamiji, Kali is the Vision of *Śiva*! Is She?" He looked at me for a moment. "Well! Well! Express it in your own way", he said gently, "Express it in your own way!"

A Born Educator

Another day he was going with me to visit the old Maharshi Devendra Nath Tagore, in the seclusion of his home in Jorasanko, and before we started, he questioned me about a death scene at which I had been present the night before. I told him eagerly of the sudden realisation that had come to me, that religions were only languages, and we must speak to a man in his own language. His whole face lighted up at the thought. "Yes!" he exclaimed, "and Ramakrishna Paramahamsa was the only man who taught that! He was the only man who ever had the courage to say that we must speak to all men in their own language!"

Yet there came a day when he found it necessary to lay down with unmistakable clearness his own position in the matter of Mother-worship. I was about to lecture at the Kalighat, and he came to instruct me that if any foreign friends should wish to be present, they were to remove their shoes, and sit on the floor, like the rest of the audience. In that Presence, no exceptions were to be made. I was myself to be responsible for this.*

After saying all this, however, he lingered before going, and then, making a shy reference to Colonel Hay's poem of the 'Guardian Angels', he said, "That is precisely my position about Brahman and the gods! I believe in Brahman *and* the gods, and not in anything else!"

He was evidently afraid that my intellectual difficulty would lie where his own must have done, in the incompatibility of the exaltation

---

* In no temple anywhere ought there to be any exception. No one has any respect for a man who cannot stand for the dignity and sacredness of his own place of worship.—N.

of one definite scheme of worship with the highest Vedantic theory of Brahman. He did not understand that to us who stood about him, he was himself the reconciliation of these opposites, and the witness to the truth of each. Following up this train of thought, therefore, he dropped into a mood of half-soliloquy, and sat for a while talking disjointedly, answering questions, trying to make himself clear, yet always half-absorbed in something within, as if held by some spell he could not break.

The Kali and Vedanta

"How I used to hate Kali!" he said, "and all Her ways! That was the ground of my six years' fight—that I would not accept Her. But I had to accept Her at last. Ramakrishna Paramahamsa dedicated me to Her, and now I believe that She guides me in every little thing I do, and does with me what She will! ... Yet I fought so long! I loved him, you see, and that was what held me. I saw his marvellous purity ... I felt his wonderful love ... His greatness had not dawned on me then. All that came afterwards, when I had given in. At that time I thought him a brain-sick baby, always seeing visions and the rest. I hated it. And then I too had to accept Her!"

The Dedication

"No, the thing that made me do it is a secret that will die with me. I had great misfortunes at that time ... It was on opportunity ... She made a slave of me. Those were the very words—'a slave of you'. And Ramakrishna Paramahamsa made me over to Her ... Strange! He lived only two years after doing that, and most of the time he was suffering. Not more than six months did he keep his own health and brightness.

"Guru Nanak was like that, you know, looking for the one disciple to whom he would give his power. And he passed over all his own family—his children were as nothing to him—till he came upon the boy to whom he gave it, and then he could die.

"The future, you say, will call Ramakrishna Paramahamsa on Incarnation of Kali? Yes, I think there's no doubt that She worked up the body of Ramakrishna for Her own ends.

"*You see, I cannot but believe that there is somewhere a great Power That thinks of Herself as feminine, and called Kali, and Mother* ... And I believe in Brahman too ... But is it not always like that? Is it not the multitude of cells in the body that make up the personality, the many brain centres, not the one, that produce consciousness? ... Unity in complexity! Just so! And why should it be different with Brahman? It *is* Brahman. It *is* the One. And yet—and yet—it is the gods too!"

Similarly, he had returned from a pilgrimage in Kashmir saying, "These gods are not merely symbols! They are the forms that the *Bhaktas* have seen!" And it is told of Sri Ramakrishna that he would sometimes speak, coming out of

Samādhi, of the past experience of that soul that dwelt within him—"He who came as Rama, as Krishna, as Jesus dwells here"—and then would add playfully, turning to his chief disciple, "but not in your Vedanta sense, Noren!"

Thus we are admitted to a glimpse of the struggle that goes on in great souls, for the correlation and mutual adjustment of the different realisations of different times. On the one side the Mother, on the other side Brahman. We are reminded of the Swami's own words, heard long ago, "The impersonal God, seen through the mists of sense, is personal." In truth, it might well be that the two ideas could not be reconciled. Both conceptions could not be equally true at the same time. It is clear enough that in the end, as a subjective realisation, either the Mother must become Brahman, or Brahman the Mother. One of the two must melt into the other, the question of which, in any particular case, depends on the destiny and the past of the worshipping soul.

The Trust Carried

For my own part, the conversation I have related marked an epoch. Ever since it took place, I have thought I saw in my Master's attitude a certain element of one who carried for another a trust confided to him. He would always, when asked to explain the image of Kali, speak of it as the book of experience, in which the soul turns page after page, only to find that there is nothing in it, after all. And this, to my own mind, is the final explanation. Kali the mother is to be the worship of the Indian future. In Her name will her sons find it possible to sound many experiences to their depths. And yet, in the end, their hearts will return to the ancient wisdom, and each man will know, when his hour comes, that all his life was but a dream.

Who does not remember the Veda-like words of the Gita?—"Not, verily, by avoiding action, can a man rise to this inaction!" May we not, similarly, know for a certainty that not without going through this experience can we reach the realisation at the end? Through the Mother to Brahman, through new life and knowledge, and many changes, through the struggles, the victories, and the defeats of the immediate future, to that safe haven of the soul where all is One and all is peace? As I look more and more closely into the life of the great Teacher whom I have followed, I see each day with growing clearness, how he himself was turning the pages of the book of experience, and that it was only when he had come to the last word that he could lie back like a weary child, in the arms of his Mother, to be wrapped away at last into the Supreme Revelation, knowing that 'all this was but a dream!'

The play of the Mother

XII

Half-Way Across the World

On the 20th of June 1899, I left Calcutta by the same steamer as the Swami, and his *gurubhai* Turiyananda, for London, which we reached on the morning of July 31st. A few weeks later he left England for America, where I met him once more, late in September. After the five or six weeks which I spent there, as a guest in the same house as he, and a fortnight in Brittany in the following year, 1900, I never again enjoyed any long unbroken opportunity of being with him. Towards the end of 1900, he returned to India, but I remained in the West until the beginning of 1902. And when I then reached India, it was only as if to be present at the closing scene, to receive the last benediction. To this voyage of six weeks, I look back on it as the greatest occasion of my life. I missed no opportunity of the Swami's society that presented itself, and accepted practically no other, filling up the time with quiet writing and needlework; thus I received one long continuous impression of his mind and personality, for which I can never be sufficiently thankful.

Vindication of Man

From the beginning of the voyage to the end, the flow of thought and story went on. One never knew what moment would see the flash of intuition, and hear the ringing utterance of some fresh truth. It was while we sat chatting in the River on the first afternoon, that he suddenly exclaimed, "Yes! the older I grow, the more everything seems to me to lie in manliness. This is my new gospel. Do even evil like a man! Be wicked, if you must, on a great scale!" And these words link themselves in my memory with those of another day, when I had been reminding him of the rareness of criminality of India. And he turned on me, full of sorrowful protest. "Would God it were otherwise in my land!" he said, "for this is verily the virtuousness of death!" Stories of the *Śivarātri* or Dark Night of *Śiva*, of Prithi Rai, of the judgement seat of Vikramaditya, of Buddha and Yasodhara, and a thousand more, were constantly coming up. And a noticeable point was, that one never heard the same thing twice. There was the perpetual study of caste; the constant examination and restatement of ideas; the talk of work, past, present, and future; and above all the vindication of Humanity, never abandoned, never weakened, always rising

Indian History

to new heights of defence of the undefended, of chivalry for the weak. Our Master has come and he has gone, and in the priceless memory he has left with us who knew him, there is no other thing so great, as this his love of man.

I cannot forget his indignation when he heard some European reference to cannibalism, as if it were a normal part of life in some societies. "That is not true!" he said, when he had heard to the end. "No nation ever ate human flesh, save as a religious sacrifice, or in war, out of revenge. Don't you see? That's not the way of gregarious animals! It would cut at the roots of social life!" Kropotkin's great work on 'Mutual Aid' had not yet appeared, when these words were said. It was his love of Humanity, and his instinct on behalf of each in his own place, that gave the Swami so clear an insight.

Again he talked of the religious impulse, "Sex-love and creation!" he cried, "these are at the root of most religions. And these in India are called Vaishnavism, and in the West Christianity. How few have dared to worship Death, or Kali! Let us worship Death! Let us embrace the Terrible, because it is terrible! Not asking that it be toned down. Let us take misery, for misery's own sake!"

As we came to the place where the river water met the ocean, we could see why the sea had been called 'Kali Pani' or black water, while the river was 'Sadha Pani' or white, and the Swami explained how it was the great reverence of Hindus for the ocean, forbidding them to defile it by crossing it, that had made such journeys equal to outcasting for so many centuries. Then, as the ship crossed the line, touching the sea for the first time, he chanted "*Namo Śivāya*! *Namo Śivāya*! Passing from the Land of Renunciation to the Land of the Enjoyment of the World!"

He was talking again, of the fact that he who would be great must suffer, and how some were fated to see every joy of the senses turn to ashes, and he said, "The whole of life is only a swan-song! Never forget those lines—

"The lion, when stricken to the heart,
gives out his mightiest roar.
When smitten on the head,
the cobra lifts its hood.
And the majesty of the soul comes forth,
only when a man is wounded to his depths."

Now he would answer a question, with infinite patience, and again he would play with historic and literary speculations. Again and again, his mind would return to the Buddhist period, as the *crux* of the real understanding of Indian History.

"The three cycles of Buddhism," he said one day, "were five hundred years of the Law, five hundred years of Images, and five hundred years of Tantras. You must not imagine that there was ever a religion in India called Buddhism, with temples and priests of its own order! Nothing of the sort. It was always within Hinduism. Only at one time, the influence of Buddha was paramount, and this made the nation monastic." He had been discussing the question of the adoption into Buddhism, as its saints, of the Nags of Kashmir (the great serpents who were supposed to dwell within the springs), after the terrible winter that followed their deposition as deities.

Buddhism in Hinduism

And he drifted on to talk about the Soma plant, picturing how, for a thousand years after the Himalayan period, it was annually received in Indian villages as if it were a king, the people going out to meet it on a given day, and bringing it in rejoicing. And now it cannot even be identified!

Again it was Sher Shah, of whom he talked—Sher Shah, making a thirty [13?] years' interim in the reign of Humayoon. I remember the accession of delight with which he began the subject, saying, "He was once a boy, running about the streets of Bengal!" He ended by showing how the Grand Trunk Road from Chittagong to Peshawar, the Postal system, and the Government Bank, were all his work. And then there were a few minutes of silence, and

Salutation to the Guru

Conservative and Liberal

he began reciting lines from the Guru Gita. "To that Guru who is Brahman, to that Guru who is Vishnu, to that Guru who is *Śiva*, to that Guru who is Para Brahman, I bow down to that Guru. From the Guru is the beginning, yet is he without beginning; to that Guru who is greatest among the gods, to that Guru who is Para Brahman, I bow down to that Guru." He was pursuing some train of thought within to which these snatches of prayer bore some relation. A moment or two went by, and suddenly he broke his reverie, saying: "Yes, Buddha was right! It *must* be cause and effect in *Karma*. This individuality cannot but be an illusion!" It was the next morning, and I had supposed him to be dozing in his chair, when he suddenly exclaimed, "Why the memory of one life is like millions of years of confinement, and they want to wake up the memory of many lives! Sufficient unto the day is the evil thereof!"

"I have just been talking to Turiyananda about conservative and liberal ideas," he said, as he met me on deck before breakfast one morning, and straight-way plunged into the subject.

"The conservative's whole ideal is *submission*. Your ideal is struggle. Consequently it is *we* who enjoy life, and never you! You are always striving to change yours to something better, and before a millionth part of the change is carried out, you die. The Western ideal is to be doing; the Eastern to be suffering. The perfect life would be a wonderful harmony between doing and suffering. But that can never be.

"In our system, it is accepted that a man cannot have all he desires. Life is subjected to many restraints. This is ugly, yet it brings out points of light and strength. Our liberals see only the ugliness, and try to throw it off. But they substitute something quite as bad, and the new custom takes as long as the old, for us to work to its centres of strength.

"Will is not strengthened by change. It is weakened and enslaved by it. But we must be always absorbing. Will grows stronger by absorption. And consciously or unconsciously, will is the one thing in the world that we admire. *Suttee* is great, in the eyes of the whole world, because of the will that it manifests.

"It is selfishness that we must seek to eliminate! I find that whenever I have made a mistake in my life, it has always been because *self* entered into the calculation. Where self has not been involved, my judgement has gone straight to the mark.

"Without this self, there would have been no religious systems. If man had not wanted anything for himself, do you think he would have had all this praying and worship? Why! He would never have thought of God at all, except perhaps for a little praise now and then, at the sight of a beautiful landscape or something. And that is the only attitude there ought to be. All praise and thanks. If only we were rid of self!"

"You are quite wrong," he said again, "when you think that fighting is a sign of growth. It is not so at all. Absorption is the sign. Hinduism is a very genius of absorption. We have never cared for fighting. Of course, we could strike a blow now and then, in defence of our homes! That was right. But we never cared for fighting for its own sake. Everyone has to learn that. So let these races of newcomers whirl on! They'll all be taken into Hinduism in the end!"

He never thought of his Mother-Church or his Motherland except as dominant; and again and again, when thinking of definite schemes, he would ejaculate, in his whimsical way, "Yes, it is true! If European men or women are to work in India, it must be under the black man!"

Indian Achievements

He brooded much over the national achievement. "Well! Well!" he would say, "We have done one thing that no other people ever did. We have converted a whole nation to one or two ideas. Non-beef-eating for instance. Not one Hindu eats beef. No, no!"—turning sharply round—"it's not at all like European non-cat-eating; for beef was formerly the food of the country!"

We were discussing a certain opponent of his own, and I suggested that he was guilty of putting his sect above his country. "That is Asiatic," retorted the Swami warmly, "and it is grand! Only he had not the brain to conceive, nor the patience to wait!" And then he went off into a musing on Kali

"I am not one of those," he chanted,
"Who put the garland of skulls, round
Thy neck,
And then look back in terror
And call Thee 'The Merciful'!
The heart must become a
burial ground,
Pride, selfishness, and desire all
broken into dust,
Then and then alone will the Mother
dance there!"

"I love terror for its own sake" he went on, "despair for its own sake, misery for its own sake. Fight always. Fight and fight on, though always in defeat. That's the ideal. That's the ideal."

"The totality of all souls, not the human alone," he said once, "is the Personal God. The will of the Totality nothing can resist. It is what we know as Law. And this is what we mean by *Śiva* and Kali, and so on."

Some of the most beautiful scenes in the world have been made for me more beautiful, by listening, in their midst, to these long soliloquies.

It was dark when we approached Sicily, and against the sunset sky, Etna was in slight eruption. As we entered the straits of Messina, the moon rose, and I walked up and down the deck beside the Swami, while he dwelt on the fact that beauty is not external, but already in the mind. On one side frowned the dark crags of the Italian coast, on the other, the island was touched with silver light. "Messina must thank *me*!" he said. "It is I who give her all her beauty!"

Then he talked of the fever of longing to reach God, that had wakened in him as a boy, and of how he would begin repeating a text before sunrise, and remain all day repeating it, without stirring. He was trying here to explain the idea of *tapasya*, in answer to my questions, and he spoke of the old way of lighting four fires, and sitting in the midst, hour after hour, with the sun overhead, reining in the mind. "Worship the terrible!" he ended, "Worship Death! All else is vain. All struggle is vain. That is the last lesson. Yet this is not the coward's love of death, not the love of the weak, or the suicide. It is the welcome of the strong man, who has sounded everything to its depths, and *knows* that there is no alternative."

Religious Austerity

XIII

Glimpses of the Saints

The Swami talked with me one day, of the saints he had seen. The subject began perhaps with that Nag Mahashoy, who had paid him a visit in Calcutta, only a few weeks before, and whose death must have occurred a day or two previous to our leaving.* The news reached him, while the ship was still in the river. Nag Mahashoy, he said repeatedly, was "one of the greatest of the works of Ramakrishna Paramahamsa". He described his impassioned idea of the necessity of *Bhakti,* and how he would refuse to give food, to the body of one so worthless and unfortunate as he himself was, in never yet having loved God. He told me, too, how on one occasion Nag Mahashoy had cut down the ridge pole of his cottage, in order to make the fire to cook food for a guest.

The talk passed perhaps, to the story of that youth who was touched by Sri Ramakrishna's

*Nag Mahashoy died in the last week of December, 1899, not as stated in the text—Ed.

hand, and who never afterwards spoke, save to say "My Beloved! My Beloved!" He lived ten years, without other speech than this.

A vision of the Madonna

There were many stories current amongst the monks, of persons who had come to *Dakshineshwar* during the lifetime of their Master, and being touched by his hand, went immediately into *Samadhi*. In many cases, nothing more was known of the visitants than this. This was notably true of a certain woman, who had driven to the Temple and of whom Sri Ramakrishna had said at once that she was "a fragment of the Madonnahood of the worlds". He had offered salutation to this guest, in the name of the Mother, throwing flowers on her feet and burning incense before her, and she, as was not perhaps surprising, had passed immediately into the deepest *Samadhi*. From this, however, to everyone's surprise, it had proved most difficult to recall her. It was two or three hours before she awoke from her ecstasy, and when this happened her whole appearance, it is said, was as that of one who had been intoxicated. Much relieved that all was ending thus well, however—for it had been feared that her *Samadhi* might last much longer, and her family, wherever they were, feel justly disturbed—all lent their aid to the departure of the stranger from the temple, and none had the forethought to make a single enquiry as to her name or abode. She never came again. Thus her memory became like some beautiful legend, treasured in the Order as a witness to the worship of Sri Ramakrishna for gracious and noble wifehood and motherhood. Had he not said of this woman, "a fragment of the eternal Madonnahood?"

In my own ignorance of religious matters in general, my mind felt out much after these stray children of the central impulse, shining like distant stars in their own orbits, as it were, and never returning upon us or ours. I wanted to know whether, even in lives so fair as theirs, it might perhaps be possible to forget the great experience of a day long years ago, so that the memory of the great Teacher and his touch would become to them also a far-away incident, a story heard in a dream, even as their visits had become to those who saw them pass. I wanted in fact to be able to measure the relative values of many things, and I left out of sight at that time altogether—having not yet begun to consider it—the preparedness which the national idea had produced in every Hindu for such experiences. But the Swami could not understand my mental twilight. "Was it a joke," he said, "that Ramakrishna Paramahamsa should touch a life? Of course he made new men and new women of those who came to him, even in these fleeting

Lives Transformed

contacts!" And then he would tell story after story of different disciples. How one came and came again, and struggled to understand. And suddenly to this one, he turned and said, "Go away now, and make some money! Then come again!" And that man today was succeeding in the world, but the old love was proving itself ever alight. There was no mention of the defects of this, or any other of whom he told. As one listened, it was the courage and nobility of each man's struggle that one felt. Why should every man force himself to be a monk? Nay, how *could* every man, till his other work was done? But there would be no mistake in the end. All these would be his at last.

Similarly, of the saints. His whole soul went to the interpretation of each, as he rose before him, and it would have been impossible at that moment for the listener to think of any other as higher. Of Pavhari Baba he had so striven to tell us everything, that it would have seemed scarcely delicate to press vague questions upon him further. All who had been with him at the time of the saint's death knew that he held him second only to Sri Ramakrishna, knew that there was none whose love to himself he had more valued.

Now he set himself to tell stories for an hour, of one or two others whom he had met. Trailinga Swami he had seen when very, very old, more than a hundred, apparently. He was always silent. He would lie in a *Śiva-temple* in Banares, with his feet on the image. A madcap, seemingly. He allowed people, however, to write him questions, and sometimes, if he fancied one, would write an answer in Sanskrit. This man was lately dead.

Raghunath Dass

RAGHUNATH DASS had been dead for two months when the Swami reached his ashrama. He had been a soldier originally in the British service, and as an outpost sentinel was faithful and good, and much beloved by his officers. One night, however, he heard a Ram-Ram party. He tried to do his duty, but "Jaya Bolo Ram Chunder ki jai!" maddened him. He threw away his arms and uniform, and joined the worship.

This went on for some time, till reports came to the Colonel. He sent for Raghunath Dass, and asked him whether these were true, and if he knew the penalty. Yes, he knew it. It was to be shot.

"Well," said the Colonel, "go away this time, and I shall repeat it to no one. This once I forgive you. But if the same thing happens again, you must suffer the penalty."

That night, however, the sentinel heard again the Ram-Ram party. He did his best, but it was irresistible. At last, he threw all to the winds, and joined the worshippers till morning.

Meanwhile, however, the Colonel's trust in Raghunath Dass had been so great that he found it difficult to believe anything against him, even on his own confession. So in the course of the night, he visited the outpost, to see for himself. Now Raghunath Dass was in his place, and exchanged the word with him three times. Then, being reassured, the Colonel turned in, and went to sleep.

In the morning appeared Raghunath Dass to report himself and surrender his arms. But the report was not accepted, for the Colonel told him what he had himself seen and heard.

Thunderstruck, the man insisted by some means on retiring from the service. Rama, it was who had done this for His servant. Henceforth, in very truth, he would serve no other.

"He became a Vairagi," said the Swami, "on the banks of the Saraswati. People thought him ignorant, but I knew his power. Daily he would feed thousands. Then would come the grain seller, after a while, with his bill. 'H'm!' Raghunath Dass would say, 'A thousand rupees you say? Let me see. It is a month I think since I have received anything. This will come, I fancy, to-morrow.' And it always came."

Someone asked him if the story of the Ram-Ram party was true.

"What's the use of knowing such things?" he answered.

"I do not ask for curiosity," urged the questioner, "but only to know if it is possible for such things to happen!"

"Nothing is impossible with the Lord!" answered Raghunath Dass.

At Hrishikesh

"I saw many great men," went on the Swami, "in Hrishikesh. One case that I remember was that of a man who seemed to be mad. He was coming nude down the street, with boys pursuing and throwing stones at him. The whole man was bubbling over with laughter, while blood was streaming down his face and neck. I took him, and bathed the wound, putting ashes* on it, to stop the bleeding. And all the time, with peals of laughter, he told me of the fun the boys and he had been having, throwing the stones. 'So the Father plays,' he said."

"Many of these men hide, in order to guard themselves against intrusion. People are a trouble to them. One had human bones strewn about his cave, and gave it out that he lived on corpses. Another threw stones. And so on"...

"Sometimes the thing comes upon them in a flash. There was a boy, for instance, who used to come to read the Upanishads with Abhedananda. One day he turned and said, 'Sir, is all this really true?'

* These ashes are made by burning a piece of cotton cloth—N.

'Oh yes!' said Abhedananda, 'it may be difficult to realise, but it is certainly true.'

"And the next day, that boy was a silent *Sannyāsin*, nude, on his way to Kedarnath!"

"What happened to him? You ask. He became silent!"

"But the *Sannyāsin* needs no longer to worship, or to go on pilgrimage, or perform austerities. What, then, is the motive of all this going from pilgrimage to pilgrimage, shrine to shrine, and austerity to austerity? He is acquiring merit, and giving it to the world!"

Shibi Rana

And then, perhaps, came the story of Shibi Rana. "Ah yes!" exclaimed the teller, as he ended, "these are the stories that are deep in our nation's heart! Never forget that the *Sannyāsin* takes two vows, one to realise the truth, and one to help the world, and that the most stringent of stringent requirements is that he should renounce any *thought* of heaven!"

XIV

Past and Future in India

Even a journey round the world becomes a pilgrimage, if one makes it with the *Guru*. It was late one evening, in the Red Sea, when I brought to the Swami some perplexity, of a personal nature, about the right method of helpfulness to others. It was rarely, indeed, that he would answer a question of this sort, without first turning for authority to some *dictum* of the *Shastras*. And how grateful does one become later for this fact! It was his personal opinion that one desired. But giving this, as he did, in the form of a comment on some text, it went much deeper into the mind, and became the subject of much longer thought and consideration, than if he had answered at once, in the sense required by the impatient questioner.

The Broken Vow

In the same way, when I had asked him what becomes of those who failed to keep their vows, he had gone all the way round by a beautiful Sanskrit quotation, to answer me. Even now, I hear the ring of his wonderful voice, repeating Arjuna's question :

अयतिः श्रद्धयोपेतो योगाच्चलितमानसः ।
अप्राप्य योगसंसिद्धिं कां गतिं कृष्ण गच्छति ॥
कच्चिन्नोभयविभ्रष्टश्छिन्नाभ्रमिव नश्यति ।
अप्रतिष्ठो महाबाहो विमूढो ब्रह्मणः पथि ॥

Gita, vi. 37-38.

They who begin with *Shraddha*, and afterwards become unsteady, to what end do those come, O Krishna, who fail in *Yoga*? Do they, fallen from both estates, perish—*blasted, like a summer-cloud before the wind*?

And the answer of Sri Krishna, fearless, triumphant—

पार्थ नैवेह नामुत्र विनाशस्तस्य विद्यते ।
नहि कल्याणकृत्कश्चिद्दुर्गतिं तात गच्छति ॥

Gita, vi. 40.

"Neither here nor hereafter, O son of Pritha, shall such meet with destruction, NEVER shall one who has done good, come to grief, O my son!"

And then he drifted into a talk that I can never forget. First, he explained how everything, short of the absolute control of mind, word, and deed, was but "the sowing of wild oats". Then he told how the religious who failed would sometimes be born again to a throne, 'there to sow his wild oats', in gratifying that particular desire which had led to his downfall, 'A memory of the religious habit,' he said, 'often haunts the throne.' For one of the signs of greatness was held to be the persistence of a faint memory. Akbar had had this memory. He thought of himself as *brahmacharin* who had failed in his vows. But he would be born again, in more favourable surroundings, and that time he would succeed. And then there came one of those personal glimpses which occurred so seldom with our Master. Carried away by the talk of memory, he lifted the visor for a moment, on his own soul. "And whatever you may think," he said, turning to me suddenly, and addressing me by name, "I have such a memory! When I was only two years old, I used to play with my syce, at being a *vairagi*, clothed in ashes and *kaupina*. And if a *Sadhu* came to beg, they would lock me in, upstairs, to prevent my giving too much away. I felt that I also was this, and that for some mischief I had had to be sent away from *Śiva*. No doubt my family increased this feeling, for when I was naughty they would say 'Dear, dear! so many austerities, yet *Śiva* sent us this demon after all, instead of a good soul!' Or when I was very rebellious they would empty a can of water over me, saying '*Śiva*! *Śiva*!' And then I was all right, always. Even now, when I feel mischievous, that word keeps me straight. 'No!' I say to myself, 'not this time!' "

On the present occasion, then, he went back, in similar fashion, to the Gita. "The Gita says," he answered me, "that there are three kinds of charity, the *Tāmasic*, the *Rājasic*, and the *Sāttvic*. *Tāmasic* charity is performed on an impulse. It is always making mistakes. The doer thinks of nothing but his own impulse to be kind. *Rājasic* charity is what a man does for his own glory. And *sāttvic* charity is that which is given to the right person in the right way, and at the proper time. Your own," he said, referring to the incident that had brought about my question, "was, I fear, like the *Tāmasic* charity. When it comes to the *Sāttvic*, I think more and more of a certain great Western woman, in whom I have seen that quiet giving, always to the right person in the right way, at the right time, and never making a mistake. For my own part. I have been learning that even charity can go too far."

Tamasic Charity

His voice sank into silence, and we sat looking out over the starlit sea. Then he took up the thread again. "As I grow older I find that I look more and more for greatness in *little* things. I want to know what a great man eats and wears, and how he speaks to his servants. I want to find a Sir Philip Sidney greatness! Few men would remember the thirst of others, even in the moment of death.

"But anyone will be great in a great position! Even the coward will grow brave in the glare of the footlights. The world looks on. Whose heart will not throb? Whose pulse will not quicken, till he can do his best?

True Greatness

"More and more the true greatness seems to me that of the worm, doing its duty silently, steadily, from moment to moment, and hour to hour."

How many points on the map have received a new beauty in my eyes, from the conversations they recall! As we passed up the coast of Italy, we talked of the Church. As we went through the Straits of Bonifacio, and sat looking at the south coast of Corsica, he spoke in a hushed voice of "this land of the birth of the War-Lord," and wandered far afield to talk of the strength of Robespierre, or to touch on Victor Hugo's contempt for Napoleon III, with his "*Et tu* Napoleon!"

As I came on deck, on the morning of our passing through the Straits of Gibraltar, he met me with the words "Have you seen them? Have you seen them? Landing there and crying 'Din! Din! The Faith! The Faith!' " And for half an hour I was swept away into his dramatisation of the Moorish invasions of Spain.

Or again, on a Sunday evening, he would sit and talk of Buddha, putting new life into the customary historic recital of bare facts, and interpreting the Great Renunciation as it had appeared to him who made it.

But his talks were not all entertaining, nor even all educational. Every now and then he would return, with consuming eagerness, to the great purpose of his life. And when he did this, I listened with an anxious mind, striving to treasure up each word that he let fall. For I knew that here I was but the transmitter, but the bridge, between him and that countless host of his own people, who would yet arise, and seek to make good his dreams.

His Message

One of these occasions came on a certain evening, as we neared Aden. I had asked him, in the morning, to tell me, in broad outline, what he felt to be the points of difference between his own schemes for the good of India, and those preached by others. It was impossible to draw him out on this subject. On the contrary, he expressed appreciation of certain personal characteristics and lines of conduct, adopted by some of the leaders of other schools, and I regarded the question as dismissed. Suddenly, in the evening, he returned to the subject of his own accord.

"I disagree with all those," he said, "who are giving their superstitions back to my people. Like the Egyptologist's interest in Egypt, it is easy to feel an interest in India that is purely selfish. One may desire to see again the India of one's books, one's studies, one's dreams. *My* hope is to see again the strong points of that India, reinforced by the strong points of this age, only in a natural way. The new state of things must be a *growth* from within.

Be Strong

"So I preach only the Upanishads. If you look, you will find that I have never quoted anything but the Upanishads. And of the Upanishads, it is only that one idea *strength*. The quintessence of *Vedas* and *Vedanta* and all, lies in that one word. Buddha's teaching was of Non-resistance of Non-injury. But I think this is a better way of teaching the same thing. For behind that Non-injury lay a dreadful weakness. It is weakness that conceives the idea of resistance. I do not think of punishing or escaping from a drop of sea spray. It is nothing to me. Yet to the mosquito, it would be serious. Now I would make all injuries like that. Strength and fearlessness. My own ideal is that giant of a saint whom they killed in the Mutiny, and who broke his silence, when stabbed to the heart, to say—'And thou also art He!'

"But you may ask—what is the place of Ramakrishna in this scheme?

"He is the method, that wonderful unconscious method! He did not understand himself. He knew nothing of England or the English, save that they were queer folk from over the sea. But he lived that great life—and I read the meaning. Never a word of condemnation for any! Once I had been attacking one of our sects of Diabolists. I had been raving on for three hours, and he had listened quietly. 'Well, well!' said the old man as I finished, 'perhaps every house may have a back door. Who knows?'

"Hitherto the great fault of our Indian religion has lain in its knowing only two words—*Renunciation* and *Mukti*. Only *Mukti here*! Nothing for the householder!

"But these are the very people whom I want to help. For are not all souls of the same quality? Is not the goal of all the same?

"And so strength must come to the nation through education."

I thought at the time, and I think increasingly, as I consider it, that this one talk of my Master had been well worth the whole voyage, to have heard.

XV

The Swami on Hinduism

The Swami was constantly preoccupied with the thought of Hinduism as a whole, and this fact found recurring expression in references to Vaishnavism. As a *Sannyāsin*, his own imagination was perhaps dominated by the conceptions of Shaivism. But Vaishnavism offered him a subject of perpetual interest and analysis. The thing he knew by experience was the truth of the doctrine of Advaita. The symbols under which he would seek to convey this were the monastic ideal and the Worship of the Terrible. But these were truths for heroes. By their means, one might gather an army. The bulk of mankind would always think of God as Divine Providence, a tender Preserver, and the question of questions was how to deepen the popular knowledge, of the connection between this type of belief and the highest philosophy. With regard to the West, indeed, the bridges had actually to be built.

Advaita had to be explained and preached. But in India, all this had been done long ago. The facts were universally admitted. It was only necessary to renew realisation, to remind the nation of the inter-relation of all parts of its faith, and to go again and again over the ground, in order to see that no weak point remained, in the argument by which Vaishnavism was demonstrated to be as essential to the highest philosophy, as that philosophy was acknowledged to be, to it.

Thus he loved to dwell on the spectacle of the historical emergence of Hinduism. He sought constantly for the great force *behind* the evolution of any given phenomenon. Where was the thinker behind the founder of a religion? And where, on the other hand, was the heart to complete the thought? Buddha had received his philosophy of the five categories—form, feeling, sensation, motion and knowledge—from Kapila. But Buddha has brought the love that made the philosophy live. Of no one of these, Kapila had said, can anything be declared. For each *is* not. It but was, and is gone. 'Each is but the ripple on the waters. Know, Oh man! Thou art the sea!'

The Samkhya Philosophy

Krishna, in this turn, as the preacher and creative centre of popular Hinduism, awoke in the Swami a feeling which was scarcely second to his passionate personal adoration of Buddha. Compared to His many-sidedness, the *Sannyās** of Buddha was almost a weakness. How wonderful was the Gita! Reading it, as a boy, he would be stopped every now and then by some great sentence, which would go throbbing through his brain for days and nights. 'They who find pleasure and pain the same, heat and cold the same, friend and foe the same!' And that description of the battle—a spirited battle too!—with the opening words of Krishna, 'Ill doth it befit thee, Arjuna, thus to yield to unmanliness!' How strong! But besides this, there was the beauty of it. The Gita, after the Buddhist writings, was such a relief! Buddha had constantly said, 'I am for the People!' And they had crushed, in his name, the vanity of art and learning. The great mistake committed by Buddhism lay in the destruction of the old.

For the Buddhist books were torture to read. Having been written for the ignorant, one would find only one or two thoughts in a huge volume.† It was to meet the need thus roused, that the Puranas were intended. There had been only one mind in India that had foreseen this need, that of Krishna, probably the greatest

---

* Monasticism preached by Buddha

† It is not to be supposed that the Swami here referred to the Dhammapada—a work which he always placed on a level with the Gita. The reference, I think, was rather to such books as those Jataka Birth Stories which are published in two volumes in Trubner's Oriental Series.

man who ever lived. He recognises at once the need of the People, and the desirability of preserving all that had already been gained. Nor are the Gopi story and the Gita (which speaks again and again of women and *sudras*) the only forms in which he reached the ignorant. For the whole *Mahābhārata* is his, carried out by his worshippers, and it begins with the declaration that it is for the People.

Life Reveals God

"Thus is created a religion that ends in the worship of Vishnu, as the preservation and enjoyment of life, leading to the realisation of God. Our last movement, Chaitanyaism, you remember, was for enjoyment.* At the same time, Jainism represents the other extreme, the slow destruction of the body by self-torture. Hence Buddhism, you see, is reformed Jainism, and this is the real meaning of Buddha's leaving the company of the five ascetics. In India, in every age, there is a cycle of sects which represents every gradation of physical practice, from the extreme of self-torture to the extreme of excess. And during the same period will always be developed a metaphysical cycle, which represents the realisation of God as taking place by every gradation of means, from that of using the senses as an instrument, to that of

* The Swami was characterising doctrine here : he was not speaking of the personal asceticism of Sri Chaitanya, which has probably never been surpassed.

the annihilation of the senses. Thus Hinduism always consists, as it were, of two counter-spirals, completing each other, round a single axis.

"Yes! Vaishnavism says, 'It is all right! This tremendous love for father, for mother, for brother, husband, or child! It is all right, if only you will think that Krishna is the child, and when you give him food, that you are feeding Krishna!' This was the cry of Chaitanya, 'Worship God *through* the senses!' as against the Vedantic cry, 'Control the senses! Suppress the senses!'

"At the present moment, we may see three different positions of the national religion—the orthodox, the *Arya Samāj*, and the *Brāmo Samāj*. The orthodox covers the ground taken by the Vedic Hindus of the *Mahābhārata* epoch. The *Arya Samāj* corresponds with Jainism, and the *Brāhmo Samāj* with the Buddhists.

India not Effete

"I see that India is a young and living organism. Europe also is young and living. Neither has arrived at such a stage of development that we can safely criticize its institutions. They are two great experiments, neither of which is yet complete. In India, we have social communism, with the light of Advaita—that is, spiritual individualism—playing on and around it; in Europe, you are socially individualists, but your thought is dualistic, which is spiritual communism.

Thus the one consists of socialist institutions, hedged in by individualistic thought, while the other is made up of individualist institutions, within the hedge of communistic thought.

"Now we must help the Indian experiment as it is. Movements which do not attempt to help things as they are, are, from that point of view, no good. In Europe for instance, I respect marriage as highly as non-marriage. Never forget that a man is made great and perfect as much by his faults as by his virtues. So we must not seek to rob a nation of its character, even if it could be proved that that character was all faults."

The Worship of Humanity

His mind was extraordinarily clear on the subject of what he meant by individualism. How often has he said to me "You do not yet understand India! We Indians are MAN-worshippers, after all! Our God is man!" He meant here the great individual man, the man of self-realisation—Buddha, Krishna, the Guru, the *MahaPuruśa*. But on another occasion, using the same word in an entirely different sense, he said "This idea of man-worship* exists in the nucleus in India, but it has never been expanded. You must develop it. Make poetry, make art, of it. Establish the worship of the feet of beggars, as you had it in Medieval Europe. Make man-worshippers."

* That is to say, the worship of the manhood which exists in any man, in all men, apart from their individual achievement of thought character, humanity.

He was equally clear, again, about the value of the image. "You may always say," he said, "that the image is God. The error you have to avoid, is to think God the image." He was appealed to, on one occasion, to condemn the fetichism of the Hottentot. "I do not know," he answered, "what fetichism is!"

A lurid picture was hastily put before him, of the object alternately worshipped, beaten and thanked. "*I* do that!" he exclaimed. "Don't you see," he went on, a moment later, in hot resentment of injustice done to the lowly and absent, "Don't you see that there is no fetichism? Oh, your hearts are steeled, that you cannot see that the child is right! The child sees person everywhere. Knowledge robs us of the child's vision. But at last, through higher knowledge, we win back to it. He connects a living power with rocks, sticks, trees, and the rest. And is there not a living Power behind them? It is *symbolism*, not fetichism! Can you not see?"

The Mimansakas

But while every sincere ejaculation was thus sacred to him, he never forgot for a moment the importance of the philosophy of Hinduism. And he would throw perpetual flashes of poetry into the illustration of such arguments as are known to lawyers. How lovingly he would dwell upon the *Mimānsaka* philosophy! With what pride he would remind the listener that, according to Hindu *savants*, 'the whole universe is only the *meaning of words*. After the word comes the thing. Therefore, the idea is all!' And indeed, as he expounded it, the daring of the *Mimānsaka* argument, the fearlessness of its admissions and the firmness of its inferences, appeared as the very glory of Hinduism. There is assuredly no evasion of the logical issue in a people who can say, even while they worship the image, that the image is nothing but the idea made objective, that prayer is powerful in proportion to the concentration it represents; that the gods exist only in the mind, and yet the more assuredly exist. The whole train of thought sounded like the most destructive attack of the iconoclast, yet it was being used for the exposition of a faith! One day, he told the story of Satyavama's sacrifice and how the word 'Krishna', written on a piece of paper, and thrown into the balances, made Krishna himself, on the other side, kick the beam. "Orthodox Hinduism," he began, "makes *sruti*, the sound, everything. The *thing* is but a feeble manifestation of the pre-existing and eternal Idea. So the *name* of God is everything : God Himself is merely the objectification of that idea in the eternal mind. Your own name is infinitely more perfect than the person, you! The name of God is greater than God. Guard you your speech!" Surely there has never been another religious system so fearless of truth! As he talked, one saw that the whole turned on the unspoken conviction, self-apparent to the Oriental mind, that religion is not a creed but an experience; a process, as the Swami himself has elsewhere said, of being and becoming. If it be true that this process leads inevitably from the apprehension of the manifold to the realisation of the One, then it must also be true that everything is in the mind, and that the material is nothing more than the concretising of ideas. Thus the Greek philosophy of Plato is included within the Hindu philosophy of the *Mimānsakas*, and a doctrine that sounds merely empiric on the lips of Europe, finds reason and necessity, on those of India. In the same way, as one declaring a truth self-evident, he exclaimed, on one occasion, "I would not worship even the Greek gods, for they were separate from humanity! Only those should be worshipped who are like ourselves, but greater. The difference between the gods and me must be a difference only of degree."

Indian Logic

But his references to philosophy did not by any means always consist of these epicurean titbits. He was merciless, as a rule, in the demand for intellectual effort, and would hold a group of unlearned listeners through an analysis of early systems, for a couple of hours at a stretch, without suspecting them, of weariness or difficulty. It was evident, too, at such times, that his mind was following the train of argument in another language, for his translations of technical terms would vary from time to time.

In this way, he would run over the six objects with which the mind has to deal, in making up the universe according to the Vaisheshik formulation. These were substance,* quality, action, togetherness, classification or differentiation, and inseparable inherence as between cause and effect, parts and the whole. With this, he would compare the five categories of Buddhism—form, feeling, consciousness, reaction [*i.e.* the resultant of all previous impressions], and *vidyā*, or judgment. The Buddhist made form the resultant of all the others, and nothing by itself; the goal, therefore, for Buddhism, was beyond *vidyā* [which Buddhism called *Prajnā*], and outside the five categories. Side by side with this, he would place the three illusive categories of the Vedanta (and of Kant)—time, space, and causation [*Kāla-desh-nimitta*] appearing as name-and-form, which is *Māyā*, that is to say, neither existence nor non-existence. It was clear, then, that the seen was not, according to this, a being. Rather it is an eternal, changeful process. Being is one, but the process makes this being appear

* Substance, according to the Vaisheshik consists of time, space, mind, soul and five elements (earth, water, fire, air and ether).

as many. Evolution and involution are both alike in *Māyā*. They are certainly not in Being [*Sat*], which remains eternally the same.

Nor would Western speculations pass forgotten, in this great restoration of the path the race had come by. For this was a mind which saw only the seeking, pursuing, and enquiry of man, making no arbitrary distinctions as between ancient and modern. The analysis of the modern syllogism—under the old Indian title of 'the five limbs of the argument'—would be followed by the four proofs of the *Nyāyas*. These were, (1) direct perception; (2) inference; (3) analogy; (4) testimony. According to this logic, the induction and deduction of the moderns were not recognized; inference was regarded as always from the more known to the less known, or from the less to the more. The inference from direct perception was divided into three different kinds : first, that in which the effect is inferred from the cause, second, that in which cause is inferred from effect, and thirdly, the case in which inference is determined by concomitant circumstances. Methods of inference, again, were fivefold : by agreement, by difference, by the double method of agreement and difference, by the partial method of agreement, and by the partial method of difference. The two last were sometimes classed together as the method of the residuum. It was quite clear that only the third of these could furnish a perfect inference; that is to say, 'proof is only complete when the negative has been proved, as well as the affirmative. Thus God can never be proved to be the cause of the Universe.'

"There is, again, the fact of pervasiveness. A stone falls, and crushes a worm. Hence we infer that all stones, falling, crush worms. Why do we thus immediately reapply a perception? Experience, says someone. But it happens, let us suppose, for the first time. Throw a baby into the air, and it cries. Experience from past lives? But why applied to the future? Because there is a real connection between certain things, a *pervasiveness*, only it lies with us to see that the quality neither overlaps, nor falls short of, the instance. On this discrimination depends all human knowledge.

All is Inference

"With regard to fallacies, it must be remembered that direct perception itself can only be a proof, provided the instrument, the method, and the persistence of the perception, are all maintained pure. Disease, or emotion, will have the effect of disturbing the observation. *Therefore direct perception itself is but a mode of inference.* Therefore all human knowledge is uncertain, and may be erroneous. Who is a true witness? He is a true witness to whom the thing said is a direct perception. Therefore the Vedas are true, because they consist of the evidence of competent persons. But is this power of perception peculiar to any? No! The *Rishi*, the *Aryān*, and the *Mlechha* all alike have it.

"Modern Bengal holds that evidence is only a special case of direct perception, and that analogy and parity of reasoning are only bad inferences. Therefore of actual proofs, there are only two, direct perception and inference.

"One set of persons, you see, gives priority to the external manifestation, the other to the internal idea. Which is prior, the bird to the egg, or the egg to the bird? Does the oil hold the cup or the cup the oil? That is the problem of which there is no solution. Give it up! Escape from *Māyā*!"

XVI

Glimpses in the West

On July 31st, we arrived in London, and the voyage that to myself had been so memorable, was over. The Swami spent a few weeks in Wimbledon, but at this time of the year, not many of his friends were in town, and before long he acceded to the invitations which were constantly reaching him and went on to America, there to wait in a beautiful country-home on the Hudson, for the leading that he confidently expected, to show him where his next effort was to lie. A month later, I became a guest in the same house, and continued to see him daily, until November 5th, that is to say, six or seven weeks later. After that date, when our party was broken up, the Swami paid a few visits to New York and its neighbourhood. At the end of the month, he passed through Chicago, where I then was, on his way to California. Again I met him in New York in the following June (1900). There for a few weeks, and later in Paris for a similar length of time, I saw him frequently; and in September, finally, I spent a fortnight as his fellow guest, with American friends, in Brittany. So ends the priceless memory of the years of my schooling under him. For when I next saw my Master, in India in the first half of 1902, it was only to receive his final blessing and take a last farewell.

Discipleship is always serenely passive, but it changes, at a moment's notice, into strenuous effort and activity, when the personal presence of the Teacher is withdrawn. And this last was what our Master above all expected of his disciples. He said once that whenever a young monk, received for a few weeks or months into the monastery, complained that as yet he had learnt nothing, he always sent him back for a while to the world he had left, there to find out how very much he had in fact absorbed. Every parting from his was like the entrusting of a standard for warfare. "Be the heroic Rajput wife!" he exclaimed in an undertone on one occasion, to a girl who was about to give way to emotion, at saying farewell to her betrothed. And the words acted like a charm. His last words, after my brief glimpse of him in Chicago, were "Remember! The message of India is always '*Not the soul for Nature but Nature for the soul*!' "

The Farewell Charge

When I said goodbye to him in Brittany in September 1900, I was on the eve of returning alone to England, there to find friends and means, if possible, for the Indian work. I knew nothing as yet of the length of my stay. I had no plans. And the thought may have crossed his mind that old ties were perilous to a foreign allegiance. He had seen so many betrayals of honour that he seemed always to be ready for a new desertion. In any case, the moment was critical to the fate of the disciple, and this he did not fail to realise. Suddenly, on my last evening in Brittany, when supper was some time over, and the darkness had fallen, I heard him at the door of my little arbour-study, calling me into the garden. I came out, and found him waiting to give me his blessing, before leaving with a man-friend, for the cottage where they were both housed.

"There is a peculiar sect of Mohammedans," he said, when he saw me, "who are reported to be so fanatical that they take each new-born babe, and expose it, saying, 'If God made thee, perish! If Ali made thee, live!' Now this which they say to the child, I say, but in the opposite sense, to you, tonight—'Go forth into the world, and there, if I made you, be destroyed! If Mother made you, live!' "

Yet he came again the next morning, soon after dawn, to say farewell, and in my last memory of him in Europe, I look back once more from the peasant market-cart, and see his form against the morning sky, as he stands on the road outside our cottage at Lannion, with hands uplifted, in that Eastern salutation which is also benediction.

The outstanding impression made by the Swami's bearing, during all these months of European and American life, was one of almost complete indifference to his surroundings. Current estimates of value left him entirely unaffected. He was never in any way startled or incredulous under success, being too deeply convinced of the greatness of the Power that worked through him, to be surprised by it. But neither was he unnerved by external failure. Both victory and defeat would come and go. He was their witness. "Why should I care, if the world itself were to disappear?" he said once. "According to my philosophy, that, you know, would be a very good thing! But in fact," he added, in tones suddenly graver, "all that is against me must be with me in the end. Am I not HER soldier!"

He moved fearless and unhesitant through the luxury of the West. As determinedly as I had seen him in India, dressed in the two garments of simple folk, sitting on the floor and eating with his fingers, so, equally without doubt or shrinking, was his acceptance of the complexity of the means of living in America or France. Monk and king, he said, were obverse and reverse of a single medal. From the use of the best to the renunciation of all, was but one step. India had thrown all her prestige in the past, round poverty. Some prestige was in the future to be cast round wealth.

Rapid changes of fortune, however, must always be the fate of one who wanders from door to door, accepting the hospitality of foreign peoples. These reversals he never seemed to notice. No institution, no environment, stood between him and any human heart. His confidence in that Divine-within-Man of which he talked, was as perfect, and his appeal as direct, when he talked with the imperialist aristocrat or the American millionaire, as with the exploited and oppressed. But the out-flow of his love and courtesy were always for the simple.

Love of the Lowly

When, travelling in America, he had at first in certain Southern towns been taken for a Negro, and refused admission to the hotels, he had never said that he was not of African blood, but had as quietly and gratefully availed himself of the society of the coloured race, when that was offered, as of that of the local magnates who hastened round him later, in mortified apology for what they deemed the insult put upon him. "What! Rise at the expense of another!" he was heard to say to himself, long after, when someone referred with astonishment to this silence about his race, "Rise at the expense of another! I didn't come to earth for that!" It is not for the monk to dictate terms : the monk submits. Often, in after-years, he spoke of the pathos of the confidences regarding race-exclusion, which he had received at this time. Few things ever gave him such pleasure as a negro railway servant who came up to him on one occasion, in a station, saying that he had heard how in him one of his own people had become a great man, and he would like to shake hands. Finally, it was never possible, in his presence, for the vulgar social exultation of the white man to pass unrebuked. How stern he would become at any sign of this! How scathing was his reproof! And above all, how glowing was the picture he would paint, of a possible future for these children of the race, when they should have outstripped all others, and become the leaders of Humanity! He was scornful in his repudiation of the *pseudo-ethnology* of privileged races. "If I am grateful to my white-skinned Aryan ancestor," he said, "I am far more so to my yellow-skinned Mongolian ancestor, and most so of all, to the black-skinned Negritoid!"

The Tartar Blood

He was immensely proud, in his own physiognomy, of what he called his 'Mongolian Jaw,' regarding it as a sign of 'bull-dog tenacity of purpose'; and referring to this particular race-element, which he believed to be behind every *Aryān* people, he one day exclaimed, "Don't you see? the Tartar is the wine of the race! He gives energy and power to every blood!"

In seeking to penetrate his indifference to circumstance, one has to remember that it was based on a constant effort to find the ideal thinking place. Each family, each hearth-stone was appreciated by him, in the degree in which it provided that mental and emotional poise which makes the highest intellectual life possible. One of a party who visited Mont Saint Michael with him on Michaelmas Day 1900, and happened to stand next to him, looking at the dungeon-cages of mediaeval prisoners, was startled to hear him say, under his breath, "What a wonderful place for meditation!" There are still some amongst those who entertained him in Chicago in 1893, who tell of the difficulty with which, on his first arrival in the West, he broke through the habit of falling constantly into absorption. He would enter a tram, and have to pay the fare for the whole length of the line, more than once in a single journey, perhaps, being too deeply engrossed in thought to know when he

Inactivity in Activity

had reached his destination. As years went on, and these friends met him from time to time, they saw the gradual change to an attitude of apparent readiness and actuality. But such alterations were little more than surface-deep. Beneath, the will glowed with all its old fervour, the mind held itself ever on the brink of the universal. It seemed almost as if it were by some antagonistic power, that he was 'bowled along from place to place, being broken the while,' to use his own graphic phrase. "Oh I know I have wandered over the whole earth," he cried once, "but in India, I have looked for nothing, save the cave in which to meditate!"

And yet he was a constant and keen observer. Museums, universities, institutions, and local history, found in him an eager student. It was the personal aspect of conditions that left him unaffected. Never did the contrast between two hemispheres pass before a mind better fitted to respond to its stimulus. He approached everything through the ideas which it sought to express. During the voyage to England, he came on deck one day after a sound sleep, and told me that he had in his dreams been pursuing a discussion, as between Eastern and Western ideals of marriage, and had come to the conclusion that there was something in both that the world could ill afford to lose. At the end of his last visit to America, he told me that on first seeing Western civilisation he had been greatly attracted by it, but now he saw mainly its greed and power. Like others, he had accepted without thought the assumption that machinery would be a boon to agriculture, but he could now see that while the American farmer, with his several square miles to farm, might be the better for machines, they were likely to do little but harm on the tiny farmlands of the Indian peasantry. The problem was quite different in the two cases. Of that alone, he was firmly convinced. In everything, including the problem of distribution, he listened with suspicion to all arguments that would work for the elimination of small interest, appearing in this as in so many other things, as the perfect, though unconscious expression, of the spirit of the old Indian civilisation. A strong habit of combination he was able to admire, but what beauty of combination was there, amongst a pack of wolves?

Pride of Country

He had an intense objection to discussing the grievances, or the problems of India, in a foreign country, and felt deeply humiliated when this was done in his presence. Nor did he ever fail, on the other hand, to back a fellow countryman against the world. It was useless for Europeans to talk to him of their theories, if an

Indian investigator in the same line had come to an opposite conclusion. With the simplicity and frankness of a child, he would answer that he supposed his friend would invent more delicate instruments, and make more accurate measurements, which would enable him to prove his point.

Thus, student and citizen of the world as others were proud to claim him, it was yet always on the glory of his Indian birth that he took his stand. And in the midst of the surroundings and opportunities of princes, it was more and more the monk who stood revealed.

XVII

The Swami's Mission Considered as a Whole

The mission of Buddha, in the centuries before the Christian era, was twofold. He was the source, on the one hand, of a current of energy, that swept out from the home-waters to warm and fertilise the shoes of distant lands. India, scattering his message over the Eastern world, became the maker of nations, of churches, of literatures, arts and scientific systems, in countries far beyond her own borders. But within India proper, the life of the Great Teacher was the first nationaliser. By democratising the Aryan culture of the Upanishads, Buddha determined the common Indian civilisation, and gave birth to the Indian nation of future ages.

Similarly, in the great life that I have seen, I cannot but think that a double purpose is served—one of world-moving, and another, of nation-making. As regards foreign countries, Vivekananda was the first authoritative exponent, to Western nations, of the ideas of the Vedas and Upanishads. He had no dogma of his own to set forth. "I have never," he said, "quoted anything but the Vedas and Upanishads, and from them only that the word *strength*!" He preached Mukti instead of heaven; enlightenment instead of salvation; the realisation of the Immanent Unity, Brahman, instead of God; the truth of all faiths, instead of the binding force of anyone.

Western scholars were sometimes amazed and uncomfortable, at hearing the subject of the learned researches of the study poured out as living truths with all the fervour of the pulpit, but the scholarship of the preacher proved itself easily superior to any tests they could offer. His doctrine was no academic system of metaphysics, of purely historic and linguistic interest, but the heart's faith of a living people, who have struggled continuously for its realisation, in life and in death, for twenty-five centuries. Books had been to him not the source and fountain of knowledge, but a mere commentary on, and explanation of, a Life whose brightness would, without them have dazzled him, and left him incapable of analysing it. It had been this same life of Ramakrishna Paramahamsa that had forced upon him the conviction that the theory of Advaita, as propounded by Sankaracharya—the theory that all is One and

The Focus of Books

there is no second—was ultimately the only truth. It was this life, reinforced of course by his own experience, that had convinced him that even such philosophies* as seemed to culminate at a point short of the Absolute Oneness, would prove in the end to be dealing with phases only, of this supreme realisation.

The Home a Temple

As an expression of this goal, however, every sincere belief was true. "Bow thy head and adore," had said Sri Ramakrishna, "where others worship, for in that form in which man has called on Him, God will assuredly appear," At each step between the earth and the sun, said the Swami, we might conceivably take a photograph. No two of these would be perfectly similar. Yet which could be said to be untrue? These sayings referred to the compatibility of the antagonistic religious ideas of different sects and creeds. But when the Teacher of Dakshineshwar set himself to determine the accessibility of the highest illumination through the life of woman, we are perhaps justified in feeling that he opened the door to a deeper regard for the sacredness of what is commonly considered to be merely social and secular. In a world of symbols, he proved the service of the home as true a means to God as attendance on the altar; the sacraments

* Dualism, the doctrine of the ultimate difference between soul and God, saved and Saviour; and Qualified Dualism, the mergence of the soul in the realisation of God, but not in His being.

of the temple, though served by priestly hands, not more a means of grace than the common bread of the household, broken and distributed by wife or mother. "Everything, even the name of God," said Sri Ramakrishna, "is *Māyā*. But some of this *Māyā* helps us towards freedom; the rest only leads up deeper into bondage." In showing, that the daily life of a good woman was thus blessed, that a home was a temple, that courtesy, hospitality, and the fulfilment of duty in the world might be made into one long act of worship, Sri Ramakrishna, as I think, provided basis and sanction for what was to be a predominant thought with his great disciple.

The Swami Vivekananda, in his wanderings over India during subsequent years, studied its multitude of small social formations, each embodying its central religious conviction, and found in all broken gleams of that brightness which he had seen at its fullest in his Master. But when, in 1893, he began to see the world outside India, it was by national and patriotic unities that he was confronted. And in these, as naturally as in the creeds and sects of his own land, he continued to feel the outworking of the Divine within Man. For many years, this was entirely unconscious, yet no one around him stood unimpressed by his eager study of the strong points of different peoples.

One day, in the course of my voyage to England, when he had been telling me, with the greatest delight, of the skilled seamanship and exquisite courtesy of the Turk, I drew his attention to the astonishing character of his enthusiasm. His mind seemed to turn to the thought of the ship's servants, whose childlike devotion to himself had touched him deeply. "You see, I love our Mohammedans!" he said simply, as if accused of a fault. "Yes," I answered, "but what I want to understand is this habit of seeing every people from their strongest aspect. Where did it come from? Do you recognize it in any historical character? Or is it in some way derived from Sri Ramakrishna?"

Slowly the look of puzzled surprise left his face. "It must have been the training under Ramakrishna Paramahamsa," he answered. "We all went' by his path to some extent. Of course, it was not so difficult for us as he made it for himself. He would eat and dress like the people he wanted to understand, take their initiation, and use their language. 'One must learn,' he said, 'to put oneself into another man's very soul'. And this method was his own! No one ever before in India became Christian and Mohammedan and Vaishnava by turns!"

Thus a nationality, in the Swami's eyes, had all the sacredness of a church—a church whose

The Greatness of Nations

inmost striving was to express its own conception of ideal manhood. "The longer I live," he was once heard to ejaculate, "the more I think that the whole thing is summed up in manliness!"

By a reflex of consciousness, the more he became acquainted with the strength and lovableness of other nations, the more proud he grew of his Indian birth, becoming daily more aware of those things in which his own Motherland, in her turn, stood supreme. He discussed nations, like epochs, from various points of view successively, not blinding himself to any aspect of their vast personality. The offspring of the Roman Empire he considered always to be brutal, and the Japanese notion of marriage he held in horror. Unvaryingly, nevertheless, he would sum up the case in terms of the constructive ideals, never of the defects, of a community; and in one of the last utterances I heard from him on these subjects, he said, "For patriotism, the Japanese! For patriotism, the Japanese! For purity, the Hindu! And for manliness, the European! There is no other in the world," he added with emphasis, "who understands, as does the Englishman, what should be the glory of a man!"

His object as regards India, said the Swami, in a private conversation, had always been 'to make Hinduism aggressive'. The Eternal Faith

Aggressive Hinduism

must become active and proselytising, capable of sending out special missions, of making converts, of taking back into her fold those of her own children who had been perverted from her, and of the conscious and deliberate assimilation of new elements. Did he know that any community becomes aggressive, that any faith will be made active, the moment it becomes aware of itself as an organised unity? Did he know that he himself was to make this self-recognition possible to the Church of his forefathers? At any rate, his whole work, from the first, had consisted, according to his own statement, of 'a search for the common bases of Hinduism'. He felt instinctively that to find these and reassert them, was the one way of opening to Mother-Church the joyous conviction of her own youth and strength. Had not Buddha preached renunciation and *Nirvāna*, and because these were the essentials of the national life, had not India, within two centuries of his death, become a powerful empire? So he, too, would fall back upon the essentials, and declare them, leaving results to take care of themselves.

He held that the one authority which Hinduism claimed to rest upon, the only guide she proposed to the individual soul, was 'spiritual truth'. Those laws of experience that underlie, and give birth to, all scriptures, were what she really meant by the word 'Vedas'. The books called by that name were refused by some of her children—the Jains for example—yet the Jains were nonetheless Hindus for that. All that is true is Veda, and the Jain is to the full as much bound by his view of truth as any other. For he would extend the sphere of the Hindu Church to its utmost. With her two wings, he would cover all her fledglings. "I go forth," he had said of himself before he left for America the first time, "I go forth, to preach a religion of which Buddhism is nothing but a rebel child, and Christianity, with all her pretensions, only a distant echo!" Even as books, however, he would claim that the glory of the Vedic scriptures was unique in the history of religion. And this not merely because of their great antiquity; but vastly more for the fact that they, alone amongst all the authoritative books of the world, warned man that he must go beyond all books.

The Glory of Hinduism

Truth being thus the one goal of the Hindu creeds, and this being conceived of, not as revealed truth to be accepted, but as accessible truth to be experienced, it followed that there could never be any antagonism, real or imagined, between scientific and religious conviction, in Hinduism. In this fact, the Swami saw the immense capacity of the Indian people for that organised conception of science peculiar to the modern era. No advance of knowledge had ever been resisted by the religious intellect of India. Nor had the Hindu clergy—a greater glory still!—ever been known to protest against the right of the individual to perfect freedom of thought and belief. This last fact indeed, giving birth to the doctrine of the *Ishta Devata**—the idea that the path of the soul is to be chosen by itself—he held to be the one universal *differentia* of Hinduism; making it not only tolerant, but absorbent, of every possible form of faith and culture. Even the temper of sectarianism, characterized by the conviction that God Himself is of the believer's creed, and his limited group the one true church, and allying itself, as it now and then will with every statement that man has ever formulated, was regarded by Hinduism, he pointed out, as a symptom, not of falsehood or narrowness, but only of youth. It constituted, as Sri Ramakrishna had said, the intellectual fence, so necessary to the seedling, but so inimical to the tree. The very fact that we could impose limitations, was a proof that we were still dealing with the finite. When the cup of experience should be full, the soul would dream only of the Infinite. 'All men hedge in the fields of earth, but who can hedge in the sky?' had said the Master.

* The Chosen Ideal.

Freedom of Thought

The vast *complexus* of systems which made up Hinduism, was in every case based upon the experimental realisation of religion, and characterised by an infinite inclusiveness. The only tests of conformity ever imposed by the priesthood had been social, and while this had resulted in a great rigidity of custom, it implied that to their thinking the mind was eternally free. But it could not be disputed that the thought area within Hinduism, as actually realised, had been coloured by the accumulation of a few distinctive ideas, and these were the main subjects of the Swami's Address before the Parliament of Religions, at Chicago, in 1893.

First of these special conceptions, with which India might be said to be identified, was that of the cyclic character of the cosmos. On the relation of Creator and created, as equal elements in a dualism which can never be more than a relative truth, Hinduism had a profound philosophy, which Vivekananda, with his certainty of grasp, was able to set forth in a few brief words. The next doctrine which he put forward, as distinctive of Indian thought in general, was that of reincarnation and Karma, ending in the manifestation of the divine nature of man. And finally, the universality of truth, whatever the form of thought or worship, completed his enumeration of these secondary *differentiæ*. In a few clear sentences, he had conclusively established the unity, and delineated the salient features of Hinduism. The remainder of his work in the West was, in the main, a free gift in modern and universal forms, of the great inspirations contained in the Eternal Faith. To him, as a religious teacher, the whole world was India, and man, everywhere a member of his own fold.

Contribution to Philosophy

It was on his return to India, in January 1897, that the Swami, in philosophic form, made that contribution to the thought of his people, which, it has been said elsewhere, is required by India of all her epoch-makers. Hitherto, the three philosophic systems—of Unism, Dualism, and Modified Unism or *Advaita*, *Dvaita*, and *Visishtādvaita*—had been regarded as offering to the soul, three different ideals of liberation. No attempt had ever before been made to reconcile these schools. On reaching Madras, however, in 1897, Vivekananda boldly claimed that even the utmost realisations of Dualism and Modified Unism, were but stages on the way to Unism itself; and the final bliss, for all alike, was the mergence in One without a second. It is said that at one of his mid-day question-classes, a member of his audience asked him why, if this was the truth, it had never before been mentioned by any of the Masters. It was customary to give answers to these questions, first in English and then in Sanskrit, for the benefit of such scholars present as knew no modern language, and the great gathering was startled, on this occasion, to hear the reply "—Because I was born for this, and it was left for me to do!"

The *Brāhmo Samaj*

In India, the Swami was extremely jealous of any attempt to exclude from Hinduism any of her numerous branches and offshoots. A man was nonetheless a Hindu, for instance, in his eyes for being a member of the *Brāhmo* or the *Ārya Samāj*. The great Sikh *Khālsā* was one of the finest organisations ever created within the Mother-Church, and by her genius. With what ardour he painted for us, again and again, the scene in which Guru Govinda Singh uttered his call to sacrifice! There were, he held, three different stratifications to be recognized in the Faith. One was that of the old historic Orthodoxy. Another consisted of the reforming sects of the Mohammedan period. And third, came the reforming sects of the present period. But all these were equally Hindu. He never forgot that his own longing to consider the problems of his country and his religion on the grand scale had found its first fulfilment in his youthful membership of the *Sādhāran Brāhmo Samāj*. And he was so far from repudiating this membership, that he one day exclaimed—"It is for them to say whether I belong to them or not! Unless they have removed it, my name stands on their books to this day!" Thus a man was equally Hindu, in his opinion, whether he prefixed to the adjective the modification of *Ārya*, *Brāhmo*, or Orthodox. The claim of the Jain to a place within the fold, was a simple matter of social and historical demonstration. The Jains of Western India would be indignant to this day, if their right to rank as Hindus were seriously questioned. Even now they exchange daughters in marriage, with orthodox house, of caste correspondent to their own. And even now, their temples are served occasionally by ordinary *Brāhmins*. The Swami had disciples amongst all faiths, even the Mohammedan, and by the good offices of certain of his Jain friends, he was allowed to read some of their sacred books, nor usually accessible, except to members of their own congregations. From this study, he was deeply impressed with the authenticity of their doctrines and traditions, and with the important part which they had played in the evolution of Hinduism. Indian religion necessarily includes amongst its strongest ideas, a regard for the immanent humanity in dumb animals, and deep

Jainism

devotion to the ascetic ideal of sainthood. These two features had been isolated and emphasised by the Jains. In their clear pronouncements on the Germ Theory, moreover, confirmed as these have been by the researches of modern science, there was evidence sufficient of the intellectual and spiritual stature of the founders of the school. "The Jain is obviously right," said the Swami, "in claiming that his doctrines were in the first place declared by *Rishis*."

With regard to the Christianised castes of the present day, the Swami hoped that they would rise in social status by adopting the faith of the dominant political faction, and that in ages to come, when Christianity should be forgotten, they would still be able to maintain this advance. In this way, we might hope for a future oblivion of the nineteenth century, as a disintegrating force, and the permanent enrichment of the Indian system by its contributions. In evidence of the possibility of such a development, was there not the work of Chaitanya in Northern India, and the fact that he had succeeded in forming for his followers, 'a caste of very great respectability'.

Love for Islam

Christianity, in her present-day workings, was difficult to pardon. Not so the other non-Hindu faith, Islam. The picture that this name called up to our Master's mind was always of an eager confraternity, enfranchising the simple and democratising the great. As a factor in the evolution of modern India, he could never for a moment be forgetful of the loyal acceptance, by Islamic intruders, of the old Indian civilisation, and administrative system. Nor could he disregard the service they had done, not only in exalting the social rights of the lowly-born, but also in conserving and developing, in too gentle a race, the ideals of organised struggle and resistance. He constantly pointed out that Mohammedanism had its fourfold 'castes'—Syyed, Pathan, Mogul and Sheikh—and that of these the Sheikhs had an inherited right to the Indian soil and the Indian memory, as ancient and indisputable as those of any Hindu. He, told a disciple, *apropos* of an indiscreetly written word, that "Shah Jehan would have turned in his grave to hear himself called a 'foreigner.'" And finally, his highest prayer for the good of the Motherland was that she might make manifest the twofold ideal of 'an Islamic body and a Vedantic heart'.

Thus—far aloof as he stood from the political significance of such facts—India, to Vivekananda's thinking, was a unity, and a unity still more deeply to be apprehended of the heart than of the mind. His work in the world, as he saw it, was the sowing broadcast of the message of his own Master. But his personal struggles, his personal desires, were bound up in an inextinguishable passion for his country's good. He never proclaimed nationality, but he was himself the living embodiment of that idea which the word conveys. He, our Master, incarnates for us in his own person, that great mutual love which is the Indian national ideal.

True Orthodoxy

Nothing was less in his mind, be it understood, than a mere revival or restoration of the Indian past. It was to those who sought to bring this about that he had referred, when he said "Like the Egyptologist's interest in Egypt, their interest in India is a purely selfish one. They would fain see again that India of their books, their studies, and their dreams." What he himself wanted was to see the strength of that old India finding new application and undreamt-of expression, in the new age. He longed to see a 'dynamic religion'. Why should one select out all the elements of meanness and decadence and reaction, and call them 'Orthodox'? Orthodoxy was a term too grand, too strong, too vital, for any such use. It would be rightly applied only to that home where all the men were Pandava heroes, and all the women had the greatness of Sita or the fearlessness of Savitri. He stood aloof from all special questions, whether of conservatism or reform; not because he sympathized with one party more or less than with the other, but because he saw that for both alike the real question was the recapture of the ideal, and its identification with India. On behalf of Women and the People, alike, he held that the duty required of us was not to change institutions, but to put these in a position to solve their own problems.

At least equal to this dislike of ignorance was his horror of the identification of India with what is known as Occultism. He had the natural interest and curiosity of educated persons, and would at any time have been glad to undergo inconvenience, in order to put to the test alleged cases of walking on water, handling fire and so on. We all know, however, that evidence regarding such matters is apt to vanish into the merest hearsay, when followed up. And in any case, such occurrences would have had no significance for him, beyond pointing the simple moral that our present classification of phenomena was incomplete, and must be revised, to include some unfamiliar possibilities. They would have had no supernatural character whatsoever. Few things in the life of Buddha moved him so deeply as the tale of the unfrocking of the monk who had worked a miracle. And he said of the Figure that moves through the Christian Gospels that its perfection would have seemed to him greater, had there then a refusal to gain credence by the 'doing of mighty works'. In this matter, it is probably true as I have heard it pointed out in later years, by the Swami Sadananda, that there is a temperamental, as well as intellectual, divergence between Eastern and Western Asia, the one always despising, and the other seeking for 'a sign'. In this respect, according to Sadananda, the Mongolian and Semitic conceptions are sharply opposed, while the Aryan stands between, weighing the two. However this may be, it will be admitted by many of us that the modern interest in so-called occult phenomena has been largely instrumental in creating a mischievous idea that the Oriental is a being of mysterious nature, remote from the ordinary motives of mankind, and charged with secret batteries of supernatural powers. All this was hateful to the Swami. He desired to see it understood that India was peopled with human beings, who have indeed an intensely individual character, and a distinctive culture, but who are in all respects men amongst men, with all the duties, claims, and emotions of common humanity.

India and Miracles

He, indeed, had the generosity to extend to the West, the same gospel that the Indian sages had preached in the past to the Indian people—the doctrine of the Divinity in man, to be realised by faithful service, through whatever forms. The life of externals, with its concentration of interest in sense impressions, was, according to him, a mere hypnotism, a dream, of no exalted character. And for Western, as for Eastern, the soul's quest was the breaking of this dream, the awakening

No Mystery

to a more profound and powerful reality. He was forever finding new ways to express his belief that all men alike had the same vast potential. "Yes! my own life is guided by the enthusiasm of a certain great Personality," he said once, "but what of that? Inspiration was never filtered out to the world through one man!"

Again he said, "It is true that I believe Ramakrishna Paramahamsa to have been inspired. But then I am myself inspired also. And you are inspired. And your disciples will be; and theirs after them; and so on, to the end of time!"

And on another occasion, to one who questioned him about the old rule of the teachers, that truth should be taught only to those of proved and tested fitness, be exclaimed impatiently, "Don't you see that the age for esoteric interpretations is over? For good or for ill, that day is vanished, never to return. Truth, in the future, is to be open to the world!"

He would speak, with whimsical amusement, of attempts to offer to India religious ideas and organisations which were European-led, as a culminating effort in the long attempt to exploit one race for the good of another. But he never took such European leading seriously, in matters of religion

Finally, there was no event in the history of his own people to which he returned more constantly than the great Charge of Asoka to his missionaries, in the third century before

Christ. 'Remember,' said the mighty Emperor to those who were to carry the Law to various countries, 'Remember that everywhere you will find some root of faith and righteousness. *See that you foster this, and do not destroy*!" Asoka had thus dreamt of the whole world, as federated by ideas—ideas everywhere guided and permeated by the striving towards absolute truth and perfection of conduct. But this dream of Asoka had had to contend with ancient difficulties of communication and transport, with half-known continents and a vast diversity of races. The preliminary steps, therefore, in his world-federation, would necessarily take so long that the primal impulse of faith and energy might in the meantime be forgotten. It must have been from the consideration of this question that the Swami one day looked up—as we all entered the mountain-pass that lies beyond the village of Kathgodam—and exclaimed, breaking a long reverie, "Yes! The idea of the Buddhists was one for which only the modern world is ready! None before us has had the opportunity of its realisation!"

XVIII

The Swami Vivekananda's Attitude to Buddha

Chief of intellectual passions with the Swami, was his reverence for Buddha. It was perhaps the historical authenticity of this Indian life that was the basis of the delight it roused in him. "We are sure of Buddha and Mohammed, alone amongst religious teachers," he was wont to say, "for they alone had the good fortune to possess enemies as well as friends!" Again and again, he would return upon that note of perfect rationality in his hero. Buddha was to him not only the greatest of Aryans but also "the one absolutely sane man" that the world had ever seen. How he had refused worship! Yet he drew no attention to the fact that it had been offered. 'Buddha,' he said, 'was not a man, but a realisation. Enter, all ye, into it! Here receive the key!'

The Sane Man

He had been so untouched by the vulgar craving for wonders, that he coldly excommunicated the lad who had by a word brought down a jewelled cup from the top of a pole, in the presence of the crowd. Religion, he said, had nothing to do with jugglery!

How vast had been the freedom and humility of the Blessed One! He attended the banquet of Ambapali, the courtesan. Knowing that it would kill him, but desiring that his last act should be one of communion with the lowly, he received the food of the pariah, and afterwards sent a courteous message to his host, thanking him for the Great Deliverance. How calm! How masculine! Verily was he the bull in the herd and a moon amongst men!

And perfect as he was in reason, he was at least as wondrous in compassion. To save the goats at Rajgir, he would have given his life. He had once offered himself up, to stay the hunger of a tigress. Out of five hundred lives renounced for others, had been distilled the pity that had made him Buddha.

There comes to us a touch of his humour across the ages when he tells the tale of the youth, sobbing out his love for one he has never seen, whose very name he does not know, and likens his plight to the iterations of humanity about God. He alone was able to free religion entirely from the argument of the supernatural, and yet make it as binding in its force, and as living in its appeal, as it had ever been. This was done by the power of his own great personality, and the impression it made on the men of his generation.

The Great Farewell

For some of us, one evening, the Swami sat reconstructing the story, as it must have appeared to Jasodhara, the wife of Buddha, and never have I heard the dry bones of history clothed with such fullness or convincingness of life. Hindu monk as he himself was, it seemed to Vivekananda natural enough that a strong personality should have what he conveniently described as 'European ideas about marriage,' and should insist, as did Buddha, on seeing and choosing his bride for himself. Each detail of the week of festivities and betrothal was dwelt on tenderly. Then came the picture of the two, long wedded, and the great night of farewell. The gods sang, 'Awake! thou that art awakened! Arise! And help the world!' and the struggling prince returned again and again to the bedside of his sleeping wife. "What was the problem that vexed him? Why! It was *she* whom he was about to sacrifice for the world! *That* was the struggle! He cared nothing for himself!"

Then the victory, with its inevitable farewell, and the kiss, imprinted so gently on the foot of the princess that she never woke. "Have you never thought," said the Swami, "of the hearts of the heroes? How they were great, great, great, and soft as butter?"

It was seven years later, when the prince, now Buddha, returned to Kapilavastu, where Jasodhara had lived—clad in the yellow cloth, eating only roots and fruits, sleeping in no bed, under no roof—from the day he had left her, sharing the religious life also, in her woman's way. And he entered, and she took the hem of his garment, 'as a wife should do,' while he told, to her and to his son, the Truth.

Buddha and Jasodhara

But when he had ended, and would have departed to his garden, she turned, startled, to her son, and said "Quick! Go and ask your father for your patrimony!"

And when the child asked, "Mother, which is my father?" she disdained to give any answer, save "The lion that passes down the street, lo, he is thy father!"

And the lad, heir of the *Sākya* line, went, saying "Father, give me my inheritance!"

Three times he had to ask, before Buddha, turning to Ananda, said "Give it!" and the *gerua* cloth was thrown over the child.

Then, seeing Jasodhara, and realising that she, too, longed to be near her husband, the chief disciple said, "May women enter the Order? Shall we give to her also the yellow cloth?"

And Buddha said "Can there be sex in knowledge? Have I ever said that a woman could not enter? But this, O Ananda, was for thee to ask!"

Thus Jasodhara also became a disciple. And then all the pent-up love and pity of those seven years, welled forth in the Jataka Birth-stories! For they were all for her! Five hundred times each had forgotten self. And now they would enter into perfection together.

"—Yes, yes, so it was! For Jasodhara and for Sita, a hundred years would not have been enough to try their faith!"

"No! no!" mused the teller, after a pause, as he ended the tale, "Let us all own that we have passions still! Let each one say 'I am not the ideal!' Let none ever venture to compare another with Him!"

Study of Buddhism

During the years of our Master's boyhood at Dakshineshwar, the attention of the world had been much concentrated on the story of Buddhism. The restoration of the great shrine of Bodh-Gaya was carried out about this time* under the orders of the English Government, and the share taken in this work by Rajendra Lal Mitra, the Bengali scholar, kept Indian interest intense throughout the country. In 1879, moreover, the imagination even of the unlearned classes in English-speaking countries was deeply stirred, by the appearance of Sir Edwin Arnold's 'Light of Asia,' said to be in many parts an almost

* The excavations round the great shrine were first commenced by the Burmese Government in 1874. The British Government took them in hand in 1879 and completed the work in 1894.

literal translation from the 'Buddha Charita' of *Aśvaghosha.* But the Swami was never satisfied with taking things at secondhand, and in this too could not rest contented until in 1887 he, with his brethren, contrived to read together, not only the '*Lalita Vistāra,*' but also the great book of the Mahayana school of Buddhism, the '*Prajnā Pāramitā,*'* in the original.†

Their knowledge of Sanskrit was their key to the understanding of the daughter-language. The study of Dr. Rajendra Lal Mitra's writings and the 'Light of Asia,' could never be a mere passing event in the Swami's life, and the seed that thus fell on the sensitive mind of Sri Ramakrishna's chief disciple, during the years of his discipleship, came to blossom the moment he was initiated into *Sannyās,* for his first act then was to hurry to Bodh-Gaya, and sit under the great tree, saying to himself 'Is it possible that I breathe the air He breathed? That I touch the earth He trod?'

At the end of his life again, similarly, he arrived at Bodh-Gaya, on the morning of his thirty-ninth birthday'; and this journey ending with a visit to Benares, was the last he ever made.

---

* Lit. That which leads one beyond intellect—to the realms of super-consciousness.

† These two books were then being published by the Asiatic Society, under the able editing of Dr. Rajendra Lal Mitra. The original text appeared in Sanskrit characters, and not in *Pāli,* to help the general reader, who familiar with the former but not with the latter.

—Saradananda.

At some time in the years of his Indian wanderings, the Swami was allowed to touch the relics of Buddha, probably near the place where they were first discovered. And he was never afterwards able to refer to this, without some return of that passion of reverence and certitude which must then have overwhelmed him. Well might he exclaim, to someone who questioned him about the personal worship of the Avatars, "In truth, Madam, had I lived in *Judæa* in the days of Jesus of Nazareth, I would have washed His feet, not with my tears, but with my heart's blood!"

"A Buddhist!" he said, to one who made a mistake about the name of his faith, "I am the servant of the servants of the servants of Buddha!" as if even the title of a believer would seem, to his veneration, too exalted to claim.

But it was not only the historic authenticity of the personality of Buddha that held him spellbound. Another factor, at least as powerful, was the spectacle of the constant tallying of his own Master's life, lived before his eyes, with this world-attested story of twenty-five centuries before. In Buddha, he saw Ramakrishna Paramahamsa : in Ramakrishna, he saw Buddha.

In a flash, this train of thought was revealed, one day when he was describing the scene of the death of Buddha. He told how the blanket had been spread for him beneath the tree, and how the Blessed One had lain down, 'resting on his right side, like a lion,' to die, when suddenly there came to him one who ran, for instruction. The disciples would have treated the man as an intruder, maintaining peace at any cost about their Master's death-bed, but the Blessed One overheard, and saying 'No, no! He who was sent* in ever ready,' he raised himself on his elbow, and taught. This happened four times, and then, and then only, Buddha held himself free to die. 'But first he spoke to reprove Ananda for weeping. The Buddha was not a person, he said, but a realisation, and to that, anyone of them might attain. And with his last breath he forbade them to worship any.'

The Name of a Disciple

The immortal story went on to its end. But to one who listened, the most significant moment had been that in which the teller paused—at his own words 'raised himself on his elbow and taught'—and said, in brief parenthesis, "*I* saw this, you know, in the case of Ramakrishna Paramahamsa!" And there rose before the mind the story of one, destined to learn from that Teacher, who had travelled a hundred miles, and arrived at Cossipore† only when he lay dying. Here

* *Lit. The Tathagata*, 'A word', explained the Swami, "which is very like your 'Messiah.'"

† Sri Ramakrishna entered into *Mahāsamādhi* at the garden house of Krishna Gopal Ghosh in Cossipore, 1886.

also the disciples would have refused admission, but Sri Ramakrishna intervened, insisting on receiving the newcomer, and teaching him.

The Teachings of Buddha

The Swami was always deeply preoccupied with the historic and philosophic significance of Buddhistic doctrine. Sudden references and abrupt allusions would show that his thoughts were constantly with it. " 'Form, feeling, sensation, motion and knowledge are the five categories,' " he quoted one day, from Buddha's teachings,* " 'in perpetual flux and fusion. And in these lies *Māyā*, Of any one wave, nothing can be predicated, for it is not. It but was, and is gone. *Know, O Man thou art the sea*!' Ah, this was Kapila's philosophy," he went on, "but his great Disciple brought the heart to make it live!"

And then, as the accents of that Disciple himself broke upon the inner ear, he paused a moment and fell back on the deathless charge of the Dhamapada to the soul :

"Go forward without a path!
Fearing nothing, caring for nothing,
Wander alone, like the rhinoceros!
"Even as the lion, not trembling at noises,
Even as the wind, not caught in a net,
Even as the lotus-leaf, unstained by the water,
Do thou wander alone, like the rhinoceros!"

---

* *Vide* Vinaya Pitaka, Part I, Sacred Books of the East Series.

"Can you *imagine*, what their strength was?" he said one day, as he dwelt on the picture of the First Council, and the dispute as to the President. "One said, it should be Ananda, because He had loved him most. But someone else stepped forward, and said no! for Ananda had been guilty of weeping at the death-bed. And so he was passed over!"

No Compromise

"But Buddha," he went on, "made the fatal mistake of thinking that the whole world could be lifted to the height of the Upanishads. And self-interest spoiled all. Krishna was wiser, because He was more politic. But Buddha would have no compromise. The world before now has seen even the Avatar ruined by compromise, tortured to death for want of recognition, and lost. But Buddha would have been worshipped as God in his own lifetime, all over Asia, for a moment's compromise. And his reply was only 'Buddhahood is an achievement, not a person!' Verily was He the only man in the world who was ever quite sane, the only sane man ever born!"

Indian clearness of thought spoke in the Swami's contempt for our Christian leaning towards the worship of suffering. People had told him in the West that the greatness of Buddha would have been more appealing, had he been crucified! This he had no hesitation in stigmatising as 'Roman brutality'. "The lowest and most animal liking," he pointed out. "is for action. Therefore the world will always love the epic. Fortunately for India, however, she has never produced a Milton, with his 'hurled headlong down the steep abyss!' The whole of that was well exchanged for a couple of lines of Browning!" It had been this epic vigour of the story, in his opinion, that had appealed to the Roman. The crucifixion it was, that had carried Christianity over the Roman world. "Yes Yes!" he reiterated, "You Western folk want *action*! You cannot yet perceive the poetry of every common little incident in life! What beauty could be greater than that of the story of the young mother, coming to Buddha with her dead boy? Or the incident of the goats? You see the Great Renunciation was not new in India! Gautama was the son of a petty chieftain. As much had been left many times before. But *after Nirvāna*, look at the poetry!

The Song of the Cowhard

*"It is a wet night, and he comes to the cowherd's hut and gathers in to the wall under the dripping eaves. The rain is pouring down, and the wind rising.

"Within, the cowherd catches a glimpse of a face, through the window, and thinks 'Ha, ha!

* The Swami was here making a rough paraphrase, from memory, of Rhys Davids' metrical rendering of the Dhaniya Sutta, from the Sutta Nipata, in Fausboll's translation of the Dhammapada. See Rhys Davids' American Lectures.

Yellow Garb! Stay there! It's good enough for you!' And then he begins to sing.

'My cattle are housed, and the fire burns bright. My wife is safe and my babes sleep sweet! Therefore ye may rain, if ye will, O clouds, tonight!'

"And the Buddha answers from without, 'My mind is controlled. My senses are all gathered in. My heart is firm. Therefore ye may rain, if ye will, O clouds, tonight!'

"Again the cowherd—'The fields are reaped, and the hay is all fast in the barn. The stream is full, and, the roads are firm. Therefore ye may rain, if ye will, O clouds, tonight.'

"And so it goes on, till at last the cowherd rises, in contrition and wonder, and becomes a disciple.

The Barber's Story

"Or what could be more beautiful than the Barber's story?

*"The Blessed One passed by my house, *my* house—the Barbers!

'I ran, but He turned and awaited me. Awaited *me*—the Barber!

'I said, 'May I speak, O Lord, with Thee?'

'And He said 'Yes!'

---

* The original form of this anecdote, as it appeared in the Buddhist texts in old times, under the name of Upali Prichcha (The Questions of Upali, the Barber) has been lost, but the fact that there was such a writing in existence, is known from its mention is other Buddhist books, e.g., the Vinaya Pitaka.

'Yes!' to *me*—the Barber!
'And I said 'Is Nirvāna for such as I?'
'And He said 'Yes!'
Even for *me*—the Barber!
'And I said 'May I follow after Thee!'
'And He said 'Oh yes!'
Even *I*—the Barber!
'And I said 'May I stay, O Lord, near Thee?'
'And He said 'Thou mayest!'
Even to *me*—the poor Barber!'"

He was epitomising the history of Buddhism one day, with its three cycles—five hundred years of law, five hundred of images, and five hundred of *tantras*—when suddenly he broke off, to say, "You must not imagine that there was ever a religion in India called Buddhism, with temples and priests of its own order! Nothing of the sort! The idea was always within Hinduism. Only the influence of Buddha was paramount at one time, and made the nation monastic." And the truth of the view so expressed can only, as I believe, become increasingly apparent to scholars, with time and study. According to it, Buddhism formed complete churches only in the circle of missionary countries, of which Kashmir was one. And an interesting morsel of history dwelt on by the Swami, was that of the adoption of the Indian apostolate in that country, with its inevitable deposition of the local *Nāgs*, or mysterious serpents living beneath the springs, from their position of deities. Strange to say, a terrible winter followed their disestablishment, and the terrified people hastened to make a compromise between the new truth and the old superstition, by reinstating the *Nāgs* as saints, or minor divinities of the new faith—a piece of human nature not without parallels elsewhere!

Re-incarnation —an illusion

One of the great contrasts between Buddhism and the Mother-church lies in the fact that the Hindu believes in the accumulation of Karma by a single ego, through repeated incarnations, while Buddhism teaches that this seeming identity is but illusory and impermanent. It is in truth another soul which inherits what we have amassed for it, and proceeds, out of our experience, to the sowing of fresh seed. On the merits of these rival theories, the Swami would often sit and ponder. By those to whom, as to him, the great life of superconsciousness has ever opened, as also in a lesser degree to those who have only dwelt in its shadow, the condition of the embodied spirit is seen as an ever-fretting limitation. The encaged soul beats wings of rebellion ceaselessly, against the prisoning bars of the body, seeing outside and beyond them that existence of pure ideas, of concentrated emotion, of changeless bliss and unshadowed light, which is its ideal and its goal. To these, then, the body is a veil and a barrier, instead of a means to mutual communing. Pleasure and pain are but the Primal Light seen through the prism of personal consciousness. The one longing is to rise above them both, and find That, white, undivided, radiant. It was this train of feeling that expressed itself now and then in our Master's utterances of impatience at current conceptions, as when he broke out with the words "Why, one life in the body is like a million years of confinement, and they want to wake up the memory of many lives! Sufficient unto the day is the evil thereof!" Yet this question, of the relation to one another of the different personalities in a single long chain of experience, never failed to interest him. The doctrine of reincarnation was never treated by him as an article of faith. To himself personally, it was 'a scientific speculation' merely, but of a deeply satisfying kind. He would always bring it forward, in opposition to our Western educational doctrine that all knowledge begins with the senses, pointing out, on his side, that this beginning of knowledge is often lost in the remote past of the given person. Yet when all had been said, the question still remained whether in the end Buddhism would not be proved philosophically right. Was not the whole notion of continuous identity illusory, to give way, at the last, to the final perception that the many were all unreal, and the One alone Real? "Yes!" he exclaimed one day, after long thought in silence, "Buddhism must be right! Re-incarnation is only a mirage! But this vision is to be reached, by the path of Advaita alone!"

Buddhism and Advaita

Perhaps it gave him pleasure, thus to play off Sankaracharya against Buddha, as it were, by calling in Advaita to the aid of Buddhism. Perhaps it was the unification of history involved, that so delighted him; since the one idea was thus shown to be imperfect, apart from the other. 'The heart of Buddha and the intellect of Sankaracharya was always his definition of the highest possibility of humanity. In this vein was the attention he gave to the argument of a certain Western woman, against the Buddhistic view of *Karma.* The extraordinary sense of social responsibility involved in that rendering,* had escaped this particular mind. "I find," she said, "no motive for doing good deeds, of which someone else, and not I, will reap the fruit!"

The Swami, who was himself quite incapable of thinking in this way, was greatly struck by the remark, and a day or two later said to someone

* There is surely a sense in which the motive for doing right is much strengthened if we are to feel that another, and not oneself, will bear the punishment for our sin. We may compare with this our own sense of responsibility for the property, children, or honour of another.

near him—"That was a very impressive point that was made the other day, that there can be no reason for doing good to people, if not they, but others, are to gather the fruit of our efforts!"

"But that was not the argument!" ungraciously answered the person addressed. "The point was that someone else than myself would reap the merit of my deed!"

"I know, I know," he replied quietly, "but our friend would have done greater justice to her own idea, if she had put it in this other way. Let us suppose it to stand, that we are deceived in doing service to those who can never receive that service. Don't you see that there is but only reply—the theory of Advaita? For we are all one!"

The Modern Hindu Mind

Had he realised that the distinction between the mediæal and modern Hindu minds lay precisely here, that in the modern idea of India there would always be a place accorded to Buddhism and Buddha? Had he told himself that the *Mahābhārata* and *Rāmāyana*, which had dominated Indian education since the Guptas, were henceforth to be supplemented, in the popular mind, by the history of the Asokan and Pre-Asokan periods? Had he thought of the vast significance to Asia of such a generalisation, of the new life to be poured from Hinduism into the veins of Buddhist countries, and of the vigour and strength to be gained by India herself, from the self-recognition of the Mother-church, feeding with knowledge the daughter-nations? However this be, we must never forget that it was in *Hinduism* that he saw the keystone of the arch of the two faiths. It was this mother, and not her daughter, that he found all-inclusive. Great and beloved Mother-church as she is, she has room to all-time for the glorious form of the first and most lion-hearted of all her Avatars. She has place for his orders; understanding and reverence for his teachings; mother-love for his flock; and sympathy and welcome for the young he brought to her. But never will she say that truth is confined to his presentment; that salvation is only to be found through the monastic rule; that the path to perfection is one and one alone. That was perhaps the greatest of the Swami Vivekananda's pronouncements on Buddhism, in which he said : "The great point of contrast between Buddhism and Hinduism lies in the fact that Buddhism said 'Realise all this as illusion', while Hinduism said 'Realise that within the illusion is the Real.' *Of how* this was to be done, Hinduism never presumed to enunciate any rigid law. The Buddhist command could only be carried out through monasticism; the Hindu might be fulfilled through any state of life. All alike were roads to the One Real. One of the highest and greatest expressions of

Hinduism All-Inclusive

the Faith is put into the mouth of a butcher, preaching, by the orders of a married woman, to a *Sannyāsin*. Thus Buddhism became the religion of a monastic order, but Hinduism became the religion of a monastic order, but Hinduism, in spite of its exaltation of monasticism, remains ever the religion of faithfulness to daily duty, whatever it be, as the path by which man may attain to God."

XIX

The Swami's Estimate of Historic Christianity

Some of the deepest convictions of our lives are gathered from data which, in their very nature, can influence no one but ourselves. The instantaneous estimate of a motive or a personality, for instance, cannot be communicated, in its vividness, to any other, yet remains irresistible to the mind that makes it. It may be either true or false, that is to say, it may be based on a subtle species of observation, possible only to a few; or it may be only a vagrant impulse of emotion. Be this as it may, the strong subjective impression will colour much of the subsequent thought of him who has experienced it, and will appear to others as wisdom or caprice, according to its good or ill luck, in coinciding with fact. In the same way, if, for the sake of argument, we grant the truth of the theory of reincarnation, it immediately becomes conceivable that some minds may enjoy occasional access within themselves to stores of subconscious memory, in which others have no share. If so, it is just possible that the results of such an *excursus* might furnish clues of some value, even though the difference between it and pure imagination could only be appreciated by the exploring mind itself

Subjective Experiences

Some such train of thought is necessary, if one is to visualize no less than three striking subjective experiences, which exerted an undoubted influence over my Master's mind and thought. Chief of these probably, was that vision of an old man on the banks of the Indus, chanting Vedic riks, from which he had learnt his own peculiar method of intoning Sanskrit—a method much closer to that of Gregorian plainsong than is the ordinary singing of the Vedas. In this, he always believed himself to have recovered the musical cadences of the Aryan ancestors. He found something remarkably sympathetic to this mode in the poetry of Sankaracharya, and this fact he expressed, by saying that that master must have had a vision like his own, in which he had caught 'the rhythm of the Vedas'.*

---

* The Swami Saradananda says that this vision occurred about two years after Sri Ramakrishna had passed away, probably in January, 1888. The passage which he heard was that Salutation to *Gāyatri* which begins, "O come, Thou Effulgent!"

आयाहि वरदे देवि त्र्यक्षरे ब्रह्मवादिनि ।
गायत्रिच्छन्दसां मातः, ब्रह्मयोनि नमोऽस्तु ते ॥

It is a great happiness to know that the Swami Abhedananda

A Vision of Buddha

Another similar experience had come to him when he was quite young. It was in the days of his discipleship at Dakshineswar. He was seated at home, in the little room that formed his study, meditating, when suddenly there appeared before him a man tall and largely built, in whose face was a calm so deep and so established, that it seemed to the lad, looking up at him, as if both pain and pleasure had been forgotten during infinite time. The devotee rose from his seat, and prostrated himself before his visitant; then he stood still, lost in an awestruck gaze. Suddenly it seemed as if the form before him were about to speak. But at this, a fit of terror overcame the boy, and without waiting to hear, he slipped quietly out of the room, and closed the door behind him! This was the vision to which he had referred, when he spoke of the entrance of Buddha into his room, in his youth. 'And I fell at his feet, for I knew it was the Lord Himself.' Nor would it be easy to measure how much of the throbbing energy of his feeling about Buddha—the conviction of his overwhelming 'sanity,' the realisation of his infinite sacrifice and compassion—was born of that hour in his boyhood, when he had felt that He stood revealed before him.

has learnt and can reproduce this Sanskrit intoning of the Swami Vivekananda.

Story of Western Faiths

The third and last of these determining visions, in so far, at least, as is known to those about him—occurred to the Swami on his way home to India, in January of the year 1897. One gathers that during his travels in Catholic Europe, he had been startled, like others before him, to find the identity of Christianity with Hinduism in a thousand points of familiar detail. The Blessed Sacrament appeared to him to be only an elaboration of the Vedic *prasādam*. The priestly tonsure reminded him of the shaven head of the Indian monk; and when he came across a picture of Justinian receiving the Law from two shaven monks, he felt that he had found the origin of the tonsure, He could not but remember that even before Buddhism, India had had monks and nuns, and that Europe had taken her orders from the Thebaid. Hindu ritual had its lights, its incense, and its music. Even the sign of the cross, as he saw it practised, reminded him of the touching of different parts of the body, in certain kinds of meditation. And the culmination of this series of observations was reached, when he entered some cathedral, and found it furnished with an insufficient number of chairs and no pews! Then, at last, he was really at home. Henceforth he could not believe that Christianity was foreign.

Another train of thought that may have prepared him, unconsciously, for the dream I am about to recount, lay in the fact that he had, in America, had a Jewish disciple, by whom he had been introduced into orthodox Jewish society, and led to the more or less careful study of the Talmud. Thus he had a clearer sense of the background of thought, against which S. Paul stood forth, than is at all common.

Still an added factor in his study of Christianity, that is worth remembering, was his familiarity, in America, with the movement known as Christian Science. In examining the birth of religions, he said once, afterwards that there were three elements of which he thought we must always take account—doctrine, ritual, and a third, of the nature of magic, or miracle, which most commonly appeared as a movement of healing. The grounds for his inclusion of the last member of this triad, I find partly in his observation of Christian Science and the allied movements—coupled as this would be with his own conviction that we are now on the eve of a great new synthesis in religion—and partly in his vision itself, which was stamped on vividly on his brain-fibre as to stand in his memory amongst actual living experiences.

It was night, and the ship on which he had embarked at Naples, was still on her way to Port Said, when he had this dream. An old and bearded man appeared before him, saying "Observe well this place that I show to you. You are now in the island of Crete. This is the land in which Christianity began." In support of this origin of Christianity, the speaker gave two words—one of which was *Therāpeutæ*—

His Dream

and showed both to be derived directly from Sanskrit roots. The Swami frequently spoke of this dream in after years, and always gave the two etymologies; but the other seems* nevertheless, to be lost, beyond recovery. Of *Therāpeutæ*, the meaning advanced was, *sons of the therās*, from *therā*, and elder amongst the Buddhist monks, and *putra*, the Sanskrit word for *son*. "The proofs are all here," added the old man, pointing to the ground, "Dig, and you will find!"

The Swami woke, feeling that he had had no common dream and tumbled out on deck, to take the air. As he did so, he met a ship's officer, turning in from his watch. "What is the time?" he asked him.

"Midnight," was the answer.

"And where are we?"

"Just fifty miles off Crete!"

This unexpected coincidence startled the Swami, lending inevitable emphasis to the dream

* It is my own belief that the second word was *essene*. But alas, I cannot remember the Sanskritic derivation!—N.

Ishāniya—dedicated to God.—Ed.

itself. The experience now seemed to precipitate elements, that without it, would have lain in his mind meaningless and unrelated. He confessed afterwards that up to this time, it had never occurred to him to doubt the historic personality of Christ, and that after this, he could never rely upon it. He understood all at once that it was S. Paul alone of whom we could be sure. He saw the meaning of the fact that the Acts of the Apostles were an older record than the Gospels. And he divined that the teaching of Jesus might have originated with the Rabbi Hillel, while the ancient sect of the Nazarenes might have contributed the name and the person, with its beautiful sayings, reverberating out of some unknown antiquity.*

Ideals as Ideals

But while his vision thus exercised an undeniable influence over his own mind, he would have thought it insanity to offer it as evidence to any other. The function of such an experience, if admitted at all, was to his thinking, subjective alone. He might be led by it to doubt the historic character of Jesus of Nazareth, but he never referred to Crete as the probable birthplace of Christianity. That would be a hypothesis for secular scholarship alone, to prove or disprove. The admitted

* Or, he thought perhaps that the 'beautiful sayings' of Jesus might really have been uttered by Buddha and the tale told in the Gospels, opening thus only another vista for the seeing of Him.—N.

historic spectacle of the meeting of Indian and Egyptian elements at Alexandria was the only geographical factor of which he ever spoke. Nor did this intellectual dubiety in any way dim the brightness of his love for the Son of Mary. To Hindu thinking, it is the perfection of the ideal, as ideal, that matters, and not the truth of its setting in space and time. To the Swami it was only natural, therefore, to refuse, out of reverence, to give his blessing to a picture of the Sistine Madonna, touching the feet of the Divine child, instead; or to say, in answer to an enquirer, "Had I lived in Palestine, in the days of Jesus of Nazareth, I would have washed His feet, not with my tears, but with my heart's blood!" In this, moreover, he had the explicit sanction of Sri Ramakrishna, whom he had consulted anxiously, in his boyhood, on a similar question, to be answered, "Do you not think that they who could create such thing must themselves have *been* the ideal that they held up for worship?"

XX

Woman And The People

The temple of Dakshineshwar was built by the wealthy Rani Rashmani, a woman of the *Koiburto* caste, and in the year 1853, Sri Ramakrishna took up his residence there, as one of the Brahmins attached to its service.

These were facts which had impressed the mind of Vivekananda even more deeply, perhaps, than he himself ever knew. A woman of the people had been, in a sense, the mother of that whole movement of which all the disciples of his Master formed parts. Humanly speaking, without the Temple of Dakshineshwar there had been no Ramakrishna, without Ramakrishna no Vivekananda, and without Vivekananda, no Western Mission. The whole story rested on the building, erected on the Ganges side, a few miles above Calcutta, just before the middle of the nineteenth century. And that was the outcome of the devotion of a rich woman of the lower castes—a thing that under a purely

Hindu government, bound to the maintenance of Brahmin supremacy, would never have been possible, as the Swami himself was not slow to point out. From this, he inferred the importance of the non-cognisance of caste, by centralised governments in India.

Strong Woman

Rani Rashmani, in her time, was a woman of heroic mould. The story is still told of how she defended the fisherfolk of Calcutta against wrongful taxation, by inducing her husband to pay the enormous sum demanded, and then insist on closing the river against the heavy traffic of the foreigners. She fought a good fight over the right of her household to carry the images of the gods along the roads she owned, on the lordly Maidan, or Park. If the English objected to the religion of the Indian people, she said in effect, it was a small matter to build walls at the disputed points, to the right and left of the procession path. And this was done, with the result of breaking the continuity of the grand pleasure-drive, the Rotten Row of Calcutta. Early in her widowhood, she had to bring all her wits to bear on her bankers, in order to get into her own hands the heavy balance which she required for working-capital. This she accomplished, however, with the greatest tact and adroitness, and was mistress of her own affairs thenceforth. Later, a great lawsuit, in which the ready wit of her replies through counsel carried all before her, became a household word in Hindu Calcutta.

The husband of Rani Rashmani's daughter, 'Mathur Babu' as he was called, bears a name that figures largely in the early history of Sri Ramakrishna. It was he who protected the great devotee, when all around held him to be religion-mad. It was he who continued him in the enjoyment of residence and allowances without permitting duties to be demanded of him. In these things, Mathur Babu acted as the representative of his wife's mother. Rani Rashmani had recognized the religious genius of Sri Ramakrishna, from the beginning, and proved unfaltering in her adhesion to that first insight.

Sprung of the People

And yet, when Ramakrishna, as the young *Brāhmin* of Kamarpukur, had first come to Dakshineshwar, so orthodox had he been, that he could not tolerate the idea of a temple, built and endowed by a low-caste woman. As the younger brother of the priest-in-charge, he had to assist, hour after hour, in the religious ceremonies of the opening day. But he would eat none of the *prasādam*. And late at night, it is said, when all was over, and the guests had dispersed, he broke his fast for the first time, with a handful of fried lentils bought in the bazaar.

Surely this fact deepens the significance of the position which he subsequently occupied in the Temple-garden. It was by no oversight that he became the honoured guest and dependent of the *Koiburto* Rani. We are justified in believing that when at last he found his mission, he recognised it as subversive, rather than corroborative, of the rigid conservatism to which his childhood in the villages had accustomed him. And we may hold that his whole life declares the conviction of the equal religious importance of all men, whatever their individual rank in the social army.

Our Master, at any rate, regarded the Order to which he belonged as one whose lot was cast for all time with the cause of Woman and the People. This was the cry that rose to his lips instinctively, when he dictated to the phonograph in America, the message that he would send to the Rajah of Khetri. It was the one thought, too, with which he would turn to the disciple at his side, whenever he felt himself nearer than usual to death, in a foreign country, alone, "Never forget!" he would then say, "the word is, 'Woman and the People!' "

It is of course in moments of the formation of groups that the intensity of social power is at its greatest, and the Swami brooded much over the fact that the '*formed*' could no longer give life or inspiration. 'Formed' and 'dead', with him, were synonyms. A social formation that had become fixed, was like a tree that had ceased to grow. Only a false sentimentality (and sentimentality was, in his eyes, selfishness, 'the overflow of the senses') could cause us to return upon it, with expectation.

On Caste

Caste was an institution that he was always studying. He rarely criticized, he constantly investigated it. As an inevitable phenomenon of all human life, he could not look upon it as if it had been peculiar to Hinduism. It was on seeing an Englishman hesitate to admit, amongst gentlemen, that he had once killed cattle in Mysore, that the Swami exclaimed, "The opinion of his caste is the last and finest restraint that holds a man!" And with a few quick strokes, he created the picture of the difference between those standards which differentiate the law-abiding from the criminal, or the pious from the unbelieving, on the one hand, and on the other, those finer, more constructive moral ideals, that inspire us to strive for the respect of the smaller number of human beings whom we regard as our peers.

But remarks like this were no indication of partisanhip. It was for the monk to witness life, not to take sides in it. He ignored all the proposals that reached him, which would have pledged him to one party or another, as its leader. Only let women and the People achieve education! All further questions of their fate, they would themselves be competent to settle. This was his view of freedom, and for this he lived. As to what form that education should take, he knew enough to understand that but little was as yet determined. With all his reverence for individuality, he had a horror of what he called the crime of the unfaithful widow. "Better anything than that!" he said, and felt. The white unbordered *sari* of the lonely life was to him the symbol of all that was sacred and true. Naturally then, he could not think of any system of schooling which was out of touch with these things, as 'education'. The frivolous, the luxurious, and the de-nationalised, however splendid in appearance, was to his thinking not educated, but rather degraded. A modernised Indian woman, on the other hand, in whom he was the old-time intensity of trustful and devoted companionship to the husband, with the old-time loyalty to the wedded kindred, was still, to him, "the ideal Hindu wife." True womanhood, like true monkhood, was no matter of mere externals. And unless it held and developed the spirit of true womanhood, there could be no education of woman worthy of the name.

The True Woman

He was always watching for chance indications of the future type. A certain growth of individualism was inevitable, and must necessarily bring later marriage, and perhaps a measure of personal choice, in its train. Probably this, more than anything else, would tend to do away with the problems created by child-widowhood. At the same time, it was not to be forgotten that early marriage had, in its time, been a deliberate attempt, on the part of the community, to avoid certain other evils which they had regarded as incidental to its postponement.

He could not foresee a Hindu woman of the future, entirely without the old power of meditation. Modern science, women must learn; but not at the cost of the ancient spirituality. He saw clearly enough that the ideal education would be one that should exercise the smallest possible influence for direct change on the social body as a whole. It would be that which should best enable every woman, in time to come, to resume into herself the greatness of all the women of the Indian past.

Each separate inspiration of days gone by had done its work. The Rajput story teemed with the strength and courage of the national womanhood. But the glowing metal must flow into new moulds. Ahalya Bai Rani had been perhaps the greatest woman who ever lived. An

Indian *Sādhu*, who had come across her public works in all parts of the country, would naturally think so. Yet the greatness of the future, while including hers, would be no exact repetition of it. The mother's heart, in the women of the dawning age, must be conjoined with the hero's will. The fire on the Vedic altar, out of which arose Savitri, with her sacred calm and freedom, was ever the ideal background. But with this woman must unite a softness and sweetness, as of the south winds themselves.

Physical Exercise

Women must rise in capacity, not fall. In all his plans for a widow's home, or a girls' school and college, there were great green spaces. Physical exercise, gardening, and the care of animals, must form part of the life lived there. Religion, and an intensity of aspiration more frequent in the cloister than outside it, were to be the heart and background of this new departure. And such schools, when the winter was over, must transform themselves into pilgrimages, and study half the year in the Himalayas. Thus a race of women would be created, who should be nothing less than 'Bashi-Bazouks* of religion',

* The Bashi-Bazouks were the bodyguards of the Caliph, For many centuries, the members of the Turkish Guard consisted of soldiers who had been kidnapped in early childhood from all races and countries, and brought up in Islam. Their religion was thus their passion, and the service of their land and sovereign, their only bond of union. They were renowned throughout Europe for their fierceness and courage. Their power was broken in Egypt by Napoleon.

and they should work out the problem for women. No home, save in their work; no ties, save of religion; no love, but that for Guru, and people and motherland. Something after this sort was his dream. He saw plainly enough that what was wanted was a race of women educators, and this was how he contemplated making them. Strength, strength, strength was the one quality he called for, in woman as in man. But how stern was his discrimination of what constituted strength! Neither self-advertisement nor over-emotion roused his admiration. His mind was too full of the grand old types of silence and sweetness and steadiness to be attracted by any form of mere display. At the same time, woman had as large an inheritance as man, in all the thought and knowledge that formed the peculiar gift of the age to India. There could be no sex in truth. He would never tolerate any scheme of life and polity that tended to bind tighter on mind and soul the fetters of the body. The greater the individual, the more would she transcend the limitations of femininity in mind and character; and the more was such transcendence to be expected and admired.

The Educated Women

He looked, naturally enough, to widows as a class, to provide the first generation of abbess-like educators. But in this respect, as in all others, he made no definite plans. In his own words, he only said, " 'Awake! Awake!' Plans grow and work themselves." Yet he would have welcomed material, wherever it might have come from. He knew of no reason why it should be impossible for any woman—by strong and simple character and intellect, and uprightness of living—to make herself a vehicle of the highest ideals. Even burdens of the conscience must be held redeemable by sincerity. "All great ends must be freely pursued," says a recent writer on feminist movements, and the Swami had no fear or freedom, and no distrust of Indian womanhood. But the growth of freedom of which he dreamt, would be no fruit of agitation, clamorous and iconoclastic. It would be indirect, silent and organic. Beginning with a loyal acceptance of the standards of society, women would more and more, as they advanced in achievement, learn to understand both the commands and the opportunities, which characterised the national life. By fulfilling those demands, and availing themselves to the full of their opportunities, they would grow more Indian than ever before, even while they entered on a grandeur of development, of which the past had never dreamt.

National Continuity

In nothing, perhaps, did the personal freedom of Vivekananda show itself more plainly than in his grasp of the continuity of the national life.

The new form was always, to him, sanctified by the old consecration. To draw pictures of the goddess Saraswati was, according to him, "to worship her". To study the science of medicine was "to be down on one's knees, praying against the demons of disease and filth". The old *bhakti* of the cow showed how receptive was the spirit of Hindu society of new and scientific methods of dairy-farming, and the pasturing and care of animals. The training of the intellect to its highest perfection, he believed essential to the power of religious concentration. Study was *tapasyā*, and Hindu meditativeness an aid to scientific insight. All work was a form of renunciation. Love, even of home and family, was always capable of being wrought into a grander and more universal passion.

He delighted to point out that to the Hindu all written words were sacred, English and Persian to the full as much as Sanskrit. But he hated the tinkling sound of foreign manners and foreign accomplishments. He could not bear to listen to a criticism that concerned itself merely with the readjustment of externals. When comparisons had to be made, he dealt always with the ideals as differently expressed by different societies and measured either failure or achievement whether in modern or mediæval, by his central aim.

Above all, his conception of love was one that admitted of no differentiation between the speaker and him of whom he spoke. To refer to others as "they" was already, to his ears, almost hatred. He always united himself with the criticised or the condemned. Those about him realised that if the universe had indeed been resolvable into an ultimate formula of dualism, his own part would have been chosen, not with Michael the Archangel, but with him, eternally defeated, over whom he triumphed. And this was with him no expression of an inner conviction that he could teach or aid. It was simply the passionate determination to *share* the hardest lot to which any might be driven without escape, to defy the powers of the universe, if need be, by himself suffering the utmost to which any single consciousness anywhere might find itself irretrievably doomed.

The Basis of Service

Well might he point out, as he does in certain of his published letters, that even compassion was not motive enough, on which to build the service of others. He would have no such patronage. Compassion, he said, was that which served others with the idea that they were *Jīvas*, souls : love, on the contrary, regarded them as the *Atman*, the very Self. Love, therefore, was worship, and this worship was the vision of God. "For the *Advaitin*, therefore, the ONLY motive is love." There was no privilege to be compared with the trust of a great service. "It is the Saviour," he says, in one of his letters, "who should go on his way rejoicing; not the saved!" As priests purifying themselves for the service of the altar, with eager awe, and the will to endure all, and yet be steadfast, must they come forward, who were chosen for the sacred task of woman's education. He remembered, and often repeated, the words of *Mātāji Mahārāni*, the *Māhrāttā* woman who founded in Calcutta, the *Mahākāli Pāthshālā*. "Swamiji!" she said, pointing to the little girls whom she taught, "I have no help. But these blessed ones I worship, and they will take me to salvation!"

Education for all

A like intensity of chivalry spoke, in his attitude towards those whom he called 'the People'. Education and knowledge were the rights of these, as much as of their brothers, higher in the social scale. Having this, they would work out their own destiny, freely, from within. In this view of the task before him, the Swami was only continuing the tradition of all the great Indian teachers, from Buddha downwards. In the age when the philosophy of the Upanishads had been the exclusive privilege of the *Aryāns*, the Tathagata arose, and taught to all alike the Perfect Way, of *Nirvāna* by Renunciation. In a place and a period where the initiation of the great Masters was the cherished culture of the few, Ramanuja, from the tower of Conjeeveram, proclaimed the mystic text to all the pariahs. It is now the dawn of the modern age—with its realisation of manhood by secular knowledge—in India. Naturally then, to Vivekananda, the absorbing question was how to give secular knowledge to the People.

He saw, of course, that the energy and co-operation of the whole nation was necessary, if material prosperity was ever to be brought back to India. And he knew well enough that the restoration of material prosperity was an imperative need. A God, he said, with his accustomed vigour, who could not in this life give a crust of bread, was not to be trusted in the next for the kingdom of heaven! He also felt, probably, that only by the spread of knowledge could the country as a whole be kept steadfast in its reverence for the greatness of its own inherited culture, intellectual and religious. In any case, new life could only be poured into the veins of the higher classes, by a great movement of forth-reaching to the democracy. He believed that the one thing to be renounced was any idea of birth as the charter of leadership. The sublimated common sense that men call genius, was to the full as likely to occur in the small shopkeeper, or in the peasant taken from the plough, as in the

Brahmin or the *Kāyastha*, If the *Kshatriya* had had any monopoly of courage, where would *Tāntiā Bhil* have been? He believed that the whole of India was about to be thrown into the melting pot, and that no man could say what new forms of power and greatness would be the result.

He saw plainly that the education of the Indian working folk was properly the task of the Indian lettered classes, and of no others. The infinite danger that attended the introduction of knowledge by foreign minds from foreign sources, was never for one moment hidden from him. This is the meaning of his constant plea, in his published correspondence, for the teaching of the villages, by wandering students, who would carry the magic lantern, the camera, and some means for simple chemical experiments. Again he begs for the inclusion of some secular instruction in the intercourse of the begging friars, with the humbler classes. All this, of course, would be little more than a support and attractive invitation, to the New Learning. For that learning itself, every man would have to struggle, alone or in combination. But there can be no doubt that to bring home to a large population the idea that there is a world of thought and knowledge unattained by them, is the first step in the popularising of new culture. In such schemes, therefore, the Swami was emphatically right.

The Need of the Villages

As befitted a religious teacher, however, the work that he himself initiated and consecrated was almost always some special service for the hungry or the sick. It was he who found the money that started the special sanitation missions, first undertaken by the Order, as a measure for plague prevention, in 1899, and never since abandoned. Throughout his years in the West, he was seeking for workers 'to devote themselves to the Indian pariahs' and nothing caused him such exultation in 1897 as to see his Brahmin disciples nursing low-caste patients through cholera. "We see again," he said, referring to this, "what happened before, in the days of Buddha." And those who knew him best, feel a peculiar reverence and affection for the little hospital in Benares, that was the last-born child of his love and pity.

Means of Service

But his heart was not less bound up in other undertakings, which, though less directly his, were more purely educational. The well-being of the various magazines in which the Order was interested, and the industrial education carried on by the Orphanage at Murshidabad, were matters of the deepest import in his eyes. Under present circumstances in India, the magazine is often a kind of peripatetic school, college, and university, all in one. It has a marvellous degree of influence. It carries ideas on the one hand,

and offers a means of self-expression on the other, and it was an instinctive perception of this educational value that made the Swami so eager about the fate of various papers conducted by his brethren and disciples. The same number of a periodical will sometimes combine the loftiest transcendental abstractions on one page with comparatively faltering secular speculations of the next, and this affords an exact index to the popular mind of the Transition. The Swami himself said, referring to this paradox, "The Hindu's idea of the means of knowledge is meditation, and this serves him well, when the subject is mathematics. Unfortunately, however, his instinct would lead him to the same method in the case of geography, and not much geography comes that way!"

Problems of the Sudra

Vivekananda's passion of pity, however, did not concern itself with the Indian people only. True to his Oriental birth, he would always defend the *small* farmer or the *small* distributor, against those theorists who seem to consider that aggregations of business are justified in proportion to their size. He held that the age of humanity now dawning would occupy itself mainly with the problems of the working-folk, or, as he expressed it, with the problems of the Sudra. When he first landed in the West, he was greatly attracted, as his letters show, by the apparent democracy of conditions there. Later, in 1900, he had a clearer view of the underlying selfishness of capital and the struggle for privilege, and confided to someone that Western life now looked to him 'like hell'. At this riper stage of experience, he was inclined to believe that China had gone nearer to the ideal conception of human ethics than newer countries had ever done, or could do. Yet he never doubted that for man, the world over, the coming age would be 'for the People'. "We are to solve the problems of the Sudra," he said, one day, "but oh, through what tumults! Through what tumults!" He spoke like one gazing, direct into the future, and his voice had the ring of prophecy; but, though the listener waited, hoping eagerly for more, he only became silent, lapsing into deeper thought.

I have always believed that it was for the guiding and steadying of mean through some such age of confusion and terror, that in our Master's life and that of Ramakrishna Paramahamsa, the worship of the Mother has sounded such a mighty *Udbodhan.* She it is who unites in Herself the extremes of experience. She shines through evil as through good. She alone is the Goal, whatever be the road. Whenever the Swami would chant Her salutation, one would hear, like the subdued music of some orchestra behind a single melody, this great chorus of the historic drama. "Thou art the welfare and happiness in the homes of the virtuous,": he would recite. "And thou art the misery and wretchedness, in those of the quarrelsome and wicked!" And then, as the mingling of oppressor and oppressed in a common hope and terror, as the trampling of armies, and turmoil of nations, grew louder and clearer to the mental ear, one would hear the thunder of the great Ascription rise above it all :

Salutation to the Mother

Thou Mother of blessings,
Thou the Giver of desires,
Thou the Doer of all good,
To Thee our salutation.
Thee we salute, Thee we salute,
Thee we salute.
Thou terrible dark Night!
Thou the Night of Delusion!
Thou the Night of DEATH—
To THEE our salutation!
Thee we salute, Thee we salute,
Thee we salute.

XXI

The Swami's Method of Training a Western Worker

The Swami had once asked *Pavhāri Bābā* of Gazipur, "What was the secret of success in work?" and had been answered, "To make the end the means, and the means the end."

This is a saying that one penetrates now and again for a moment at long intervals. But if it signifies that the whole energy of the worker should be concentrated on the means, as if these were the end, while that end itself is for the time being forgotten or ignored, then it may be only another way of preaching the great lesson of the Gita, "To action man has a right : he has no right to the fruits of action." Our Master possessed, in a wonderful degree, the secret of inspiring his disciples to attempt this ideal. He had his own reasons—which every Hindu will perhaps understand—for feeling that a European who was to work on his behalf for India must do so in the Indian way. And in this demand, while he never confused essentials and non-essentials, he regarded no detail as too trivial to be important. To eat only of approved foods, and to do this with the fingers, to sit and sleep on the floor, to perform Hindu ceremonies, and bind oneself strictly by the feelings and observances of Hindu etiquette, were all, to his thinking, means of arriving at that Indian consciousness which would afterwards enable one to orientate oneself truly to the Indian aspects of larger questions. Even so trifling a matter as the use of lime juice and powdered lentils, instead of soap, appeared to him worthy of thought and effort. Even the caste-feeling that seemed crude must be appreciated and assimilated. It was tacitly understood that the time might someday come, when one would be free of all these, even, as he was; but the emancipation won by going through an experience is very different from the blindness that ignores or despises!

Indian Forms

The Swami was remarkable, however, in his power of imparting the ideal with a custom. To this day, one shudders at the impurity and roughness of blowing out a light; while to put on a *sari*, and veil the head, is always to strive for the mood of passive sweetness and acceptance, rather than that of self-confident aggression. For in how far this symbolism of externals is a fact of common Indian perception, we are not, perhaps, quite prepared to understand. "Never neglect to lower it!" said the monk Sadananda to me once, of this particular garment. "Remember that in that white veil lies the half of saintliness!"

In all this, one was led along the path that one knew already to be right. If the student was to solve any problem of Indian education, it was essential that there should first be experience of the humbler routine of teaching; and for this, the supreme and essential qualification was to have looked at the world, even if only for a moment, through the eyes of the taught. Every canon of educational science proclaims this fact. 'From known to unknown,' 'from simple to complex,' 'from concrete to abstract,' and the very term 'education' itself, are all words only, on the lips of those who can form no idea of the world as the pupil sees it, or the aims to which he would fain be aided to climb. To teach *against* the aspiration of the taught, is assuredly to court ill results instead of good.

Canons of Education

What was startling in the Swami's discipline was his instinctive assumption that the Indian consciousness was built up on the thousand and one tiny details of Indian daily life. Looking closer, one saw that this had been the method pursued by Sri Ramakrishna. Whenever he desired to apprehend a new idea, he had adopted the food, clothes, language, and general habits of those who held it. He had not merely attempted to approximate them in the use of a few religious formulæ.

The Freedom Given

But Vivekananda was too great an educator to disregard the freedom of the disciple, even in such matters as these. The aim was revealed only little by little, and always on the basis of some attempt already made. It was true that he was perpetually testing the purity of motive, always on his guard against the possible intrusion of self-interest, in himself or in others. "I trust no one," he said, "because I do not trust myself. How do I know what I may become tomorrow?" But it was also true that it was not in his nature, as he said once, to interfere with liberty, even to prevent mistakes. It was for him to point out the source of an error, only when it had been committed.

During the first six months of 1899, I denied occasionally with people of various classes, both Indian and European, in Calcutta. This fact always caused the Swami uneasiness. He feared a revulsion, probably, against the extreme simplicity of orthodox Hindu life. Undoubtedly also he thought a strong reaction possible, in favour of the associations of one's birth. He had seen a great religious movement shattered in the West, by the petty social ambition of a woman of over-much refinement. Yet he never interfered with me in this matter, though a single word of authority would have been enough at any time to have ended it. Nor did he ever show his disapproval. He took an interest, on the contrary, in every experience that one brought to his notice. He would in a general way express his fear, or utter a grave warning, not at the time understood, about 'loaves and fishes'. But seeing, perhaps, that there was a genuine need to form a concept of the whole synthesis of classes and interests in Modern India, he gave way completely to his disciple, and allowed of course of enquiry to pursue its own path.

It was only on the ship, during the voyage to England, that he fully expressed the ideal that was in him. "You must give up all visiting, and live in strict seclusion," he said one day, as he discussed the future of the women's work. "You have to set yourself to Hinduise your thoughts, your needs, your conceptions, and your habits. Your life, internal and external, has to become all that an orthodox Hindu Brahmin *Brahmachārini's* ought to be. The method will come to you, if only you desire it sufficiently. But *you have to forget your own past, and to cause it to be forgotten. You have to lose even its memory*!"

Never was a monk more passionately monastic than Vivekananda, for all his apparent ease and fearlessness. Yet here, in the case of a worker, he knew how to substitute for the walls of a convent, the Indian people and their lives. This has sometimes appeared to me as the greatest manifestation he gave, of his genius. "We shall speak to all men," he said once, "in terms of their own orthodoxy!" and went on to picture a branch of the Indian Orders in the English Church, wearing the yellow garb, going barefooted, practising the extreme of asceticism, and standing always for the supreme truth of the inter-relatedness of all religions.

Hindu Etiquette

In the special case of the Indian consciousness, however, his ideal was by no means limited to a strenuous aspiration. Step by step, point by point, he gave, as details of Hindu etiquette, those instructions which it is customary in Europe to offer the religious novice. It was in this way that he laboured to overcome that restlessness and emphasis of Western manners, which appears to the Eastern mind so crude. The constant expression of feeling, whether of pain, admiration, or surprise, was to him shocking. It was not necessary to stigmatise it as irreligious, for it was ill-bred. The oriental expects of a man that he should feel, and keep his feelings to himself. Any constant pointing out of the curious or the beautiful appears to him an unwarrantable intrusion on the privacy and self-directedness of thought. Yet that the desired repose of manner is not conceived of as merely idle, is seen in the case of that sage who was asked by a certain king to tell him about God. 'What is He like" What is He like?' And the saint replied, 'All this time I was telling you, O king! For silence is His name!'

This was a point on which the Swami was exacting. He would impose on the European disciple long periods of severe restraint. "Struggle to realise yourself," he said on a certain occasion, "without a trace of emotion!"

Watching the fall of dead leaves once, in the stillness of an autumn evening, he did not deny that there was poetry in the sight, but he declared that mental excitement, roused by what was merely an event of the external sense-world, was childish and out of place, All western people, he said, had to learn the great lesson, of holding experience and emotion apart. "Watch the fall of the leaves, but gather the sentiment of the sight from within, at some later time!"

This is neither more nor less than the conventual doctrine of recollectedness and peace, as known in Europe. Is it also a subtle method of evoking creative faculty? Does it point to a poetry which holds the world as a vast symbol, yet thrones the intellect high above the senses?

Carrying the question out of the sphere of mere good-breeding, and mental discipline, and framing the same truth again in terms of the spiritual life alone, the Swami would speak with horror of that bondage which shows itself in the quest of subtle metaphysical pleasures. In all idealism, he would say, lies the danger of idealizing merely what we have reached. Such 'covering of a corpse with flowers' would sooner or later mean, when realised in practice, the abandonment of the People, and the destruction of the work. Only they could be faithful who were beyond temptation, followers of the pure idea, regardless of self.

Be True to the People

"Mind!" he said, as he talked of future methods, "No loaves and fishes! No glamour of the world! All this must be cut short. It must be rooted out. It is sentimentality—the overflow of the senses. It comes to you in colour, sight, sound and associations. Cut it off, Learn to hate it. It is utter poison!"

Thus the common routine of the Hindu home became eloquent, on the Swami's lips, of a world of deeper truths, characteristically apprehended by the Hindu mind. He himself had been interested, from his babyhood, in monastic organisation. He had once had a copy of the *Imitation*, in which there was a preface describing the monastery and the rule followed by Jean de Gerson, the supposed author, and this preface, to his imagination, had been the jewel of the book. Not contented with reading it over and over till he knew it off by heart, it filled the dreams of his boyhood; till with a kind of surprise he awoke, in middle age, to find himself, organizing another monastic order, on the banks of the Ganges, and realised that the fascination of his childhood had been a foreshadowing of the future.

Monastic Orders

Yet it was not the conventualism of authority, or of the school, but that of the Hindu widow, following her rule freely, in the midst of the family, that he held up to a European disciple for a model. 'An orthodox Hindu Brahmin *Brahmachārini*' was his ideal for the woman of character, and no words can convey the delight with which his voice lingered over the phrase.

"Lay down the rules for your group, and formulate your ideas," he said once, dealing with this very point, "and put in a little universalism, if there is room for it. But remember that not more than half a dozen people in the whole world are ever at any one time ready for this! There must be room for sects, as well as for rising above sects. You will have to manufacture your own tools. Frame laws, but frame them in such a fashion that when people are ready to do without them, they can burst them asunder. Our originality lies in combining perfect freedom with perfect authority. This can be done, even in monasticism. For my own part, I always have an horizon."

He broke off here to follow another line of thought, which always interested him, and always appeared to him fruitful of applications. "Two different races," he said, "mix and fuse, and out of them rises one strong distinct type. This tries to save itself from admixture, and here you see the beginning of caste. Look at the apple. The best specimens have been produced by crossing, but once crossed, we try to preserve the variety intact."

The Value of Types

A few days afterwards, the same reflection came most uppermost again, and he said with great earnestness, "A strong and distinct type is always the physical basis of the horizon. It is all very well to talk of universalism, but the word will not be ready for that for millions of years!"

"Remember!" he said again, "if you want to know what a ship is like, the ship has to be specified as it is—its length, breadth, shape and material. And to understand a nation, we must do the same. India is idolatrous. You must help her *as she is*. Those who have left her can do nothing for her!"

The Swami felt that there was no task before India which could compare in importance with that of women's education. His own life had had two definite personal purposes, of which one had been the establishment of a home for the Order of Ramakrishna, while the other was the initiation of some endeavour towards the education of women. With five hundred men, he would say, the conquest of India might take fifty years : with as many women, not more than a few weeks.

In gathering widows and orphans to be trained, he was of the opinion that the limitations of birth must be steadfastly ignored. But it was essential to success that those who were chosen should be young and unformed. "Birth is nothing!' he would say, 'Environment is everything!' But above all else, he felt that impatience was inexcusable. If in twelve years any result were visible, this fact would constitute a great success. The task was one that might well take seventy years to accomplish.

Castles in the Air

For hours he would sit and talk of details building castles in the air of an ideal school, dwelling lovingly on this point and that. None of it would ever, perhaps, be carried out literally, yet all of it, surely, was precious, since it showed the freedom he would have given, and the results that, from his standpoint, would have appeared desirable.

It was natural—if only in view of my own preoccupation at the time with the religious ideas of Hinduism—that all these plans should wear a religious colour. They were more conventual than scholastic. The temper of the teaching was more the burden of his thought than the learning to be imparted. Except for a sudden exclamation once, "We must turn out the greatest intellect in India!" I scarcely remember that he ever said anything directly affecting the secular side of the women's education scheme. He took for granted that anything deserving of such a name must needs be measured in terms of depth and severity. He was no believer in that false idealism which leads to modification of knowledge or dilution of truth in the name of sex.

How to make the home-background against which the work of education must be carried on, at one thoroughly progressive and thoroughly Hindu, was the problem that engrossed him. There was the task of so translating the formulæ of the old *régime*, moreover, that they might continue to command the reverence of the modernised.

The moral and ethical failures which result from too easy an adoption of foreign ideas, without regard to their effects on social continuity and cohesion, were ever before his eyes. He knew instinctively that the bonds by which the old society had been knit together, must receive a new sanction and a deeper sanctification, in the light of modern learning, or that learning would prove only preliminary to the ruin of India. But he never made the mistake of thinking this reconciliation of old and new an easy matter. How to nationalise the modern and modernise the old, so as to make the two one, was a puzzle that occupied much of his time and thought. He rightly saw that only when it had been pieced together, could national education be in a fair way to begin.

Old and New

The way in which the existing obligations of Hindu life might be re-interpreted to include the whole of the modern conception of duty to country and history, suddenly struck him one day, and he exclaimed "How much you might do, with those five *Yajnas*!* What great things might be made of them!"

The Five Yajnas

The light had broken in a flash, but it did not leave him. He took up the thread of the idea, and went into every detail.

"Out of that old ancestor-*puja*, you might create hero-worship.

"In the worship of the gods, you must of course use images. But you can change these. Kali need not always be in one position. Encourage your girls to think of new ways of picturing Her. Have a hundred different conceptions of

* These are : (1) to the Rishis, by learning; (2) to the Ancestors by family honour; (3) to the Gods, by religion; (4) to the Animals; and (5) to Mankind.

These five sacrifices are to be performed daily by every Hindu.

Saraswati. Let them draw, model and paint their own ideas.

"In the chapel, the pitcher on the lowest step of the altar, must be always full of water, and the lights—in great Tamil butter-lamps—must be always burning. If, in addition, the maintenance of perpetual adoration could be organised, nothing could be more in accord with Hindu feeling.

"But the ceremonies employed must themselves be Vedic. There must be a Vedic altar, on which at the hour of worship to light the Vedic fire. And the children must be present to share in the service of oblation. This is a rite which would claim the respect of the whole of India.

"Gather all sorts of animals about you. The cow makes a fine beginning. But you will also have dogs and cats and birds and others. Let the children have a time for going to feed and look after these.

"Then there is the sacrifice of *learning*. That is the most beautiful of all. Do you know that every book is holy, in India? Not the Vedas alone, but the English and Mohammedan also? All are sacred.

"Revive the old arts. Teach your girls fruit-modelling with hardened milk. Give them artistic cooking and sewing. Let them learn painting, photography, the cutting of designs in paper, and gold and silver filigree and embroidery. See that everyone knows something by which she can earn a living, in case of need.

"And never forget Humanity! The idea of a humanitarian man-worship exists in the nucleus of India, but it has never been sufficiently specialised. Let your women develop it. Make poetry, make art, of it. Yes, a daily worship of the feet of beggars, after bathing and before the meal, would be a wonderful practical training of heart and hand together. On some days, again, the worship might be of children, of your own pupils. Or you might borrow babies, and nurse and feed them. What was it that Mataji said to me? 'Swamiji! I have no help. But these blessed ones I worship, and they will take me to salvation!' She feels, you see, that she is serving Uma in the Kumari, and that is a wonderful thought, with which to begin a school."

The Key to Ideals

But while he was thus prepared to work out the *minutiæ* of the task of connecting old and new, it remained always true that the very presence of the Swami acted in itself as a key to the ideal, putting into direct relation with it every sincere effort that one encountered. It was this that made evident to the crudest eye the true significance of ancient rites. It was this that gave their sudden vividness and value to the fresh applications made spontaneously by modernised Hindus. Thus the reverence of a great Indian man of science for the heroes and martyrs of European science, seemed but the modern form of the ancient salutation of the masters. The pursuit of knowledge for its own sake without regard to its concrete application, seemed an inevitable greatness in the race that had dreamt of *Jnānam*. Serene indifference to fame and wealth proved only that a worker was spiritually the monk, though he might be playing the part of citizen and householder.

Of this element in his own life, by which all else that was noble and heroic was made into a recognition, a definite illustration, of an ideal already revealed, the Swami was of course unconscious. Yet this was, as one imagines, the very quintessence of his interpretative power. With regard to the details of his educational suggestions, their pedagogic soundness had always been startling to me. Nor did I feel that this had been accounted for, even when he told me of a certain period of hardship and struggle, when he had undertaken to translate Herbert Spencer's 'Education' into Bengali, and had gone on, becoming interested in the subject, to read all he could find about Pestalozzi also, 'though that was not in the bond.'

In fact, so deeply is the Hindu versed in psychological observation, and so perfect an example of the development of faculty has he

Hindu Personality

always before him, in the religious practices of his people, that he enters the field of educational theory with immense advantages. Nor is there any reason why the very centre of scientific thought on the subject should not someday be found with him. Meanwhile, the first step towards so desired a consummation will lie in apprehending the vast possibilities of existing formulæ. Indian educators have to extend and fulfil the vision of Vivekananda. When this is done, when to his reverence and love for the past, we can add his courage and hope for the future, and his allegiance to the sacredness of all knowledge, the time will not be far distant that is to see the Indian woman take her rightful place amongst the womanhood of the world.

XXII

Monasticism and Marriage

To the conscience of the Swami, his monastic vows were incomparably precious. To him personally—as to any sincere monk marriage, or any step associated with it, would have been the first of crimes. To rise beyond the very memory of its impulse, was his ideal, and to guard himself and his disciples against the remotest danger of it, his passion. The very fact of un-marriedness counted with him as a spiritual asset. It follows from all this, that he was accompanied not only by the constant eagerness for monastic perfection, but also by the equally haunting fear, of loss of integrity. And this fear, however salutary or even necessary to his own fulfilment of the ideal, did undoubtedly, for many years, come between him and the formulation of an ultimate philosophy, on this most important subject.

It must be understood, however, that his dread was not of woman, but of temptation. As

Honourable Women

disciples, as co-workers, and even as comrades and playfellows, he was much associated with women, the world over. It happened almost always that he followed the custom of the Indian villages with these friends of his wanderings, and gave them some title of family relationship. In one place he found a group of sisters, elsewhere a mother, a daughter, and so on. Of the nobility of these, and their freedom from false or trivial ideas, he would sometimes boast, for he had in its highest degree that distinction of fine men, to seek for greatness and strength, instead of their opposites, in women. To see girls, as he had seen them in America, boating, swimming, and playing games, "without once," in his own phrase, "remembering that they were not boys," delighted him. He worshipped that ideal of purity which they thus embodied for him.

In the monastic training, he laid constant emphasis on the necessity of being neither man nor woman, because one had risen above both. Anything, even politeness, that emphasised the idea of sex, was horrible to him. The thing that the West calls 'chivalry' appeared to him as an insult to woman. The opinion of some writers that woman's knowledge ought not to be too exact, nor man's to be too sympathetic, would have sounded, in his neighbourhood, like a pitiful meanness. The effort of all alike must be the overcoming of such limitations, imposed on a defiant human spirit by our physical constitution.

The ideal of the life of the student, with its mingling of solitude, austerity, and intense concentration of thought, is known in India as *brahmacharya*. "*Brahmacharya* should be like a burning fire within the veins!" said the Swami. Concentration upon subjects of study, incidental to student-hood, was to him only one form of that negation of personal in impersonal which to his thinking formed so inevitable a part of all great lives, that for its sake he was even tempted to admire Robespierre, in his fanaticism of the Terror. The worship of Saraswati—by which he meant perfect emotional solitude and self-restraint—he believed with his whole heart to be an essential preparation for any task demanding the highest powers, whether of heart, mind or body. Such worship had been recognized in India for ages as part of the training of the athlete, and the significance of this fact was that a man must dedicate all the force at his disposal, if he were now and again to reach that height of superconscious insight, which appears to others as illumination, inspiration, or transcendent skill. Such illumination was as necessary to the highest work in art or science, as in religion. No man who was spending himself in other ways selfish or ignoble, could ever have painted

Worship of Saraswati

a great Madonna, or enunciated the Laws of Gravitation. The civic ideal called as loudly for monastic devotion as the spiritual. The vows of celibacy meant renunciation of the private for the public good. Thus he saw that true manhood could not be, without control of manhood; that the achievement of real greatness, by whatever path, meant always the superiority of the soul to the personal impulse; and finally, that the great monk was also potentially the great worker or great citizen. That he was equally clear as to the converse of this—as, for instance, that great wifehood or great citizenship can only be, where nunhood or monasticism might have been—I cannot say. I think that perhaps his own life, of monk and guide of monastic aspirants, hid from him this great truth, except in flashes, until the end came, and his summary of conclusions was complete. "It is true," he said once, "that there are women whose very presence makes a man feel driven to God. But there are equally others, who drag him down to hell."

At his side, it was impossible to think with respect of a love that sought to *use*, to appropriate, to bend to its own pleasure or good, the thing loved. Instead of this, love, to be love at all, must be a welling benediction, a free gift, 'without a reason,' and careless or return. This was what he meant, by his constant talk of 'loving without attachment'. Once, indeed, on his return from a journey, he told some of us that he had now realised that the power to attach oneself was quite as important as that of detachment. Each must be instantaneous, complete, whole-hearted. And each was only the complement of the other. "Love is always a manifestation of bliss," he said in England, "the least shadow of pain falling upon it, is always a sign of physicality and selfishness."

No Pain in Love

Furthest of all from his admiration were the pulling literature and vitiated art that are human beings primarily as bodies to be possessed, and only in the second place as mind and spirit, eternal in self-mastery and inner freedom. Much, though not all, of our Western idealism, seemed to him to be deeply tainted with this spirit, which he always spoke of as 'hiding a corpse beneath flowers'.

European Ideals

The ideal of wifehood he thought of, in Eastern fashion, as an unwavering flame of devotion to one alone. Western customs he may have regarded as polyandrous, for I find it difficult otherwise to account for his statement that he had seen women, as great and pure amongst polyandrous peoples as in the home of his birth. He had travelled in Malabar, but not in Tibet; and in Malabar, as one learns by enquiry, the so-called polyandry is really only matriarchal marriage. The husband visits the wife in her own home, and marriage is not necessarily for life, as in the rest of India; but two men are not received on an equal footing, at the same time. In any case, he had learnt, he said, that 'custom was nothing,' that use and wont could never altogether thwart or limit human development. He knew that in any country and any race the ideal might shine forth through individuals in all its fullness.

He never attacked a social ideal. He told me, a day or two before I landed in England, on my return there in 1899, that I must take back while in the West, as though I had never dropped them, the social ideals of Europe. To him, in Europe or America, the married woman was not less in honour than the unmarried. Some missionaries on board the ship, during this voyage, were displaying silver wedding bracelets bought from Tamil women in the stress of feminine, and the talk ran on the superstitious dislike of wives, East and West, to the removal of the wedding ring from fingers or wrist. "You call it a *superstition*?" exclaimed the Swami, in low pained tones of astonishment, "You cannot see the great ideal of chastity, behind?"*

* The chastity of the wife, as Hindus think of it, is a word that connotes not only faithfulness to one alone, but also *unwearying* faithfulness. In this ideal, there is no room for the slightest fluctuation of distaste.

Ideals of Marriage

The institution of marriage, however, was always seen by him in its relation to the ideal of spiritual freedom. And freedom, in the Eastern sense, must be understood, not as the right to do, but the right to refrain from doing—that highest inaction which transcends all action. "Against marriage, in order to rise beyond marriage," he admitted one day, in argument, "I have nothing to say." The perfect marriage was to his thinking, of the type that he had seen in his Master, in his brother Yogananda, and in his disciple Swarupananda. And these were what would in other countries have been regarded as merely nominal. "You see there is a difference of outlook on this point!" he said once, discussing the question. "The West regards marriage as consisting in all that lies beyond the legal tie, while in India it is thought of as a bond thrown by society round two people, to unite them together for all eternity. Those two must wed each other, whether they will or not, in life after life. Each acquires half of all the merit of the other. And if one seems in this life to have fallen hopelessly behind, it is for the other only to wait and beat time, till he or she catches up again!"

Sri Ramakrishna, it was said, had always referred to marriage as a special, and to the monastic life as a universal, service. In this he was, one supposes, alluding only to marriages of the very highest type. And this was clearly the determining concept of celibacy or *brahmacharya*, in the Swami's own mind. He called souls to take this vow as if he were calling them to the most honourable of warfare. He regarded a monastic order as 'an army' behind a leader, and the teacher whose followers were all citizens and householders, as without an army. There could be no comparison, in his mind, between the strength of a cause that had, and one that had not, this support.

A Path To Mukti

Yet in marriage itself, he was not wholly unable to see a career for the soul. I can never forget his story of an old couple who were separated, after fifty years of companionship, at the doors of the workhouse. "What!" exclaimed the old man, at the close of the first day, "Can't I see Mary and kiss her before she goes to sleep? Why, I haven't missed doing that at night, for fifty years!" "Think of it!" said the Swami, glowing with the thought of an achievement so high. "Think of it! Such self-control and steadiness as that ARE *mukti*! Marriage itself had been the path for those two souls!"

He held with unfaltering strength, that the freedom to refrain from marriage, if she wished, ought to be considered as a natural right of woman. A child, whose exclusive leaning to the devotional life was already strongly marked before she was twelve, had once appealed to him for protection against proposals of alliance that were being made by her family. And he, by using his influence with her father, and suggesting increased dowers for the younger daughters, had been successful in aiding her. Years had gone by, but she was still faithful to the life she had adopted, with its long hours of silence and retirement; and all her younger sisters were now wedded. To force such a spirit into marriage would in his eyes have been a desecration. He was proud, too, to count up the various classes—of child-widows, wives of *kulin* Brahmins, rare cases of the undowered and so on—who represent the unmarried woman in Hindu society.

He held that the faithfulness of widows was the very pillar on which social institutions rested. Only he would have liked to declare as high an ideal for men as for women in this respect. The old Aryan conception of marriage, symbolised in the fire lighted at marriage, and worshipped morning and evening by husband and wife together, pointed to no inequality of standards or responsibilities as between the two. Rama, in the epic of Valmiki, had been as true to Sita, as Sita to him.

The Swami was not unaware of the existence of social problems, in connection with marriage,

Problems in Marriage

in all parts of the world. "These unruly women," he exclaims, in the course of a lecture in the West, "from whose mind the words 'bear and forbear' are gone forever!" He could admit, also, when continuance in a marriage would involve treachery to the future of humanity, that separation was the highest and bravest course for husband or wife to take. In India, he would constantly point out that Oriental and Occidental ideals needed to be refreshed by one another. He never attacked social institutions as such, holding always that they had grown up out of a desire to avoid some evil which their critic was possibly too headstrong to perceive. But he was not blind to the over-swing of the pendulum, in one direction or the other.

"There is such pain in this country!" he said one day in India, speaking of marriage by arrangement instead of by choice. "Such pain! Some, of course, there must always have been. But now the sight of Europeans, with their different customs, has increased it. Society knows that there is another way!"

"We have exalted motherhood, and you wifehood," he said again, to a European, "and I think both might gain by some interchange."

Again, there was the dream that he recounted on board the ship, "in which I heard two voices discussing the marriage-ideals of the East and the West, and the conclusion of the whole was, that there was something in each, with which as yet, the world could ill afford to part.' It was this conviction that led him to spend so much time examining into differences of social ideals, as between East and West.

"In India," he said, "the wife must not dream of loving even a son as she loves her husband. She must be *Sati*. But the husband ought not to love his wife as he does his mother. Hence a reciprocated affection is not thought so high as one unreturned. It is 'shopkeeping'. The joy of the contact of husband and wife is not admitted in India. This we have to borrow from the West. Our ideal needs to be refreshed by yours. And you, in turn, need something of our devotion to motherhood."

The Monk Alone Free

But the overwhelming thought that his very presence carried home to the mind was of the infinite superiority of that life which seeks only the freedom of the soul and the service of all, to that which looks for comfort and the sweetness of home. He knew well enough the need that great workers may feel of being encircled by subordinated human lives. "You need not mind," he said once, turning to a disciple with great tenderness and compassion, "you need not mind, if these shadows of home and marriage cross your mind sometimes. Even to me, they come now and again!" And again, hearing of an expression of intense loneliness on the part of a friend, he exclaimed, "Every worker feels like that at times!"

But infinite danger lay, to his thinking, in a false exaltation of any social ideal at the risk of jeopardising the eternal supremacy of the super-social. "Never forget to say to all whom you teach," he charged one of his disciples solemnly, "that like a little fire-fly beside the brightness of the sun, like a grain of sand beside the vastness of Mount Meru, SO is the life of the citizen compared with that of the *Sannyāsin*!"

He knew the danger that lay here, of spiritual pride, and his own means of overcoming this lay in bowing himself down to anyone, whether monk or householder, who was disciple and devotee of his own Master, Sri Ramakrishna. But to abate the *dictum* itself, would have been, in his eyes, to have minimised the ideal, and this he could not do. Instead, he felt that one of the most important responsibilities lying, in the present age, upon the religious orders, was the preaching of monastic ideals even in marriage, in order that the more difficult might always exercise its compelling and restraining force upon the easier path; and that the false glamour of romance—obscuring the solitary grandeur and freedom of the soul, as the ultimate aim, in the name of an interesting and absorbing companionship—might be utterly destroyed.

Ideal Marriage

All the disciples of Ramakrishna believe that marriage is finally perfected by the man's acceptance of his wife as the mother; and this means, by their mutual adoption of the monastic life. It is a moment of the mergence of the human in the divine, by which all life stands thenceforward changed. The psychological justification of this ideal is said to be the fact that, up to this critical point, the relation of marriage consists in a constant succession of a twofold impulse, the waxing followed by the waning, of affection. With the abandonment of the external, however, the impulse is transcended, and there is no fluctuation. Henceforth the beloved is worshipped in perfect steadfastness of mind.

Yet in dealing with his views on this question, one cannot but remember his utterance on the contrast between Hinduism and Buddhism, that Sunday morning in Kashmir, when we walked under the avenue of poplars, and listened to him as he talked of Woman and Caste. "The glory of Hinduism," he said that day, "lies in the fact that while it has defined ideals, it has never dared to say that any one of these alone was the one true way. In this, it differs from Buddhism, which exalts monasticism above all others, as the path that must be taken by all souls to reach perfection. The story given in the *Mahābhārata* of the young saint who was made to seek enlightenment, first from a married woman, and then from a butcher, is sufficient to show this. 'By doing my duty' said each one of these when asked, 'by doing my duty in my own station, have I attained this knowledge.' There is no career then," he ended, "which might not be the path to God. The question of attainment depends only, in the last resort, on the thirst of the soul."

Thus the fact that all life is great, only in proportion to its expression of ideal purity, was not, in theory, outside the Swami's acceptance, however much, as a monk, he shrank from interpretation which might lead to the false claim that marriage was chosen as a means to spirituality.

Idealizing Self

That self-love constantly leads us to such subtle exaltation of our own acts and motives, he was well aware. He had constantly, he told us, met with persons, in Western countries, who urged that their own lives, though indolently passed in the midst of luxury, were without selfishness; that only the claims of duty kept them in the world; that in their affections, they were able to realise renunciation without a struggle. On all such illusions, he poured out his scorn. "My only answer was," he said, "that such great men are not born in India! The model in this kind was the great king Janaka, and in the whole of history he occurs but once!" In connection with this particular form of error, he would point out that there are two forms of idealism; one is the worship and exaltation of the ideal itself, and the other is the glorification of that which we have already attained. In this second case, the ideal is really subordinated to self.

In this severity, however, there was no cynicism. Those who have read our Master's work on Devotion or *Bhakti-Yoga*, will remember there the express statement that the lover always sees the ideal in the beloved. "Cling to this vision!" I have heard of his saying—to a girl whose love for another stood newly confessed—"As long as you can both see the ideal in one another, your worship and happiness will grow more instead of less."

Amongst the friends of our Master there was, however, one middle-aged woman who was never satisfied that, in his intensity of monasticism, he was able to do full justice to the sacredness and helpfulness of marriage. She had herself been long a widow, after an unusually blessed experience of married life. Very naturally, therefore, it was to this friend that he turned, when, a few weeks before the end, he arrived at what he knew to be his crowning conviction on this whole subject; and his letter was brought to her in her distant home by the same hand that was carrying also the telegraphic announcement of his death. In this letter, so solemnly destined, he says : "In my opinion, a race must first cultivate a great respect for motherhood, through the sanctification and inviolability of marriage, before it can attain to the ideal of perfect chastity. The Roman Catholics and the Hindus, holding marriage sacred and inviolate, have produced great chaste men and women of immense power. To the Arab, marriage is a contract, or a forceful possession, to be dissolved at will, and we do not find there the development of the ideal of the virgin, or the *brahmacharin*. Modern Buddhism—having fallen among races who have not even yet come up to the evolution of marriage—has made a travesty of monasticism. So, until there is developed in Japan a great and sacred ideal about marriage (apart from mutual attraction and love). I do not see how there can be great monks and nuns. As you have come to see that the glory of life is chastity, so my eyes also have been opened to the necessity of this great sanctification for the vast majority, in order that a few life-long chaste powers may be produced."

His Final Uterance

Fidelity Essential

There are some of us who feel that this letter has an even wider-reaching significance than he himself would have thought of ascribing to it. It was the last sentence in the great philosophy which saw 'in the Many and the One the same Reality'. If the inviolability of marriage be indeed the school in which a society is made ready for the highest possibilities of the life of solitude and self-control, then the honourable fulfilment of the world's work is as sacred a means to supreme self-realisation, as worship and prayer. We have here, then, a law which enables us to understand the discouragement of religious ecstasy, by Ramakrishna Paramahamsa, and his great preference for character, in his disciples. We understand, too, the inner meaning of Vivekananda's own constant preaching of strength. The reason is very simple. If 'the Many and the One be the same Reality, seen by the same mind at different times, and in different attitudes,' then, in three words, Character is Spirituality. 'Greatness' really is, as a deep thinker has affirmed, 'to take the common things of life, and walk truly amongst them; and holiness a great love and much serving.' These simple truths may prove after all, to be the very core of the new gospel. And in endorsement of this possibility, we have the Master's own words, "The highest truth is always the simplest."

XXIII

Our Master's Relation to Psychic Phenomena So-Called

India is undoubtedly the land of the understanding of psychology. To Hindus, more than to any other race, it may be said that men appear as minds. Concentration of mind is to them the ideal of life. Such differences as between talent and genius, between ordinary goodness and the highest sainthood, between moral weakness and power, are by them understood as simple differences in the degree of concentration. This preoccupation of the race is partly cause, and partly effect, doubtless, of the fact that the study of psychology has been organised in India as a science, from the earliest times. Long before the value of writing, for the notation of knowledge, was even suspected, the quiet registration of phenomena in the communal consciousness, had begun, by the interchange of ideas and observations. Millenniums before instruments and laboratories could be thought of, as having any bearing on scientific enquiry in general, the age of experiment was fully developed amongst the Indian people, with regard to this most characteristic of their sciences.

It is not surprising that in the singularly wide range of knowledge thus accumulated in India, many phenomena of the mind, which appear to the less informed West as abnormal or miraculous, should be duly noted and classified. Thus hypnotism, and many obscure forms of *hyperæsthesis* and *hyperkinesis*—the most familiar of these being healing, thought-reading, clairvoyance, and clairaudience—offer no overwhelming difficulty to the student of the ancient Indian psychology, or *Raja-Yoga* as it called.

We all know that the great value of scientific thought lies in enabling us to recognize and record phenomena. It matters little that disease is rare, if only it be once noted as within the field of medical practice. It has a place thenceforth, in the human mind. It is no miracle, only because, sooner or later, it will be classified. It has a name. The conjunction of diagnosis and treatment is now a question of time only.

Something of the same sort applies to the trust-worthy fraction of what are commonly referred to as 'psychic phenomena'. Occurrences falling under this head, when authentic, are obviously no more supernatural than the

No Supernatural

liquefaction of air, or the extraction of radium. Indeed the propriety of the word 'supernatural' is always open to dispute, inasmuch as if once a thing can be proved to occur, it is clearly within nature, and to call it supernatural becomes by that very fact, absurd. In India, the phenomena in question are regarded as cases of extension of faculty, and their explanation is sought, not in the event, but in the state of the mind witnessing it, since it is to be supposed that this will always, under given conditions, register a perception different from the accustomed.

Strange Facts

In Ramakrishna Paramahamsa, living in the garden of Dakshineshwar, his disciples had been familiar, for years, with many of those mental characteristics which are noted in the books as distinctive of the highest degree of concentration. He was so responsive that he would meet them at the door on their arrival, and begin at once to answer, without being told of them, the questions that the boys carried written in their pockets. His perceptions were so fine that he could tell by touch the character of anyone who might already have come in contact with his food, his clothes, or his mat. It 'burnt' him, he said of an impress from which he shrank; or, on another occasion, "Look! I can eat this The sender must have been some good soul!" His nervous system, again, had been so charged with certain ideas that even in sleep he shrank from the touch of metal, and his hand would, apparently of its own accord, restore a book or a fruit, whose return to its owner the conscious mind had failed to prompt.

No Indian psychologist would say of one of the world-seers that he had talked with angels, but only that he had known how to reach a mood in which he believed himself to talk with angels. Of this condition, the disciples of Sri Ramakrishna saw plentiful examples. Stories are still current amongst them, regarding the strangeness of the sensations with which they would listen to one side of a dialogue or one part in a conversation, which might seem to be carried on for hours at a time; while their Master, resting quietly, evidently believed himself to be holding communion with beings invisible to them.

Behind all these manifold experiences of Ramakrishna, binding them into one great life, was always the determination to serve mankind. Vivekananda spoke of him in after years as 'writhing on the ground' during the hours of darkness, in the agony of his prayer that he might return to earth again, even as a dog, if only he might aid a single soul. In moments less intimate and hidden than these, he would speak of the temptation of the higher realisations, to draw the soul away from conditions of service.

And his disciples connected with this such odd utterances as they would sometimes hear, at the end of a deep entrancement, when their Master seemed to be like a child coaxing his Mother to let him run away from Her to play. 'Just one more' act of service, or 'one more' little enjoyment would be urged, on such an occasion, as a motive for returning to common consciousness. That return, however, always brought with it the infinite love and insight of one who had been lost in God. When the Swami Vivekananda, on the occasion of his Harvard Address, defines this as the *differentia* between the unconsciousness of *Samādhi*, and the unconsciousness of catalepsy, we may take it that the assurance which breathes in every syllable, arose from his having constantly witnessed the transition, in his Master.

Samadhi not Catalepsy

There were still other remarkable traits in Sri Ramakrishna. He had his own nervous force so entirely under control that he could remove all consciousness from his throat, for instance, during his last illness, and allow it to be operated on, as if under a local anaesthetic. His faculties of observation, again, were quite unique. The smallest detail of the physical constitution had a meaning for him, as casting light on the personality within. He would throw the disciple who had just come to him into an hypnotic sleep, and learn from his subconscious mind, in a few minutes, all that was lodged there, concerning the far past. Each little act and word, insignificant to others, was to him like a straw, borne on the great current of character, and showing the direction of its flow. There were times, he said, when men and women seemed to him like glass, and he could look them through and through.

The Master's Touch

Above all, he could by his touch give flashes of supreme insight, which exercised a formative and compelling power over whole lives. In the matter of *Samādhi* this is well-known, especially in reference to women-visitors at Dakshineshwar. But beyond this, a story was told me by a simple soul, of a certain day during the last few weeks of Sri Ramakrishna's life, when he came out into the garden at Cossipore, and placed his hand on the head of a row of persons, one after another, saying in one case, "*Āj thāk*!" "Today let be!" in another, "*Chaitanya houk*!" "Be awakened!" and so on. And after this, a different gift came to each one thus blessed. In one there awoke and infinite sorrow. To another, everything about him became symbolic, and suggested ideas. With a third, the benediction was realised as over-welling bliss. And one saw a great light, which never thereafter left him, but accompanied him always everywhere, so that never could he pass a temple or a wayside shrine, without seeming to see there, seated in the midst of this effulgence—smiling or sorrowful as he at the moment might deserve—a Form that he knew and talked of as 'the Spirit that dwells in the images'.

By such stimulating of each man to his own highest and best, or by such communication of experience as one and another could bear at the time, Ramakrishna Paramahamsa built up the rigorous integrity and strong discrimination that one sees in all who were made by his hand. "We believe nothing without testing it," says one—Ramakrishnananda by name—"we have been trained to this." And when I enquired from another of the disciples what particular form this training took, he answered, after deep thought, that it lay in some experience given of the Reality, from which each gained a knowledge that could never be deceived. "By our own effort," says Vivekananda, in one of his earlier lectures, "*or by the mercy of some great perfected soul*, we reach the highest."

Limits of Consciousness

Now the life of the Guru is the disciple's treasure in hand; and it was undoubtedly by an instantaneous analysis of all that he had seen and shared, of the extensions possible to human faculty, that the Swami was able, on his arrival in the Western sphere of psychical enquiry, to classify all knowledge as subconscious, conscious, and superconscious. The two first terms were in common enough use, in Europe and America. The third, he himself added to the psychological vocabulary, with a masterly stroke of insight, authenticated by his own personal knowledge. "Consciousness," he said on one occasion, "is a mere film between two oceans, the sub-conscious and the super-conscious." Again he exclaimed "I could not believe my own ears, when I heard Western people talking so much of *consciousness!* Consciousness? What does consciousness matter! Why, it is NOTHING, as compared with the unfathomable depths of the subconscious, and the heights of the super-conscious! In this I could never be misled, for had I not seen Ramakrishna Paramahamsa gather in ten minutes, from a man's subconscious mind, the whole of his past, and determine from that his future and his powers!"

The certainty of the *dictum* had down in *Rāja-Yoga* that intuition, when genuine, can never contradict reason, is also indisputably due to the same comprehensive range of experience. The ascetic of Daskhineshwar might be capable of unusual modes of insight, but he was no victim of the vanity born thereof, to be seeking for uncommon ways of arriving at facts that were accessible enough by ordinary methods. When a strange religious came to visit the garden, professing to be able to live without food, Ramakrishna Paramahamsa attempted no clairvoyant mode of testing him, but simply set shrewd observers to watch and bring him word as to what and where he was in the habit of eating.

Nothing was to be accepted, unproven, and the Swami Vivekananda, to his dying day, had a horror of those dreams, previsions, and prophecies by which ordinary folk are so apt to try to dominate one another. These things, as was inevitable, were offered to him in abundance, but he invariably met them with defiance, leaving them to work themselves out, if they were true, in spite of him. Whether a given foretelling would eventually be verified or not, it was impossible for him, he said, to know : the one thing of which he was sure was, that if he once obeyed it, he would never again be allowed to go free.

Value of the Psychic

In the case of Sri Ramakrishna, it invariably happened that visions and intuitions were directed to things of the spirit; gipsylike prognostications were far from him and in the opinion of his disciples, such prognostications are always indicative of a greater or less misusing of energy. "All these are side issues." Said the Swami, "they are not true Yoga. They may have a certain usefulness, in establishing indirectly the truth of our statements. Even a little glimpse gives faith that there is something beyond gross matter. Yet those who spend time on such things run into grave dangers." "These are *frontier questions*!" he exclaimed impatiently, on another occasion, "there can never be any certainty or stability of knowledge, reached by their means. Did I not say they were 'frontier questions'? The boundary line is always shifting!"

In all that might come before us, the attempt at discrimination was to be maintained. "I shall accept it when I have experienced it,' was to be the reply to statements of the extraordinary. But our own experience was to be sifted thoroughly. We were not to run away with the first explanation of a phenomenon that might occur to us. In spite of his reluctance to accept easy conclusions, however, the Swami became convinced, in the course of years, of the occasional return of persons from the dead. "I have several times in my life seen ghosts," he said once, with great deliberateness, "and once, in the week after the death of Sri Ramakrishna, I saw a luminous ghost." But this did not imply the smallest respect on his part, for the bulk of the experiments known as spiritualistic *séances*. Of a famous convert whom he met on one such occasion, he said that it was sad to find a man of extraordinary intelligence in matters of the world, leaving all his intelligence behind him at the doors of a so-called medium. In America, he had been present at a number of *séances* as a witness, and he regarded the great majority of the phenomena displayed as grossly fraudulent. "Always the greatest fraud by the simplest means," he said, summing up his observations. Another large fraction of the total he thought, were better explained by subjective methods,* than as objectively true. If, after all these deductions had been made, any residuum remained, it was possible that this might be genuinely what it professed.

Fraudulent Methods

But even if so, knowledge of the phenomenal could never be the goal of effort. The return of wandering wills from one plane of physical tension to another could throw but little light on any true concept of immortality. Only by renunciation could this be reached. Any dwelling upon the occult led inevitably, in the Swami's opinion, to increase of desire, to increase of egotism, and to the fall into untruth. If the ordinary good life was to be given up, for the sake of the soul, how much more assuredly

* Thus a well-known thought reader in Southern India claimed that an invisible female figure stood beside him, and told him what to say. "I did not like this explanation," said the Swami, "and set myself to find another." He came to the conclusion that the source of information was subjective.

so, these vanities of supernatural power! Even Christianity would have seemed to him a higher creed, if it had had no miracles. Buddha's abhorrence of wonders was the eternal glory of Buddhism. At best their value could only be to give a little confidence, and that only for the first steps. 'If there be powers, they shall vanish away; charity alone remaineth.' Only to the soul that is strong enough to avoid these temptations does the door stand open. In the words of Patanjali, 'To him who is able to reject all the powers, comes the cloud of virtue.' He alone attains the very highest.

XXIV

The Swami's Teaching About Death

One of the most impressive forms of teaching practised by our Master was a certain silent change wrought in the disciple unawares, by his presence. One's whole attitude to things was reversed; one took fire, as it were, with a given idea; or one suddenly found that a whole habit of thought had left one, and a new opinion grown up in its place, without the interchange of a single word on the subject. It seemed as if a thing had passed beyond the realm of discussion, and knowledge had grown, by the mere fact of nearness to him. It was in this way that questions of taste and value became indifferent. It was in this way that the longing for renunciation was lighted, like a devouring flame, in the hearts of those about him. And to nothing could this statement be more applicable, than to the idea of death that one seemed to imbibe from him.

Teaching by Silence

In his own lifetime, he became more and more averse to any definite laying down of the law, on this subject. "I suppose so, I do not know," would be his answer, to one who was striving to piece out the eternal puzzle. He probably felt that one of the subtlest forms of self-interest lay in delightful dreams of a future happiness, and he dreaded adding to the ignorance of desire, by any emphasis laid on the conditions of life outside the body. In death, as in life, for himself, God was the only means, and *Nirvāna* was the goal. 'The highest *Samādhi* was all that counted : all the rest was wild oats,' Yet this very fact sheds all the brighter light on the way in which one's thought of death changed under him; and makes the more precious, those two or three letters, in which personal experience and sympathy strike from him a definite expression of opinion.

For my own part, when I first met the Swami, I had felt driven, for many years past, to hold that whatever our wishes might be, we had no actual reason to imagine any survival of personality, beyond the death of the body. Such a thing was either impossible or unthinkable. If we had no personal experience of the body without mind—the experiencing medium—it was equally true that we knew nothing whatever of mind without body. Hence, if mind were not actually the result of body—'a note struck upon the harp strings'—we must suppose it, at best, to be only the opposite pole of a single substance. The two—body and mind, not matter and mind—were one, and the idea of the persistence of personality was a mere shadow, born of animal instinct. Ethical conduct, rising even to supreme self-sacrifice, was determined at bottom, by our personal preference for gratifications that were socially beneficent.*

European Thought

These positions were undermined, in my own case, by the weight and emphasis which the Indian thinker habitually threw on MIND, as the pivot of life. What the modern really believes is that *man is a body*. Here the Oriental stands in sharp and instinctive contrast to him. As the Swami pointed out, 'Western languages declare that man

---

* Something like this may be taken as the characteristic thought of Europe about death, during the second half of the nineteenth century. "Is the soul," said one thinker, "a note struck upon the harp strings, or the rower seated in a boat?" Recent talk of the disintegration of matter, has now made it easy, even for scientific workers, to conceive of a cycle—call is mind—in which matter practically is not.' But even so, there remains yet to be worked out, as far as the West is concerned, the transition, from the individual mind and body to this sum of mind and matter into which both may be resumed. It is not intended, here, to imply that ethical conduct ultimately rests, in any creed, on a belief in the immortality of the soul; but only to contrast the agnostic view of a spiritual life built up from below, and the Hindu idea of a physical consciousness, which is after all, merely an expression and mask of the spiritual life, with its insatiable thirst, not for self-preservation, but for self-immolation. The modern reasons from seen to unseen; from detail to general; the Hindu reasons from universal to particular, and maintains that in this specific case that is the true method of reasoning the life of the soul being, in fact, the only known.

is a body, and has soul : Eastern languages declare that he is a soul, and has a body.'

As a result of the new hypothesis, I began to speak to people, first postulating to myself experimentally, that I was addressing the mind within, not the ear without. The immense increase of response that this evoked, led me from step to step till twelve months later, I suddenly found that I had fallen into the habit of thinking of mind as dominant, and could no longer imagine its being extinguished by the death of the body! Every new practice deepened this conviction, and I became gradually possessed of a conception of the world about us as mind-born, while the occurrence of any great and sudden change in our thought-world, at a definite physical moment, began to seem absurd.

Man not Body

The Swami's thought on the question went, however, much deeper than this. His was the perpetual effort to avoid slipping into any identification of himself with the body. He would never even use the word 'I' in any sense that might be so construed, preferring, rather quaintly to an English ear, to give a slight gesture, with the words 'all this'. But he also fought shy of the danger of admitting that the life of the senses, limited as this is by the alternating opposites, was '*life*' at all. Victory or defeat, love or hate, efficiency or ineffectiveness, being each only a partial apprehension, could never, amongst them, make up absolute existence. Hundreds of lives like the present, each bound, in its own time, to have an end, could never, as he expressed it, satisfy our hunger for immortality. For that, nothing would do but the attainment of *deathlessness*, and this could never be interpreted as in any sense the multiplication or exaltation of life within the senses. To be of any security, it must be possible to realise such deathlessness during this present life, for how else could the transcendence of bodily experience be assured? Western people were in the habit of saying that 'the soul comes and goes', thus betraying their own tendency to identify themselves with the body, watching the entrance and exit of a higher entity. The speech of the Kentish Druid who welcomed Augustine was typical of all who held this world to be the warm and lighted hall, and the soul a sparrow, taking brief refuge there, from the wintry storms without. Yet in this concept, there were to the full as many assumptions, as in its opposite. To one who was impelled irresistibly upon the hypothesis that we are not an aggregate of physical units at all, but a hyper-physical unity, holding these in suspension, to such a one it was equally clear that we really know only that '*the body comes and goes*'.

By this constant insistence on man as mind, not body, those with whom the Swami was associated were brought to see death as no terminal fatality, but only a link from the midst of a chain, in the experience of the soul. Our whole centre of vision was thus shifted. Instead of the lighted hall, this life became for us the prison of a hypnotic trance, a broken somnambulistic dream. What! was utterance to be forever limited and conditioned by human language? Were there not flashes, even as it was, of something that transcended this, something that compelled without words; that illuminated without teaching; communion direct, profound? Must knowledge remain forever relative, for based on the dim and commonplace perceptions of the senses, for ever finding expression, in the hard and narrow issues of conduct? Well might the Swami exclaim, as he did in the course of a New York lecture, almost with a groan, "Man, the infinite dreamer, dreaming finite dreams!"

The Prisoning Body

By his scorn of such, by his own passionate longing to wander off, silent and nude, along the banks of the Ganges, by his constant turning to the superconscious as the only content of consciousness to be desired, by his personal attitude to the relationships of life as so many fetters and impedimenta to the freedom of the soul, Vivekananda built up in those about him some sort of measure of Real Existence, and the idea that the mere fall of the body could seriously interrupt this, became impossible. We were saturated with the thought that the accessories of life were but so many externals of a passing dream, and it seemed obvious that we should go onwards, after death, much as we were doing before it, with only such added intensity and speed as might be due to the subtler medium in which we should find ourselves. It seemed obvious too, that, as he declared, an eternal heaven or hell, based on the deeds of this present life, was an absurdity, since a finite cause could not, by any means, have an infinite effect.

Yet the Swami laid down no hard and fast conclusions on these subjects, for others to accept. He carried those about him at any given time, as far as they could go, by the force of his own vision, by the energy of his effort to express in words the things he himself saw. But he would have nothing to do with dogma, and he was exceedingly averse to making promises about the future. As already said, 'I do not know' became more and more his answer, as years went on to questions about the fate of the soul in death. Each one, to his thinking, must work out his own belief, basing it on the data of his own experience. Nothing that he should

No Dogma

say must ever interfere with the free growth of personal conviction.

Some things, however, were noticeable. He appeared to share the common assumption that after death we meet again and 'talk things out', so to speak, with those who have preceded us. "When I stand before the old man," he would say with a smile of whimsical tenderness, "I must not have to tell him so and so!" Nor did I ever see in him any struggle against this assumption. He appeared to take it simply, as one of the facts of life.

A Requiem

A man who has once reached the *Nirvikalpa Samādhi* must have passed through many psychological conditions on the way, correspondent to disembodiment. He must be accessible, during such phases, to experience from which we are ordinarily debarred. Now and again, as the Swami believed, he had met and held converse with the spirits of the dead. To someone who spoke of the terror of the supernatural, he said, "This is always a sign of imagination. On that day when you really meet what we call a ghost, you will know no fear!" There is a story told, amongst his brethren, of certain suicides who came to him at Madras, urging him to join them, and disturbing him greatly by the statement that his mother was dead. Having ascertained by enquiry that his mother was well, he remonstrated with these souls for their untruthfulness, but was answered that they were now in such unrest and distress that the telling of truth or falsehood was indifferent to them. They begged him to set them at peace, and he went out to the seashore at night, to perform a *Shrāddha* for them. But when he came to that place, in the service, where offerings should be made, he had nothing to offer, and knew not what to do. Then he remembered an old book that said, in the absence of all other means of sacrifice, sand might be used, and taking up great handfuls of sand, he stood there on the shore casting it into the sea, and with his whole mind sending benediction to the dead. And those souls had rest. They troubled him no more.

Another experience that he could never forget, was his glimpse of Sri Ramakrishna, in the week succeeding his death. It was night. He, and one other were sitting outside the house at Cossipore, talking, no doubt, of that loss of which their heart at the moment were so full. Their Master had left them, only a few days before. Suddenly, the Swami saw a shining form enter the garden, and draw near to them. "What was that? What was that?" said his friend, in a hoarse whisper, a few minutes later. It had been one of those rare cases in which an apparition is seen by two persons at once.

Experiences like these could not fail to create a body of belief in the mind that went through them, and in a letter written from Thousand Island Park, dated August 1895, the Swami gives expression to this conviction. He says : "The older I grow, the deeper I see into the idea of the Hindus that *man* is the greatest of all beings. The only so-called higher beings are the departed, and these are nothing but men who have taken another body. This is finer, it is true, but still a *man-body*, with hands and feet and so on. And they live on this earth, in another *Ākāśa*,* without being absolutely invisible. They also think, and have consciousness, and everything else, like us. So they also are men. So are the *devas*, the angels. But man alone becomes God, and they have all to become men again, in order to become God."

Man the Highest Being

To those who believe in our Master as a 'competent witness', all this will have its own value. They will feel, even where he expresses what is only an inference, only an opinion, that it is yet an opinion based upon unique opportunity of experience.

By the time his first period of work in America was finished, on the eve of coming to England in 1896, he seemed to have felt the necessity of systematising his religious teaching. Having at first given forth his wealth of

* May be translated *sky, space,* or (in the present case) *plane* or *dimension.*

knowledge and thought without stint, we may suppose that he had now become aware of the vastness of his output, that he saw its distinctive features clearly and that he felt the possibility of unifying and condensing it, round a few leading ideas. Once started on this attempt, he would realise, in all probability, that some statement regarding the fate of the soul was essential to a universal acceptance of the Vedanta. A letter written to an English friend, during his first visit to England, in October 1895, showed plainly enough that he was awake to the question of the definite area to be covered by a religious system. On this particular occasion, a visit from a couple of young men who belonged to a 'class philosophically religious, without the least mystery-mongering', had called his attention to the need of ritual. "This," he wrote, "has opened my eyes. The world in general must have some form. In fact religion itself, in the ordinary sense, is simply philosophy concreted, by means of symbols and rituals. A mere loose system of philosophy takes no hold on mankind."

Need of Ritual

The constructive imagination thus roused was seen in two or three subsequent letters to the same friend; and in one of these, while still under the mental stimulus of conversation with a distinguished electrician, he attacks the whole problem of the relation between force and matter, making at the same time a brief but pregnant epitome of what he regards as significant, in Hindu lore about death. It is easy, as one reads this letter, to see how he has been thrilled by the congruity of ancient Indian thought with modern science. "Our friend," he writes, "was charmed to hear about the Vedantic *Prāna* and *Ākāśa* and the *Kalpas*, which, according to him, are the only theories modern science can entertain. Now both *Ākāśa* and *Prāna* again, are produced from the cosmic *Mahat*, the universal mind, the *Brahmā*, or *Iśwara*. He thinks he can demonstrate mathematically that force and matter are reducible to potential energy. I am to go and see him next week, to get this new mathematical demonstration.

Vedanta and Science

"In that case, the Vedantic cosmology will be placed on the surest of foundation. I am working a good deal now, upon the cosmology and eschatology* of the Vedanta. I clearly see their perfect unison with modern science, and the elucidation of the one will be followed by that of the other. I intend to write a work later on, in the form of questions and answers. The first chapter will be on cosmology, showing the harmony between Vedantic theories and modern science.

* *Eschatology* means the doctrine of the last things; according to Christianity, Death, Judgment, Heaven and Hell. In other words, the fate of the soul.

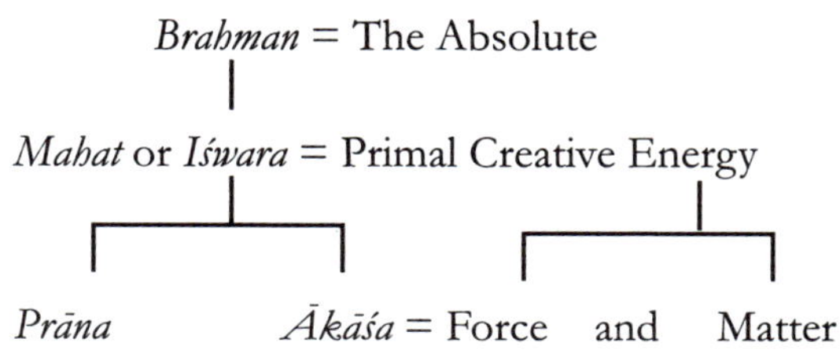

"The eschatology will be explained from the Advaitic standpoint only. That is to say, the dualist claims that the soul after death passes on to the Solar Sphere, thence to the Lunar Sphere, thence to the Electric Sphere. Thence he is accompanied by a *Puruśa* to *Brahmaloka* (thence, says the Advaitist, he goes to *Nirvāna*).

"Now on the Advaitic side, it is held that the Soul neither comes nor goes, and that all these spheres or layers of the universe are only so many varying products of *Ākāśa* and *Prāna*. That is to say, the lowest or most condensed is the Solar Sphere, consisting of the visible universe, in which *Prāna* appears as physical force, and *Ākāśa* as sensible matter. The next is called the Lunar Sphere, which surrounds the Solar Sphere. This is not the moon at all, but the habitation of the gods, that is to say, *Prāna* appears in it as psychic forces, and *Ākāśa* as *Tanmātras*, or fine particles. Beyond this is the Electric Sphere, that is to say, a condition in which the *Prāna* is almost inseparable from *Ākāśa*, and you can hardly tell whether Electricity is force or matter. Next is the *Brahmaloka*, where there is neither *Prāna* nor *Ākāśa*, but both are merged into the Mind-stuff, the primal energy. And here—there being neither *Prāna* nor *Ākāśa*—the *Jīva* contemplates the whole universe as Samasti, or the sum total of *Mahat*, or mind. This appears as a *Puruśa*, an abstract universal Soul, yet not the Absolute, for still there is multiplicity. From this, the *Jīva* finds at last that Unity which is the end. Advaitism says that these are the visions which arise in succession before the *Jīva*, who, himself, neither goes nor comes, and that in the same way, this present vision has been projected. The projection (*Sṛṣṭi*) and dissolution must take place in the same order, only one means going backward and the other coming out.

The Theory of Daulism

"Now, as each individual can only see his own universe, that universe is created with his bondage, and goes away with his liberation, although it remains for others who are in bondage. Now name and form constitute the universe. A wave in the ocean is a wave, only in so far as it is bound by name and form. If the wave subsides, it is the ocean, but that name and form have immediately vanished forever. So that the name and form of a wave could never be, without the water that was fashioned into the wave by them, yet the name and form themselves were not the wave. They die as soon as ever it returns to the water. But other names and forms live on, in relation to other waves. This name and form is called *Māyā*, and the water in *Brahman*. The wave was nothing but water all the time, yet as a wave it had the name and form. Again this name and form cannot remain for one moment separated from the wave, although the wave, as water, can remain eternally separate from name and form. But because the name and form can never be *separated*, they can never be said to exist. Yet they are not *zero*. This is called *Māyā*.

"I want to work all this out carefully, but you will see at a glance that I am on the right track. It will take more study in physiology, on the relations between the higher and lower centres, to fill out the psychology of mind, *Chitta* and *Buddhi*, and so on. But I have clear light now, free from all hocus-pocus."

Synthesis of Beliefs

Once more in this letter, as so often elsewhere, we see the reconciling and organising force of the Swami's genius. The standard of Sankaracharya shall not be moved. That 'the soul neither comes nor goes' remains to all time the dominant truth. But the labours of those who began their work at the opposite end shall not be wasted either. The Advaitin, with his philosophic insight, and the Dualist, with his scientific observation of successive phases of consciousness—both are necessary, to each other and to the new formulation.*

Death, however, is pre-eminently a matter which is best envisaged from without. Not even under personal bereavement can we see so clearly into the great truths of eternal destiny, as when depth of friendship and affection leads us to dramatise our sympathy for the sorrow of another. The comfort that we dared not lean on for ourselves becomes conviction clear as the noonday sun, when we seek it for others. To this rule, the Swami was no exception, and many of us, it may be, will think the greatest of all his utterances on this subject, a certain letter which he wrote to that American woman whom he called '*Dhīrā Mātā*, the Steady Mother,' on the occasion of the loss of her father. In this, we have the very heart of his belief, made warm and personal, and are made to apprehend its bearing, on the fate of our own beloved dead.

A Letter

"I had a premonition," he writes from Brooklyn, to his bereaved friend, in January 1895, "of your father's giving up the old body, and it is not my custom to write to anyone when

* The Swami's plan, of writing a book in the form of questions and answers, was never carried out. But in studying the lectures he delivered in London in the year 1896, it is easy to see that his mind was still working on the ideas here announced. See especially his lectures—'The Absolute and Manifestation'; 'The Cosmos : the Macrocosm'; and his American lectures, 'The Real and the Apparent Man'; and 'Cosmology'.

a wave of would- be inharmonious *Māyā* strikes him. But these are the great turning points in life, and I know that you are unmoved. The surface of the sea rises and sinks alternately, but to the observant soul, the child of light, each sinking reveals more and more of the depth, and of the beds of pearl and coral at the bottom. Coming and going is all pure delusion. The soul never comes nor goes. Where is the place to which it shall go, when all space *is in the soul*? When shall be the time for entering and departing when all time *is in the soul*?

"The earth moves, causing the illusion of the movement of the sun; but the sum does not move. So *Prakṛti*, or *Māyā*, or Nature, is moving, changing, unfolding veil after veil, turning over leaf after leaf of this grand book—while the witnessing soul drinks in knowledge, unmoved, unchanged. All souls that ever have been, are, or shall be, are all in the present tense, and—to use a material simile—are all standing at one geometrical point. Because the idea of space does not occur in the soul, therefore all that were ours, are ours, and will be ours; *are* always with us, *were* always with us, and *will be* always with us. We are in them. They are in us.

"Take these cells. Though each separate, they are all, nevertheless, inseparable joined at A B. There they are one. Each is an individual, yet

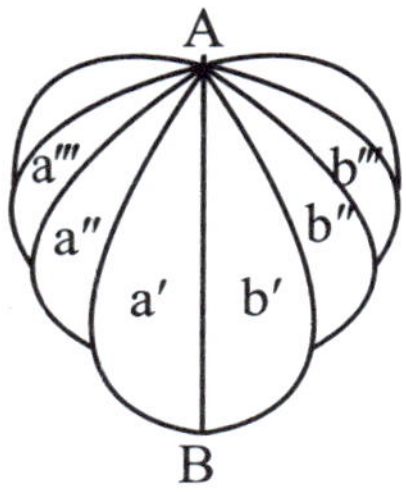

all are one at the axis A B. None can escape from that axis, and however one may strive to escape from it, yet by standing at the axis, we may enter any one of the chambers. This axis is the Lord. There, we are one with Him, all in all, and all in God.

"The cloud moves across the face of the moon, creating the illusion that the moon is moving. So nature, body, matter, moves on, creating the illusion that the soul is moving. Thus we find at last that that instinct (or inspiration?) which men of every race, whether high or low, have had, to feel the presence of the departed,' about them, is true intellectually also.

"Each soul is a star, and all stars are set in that infinite azure, that eternal sky, the Lord. There is the root, the reality, the real individuality, of each and all. Religion began with the search after some of these stars that had passed beyond our horizon, and ended in finding them all in God, and ourselves in the same place. The whole secret is, then, that your father has given up the old garment he was wearing, and is standing where he was, through all eternity. Will he manifest another such garment, in this or any other world? I sincerely pray that he may not,

All One in God

until he does so in full consciousness. I pray that none may be dragged anywhither by the unseen power of his own past actions. I pray that all may be free, that is to say, may know that they are free. And if they are to dream again, let us pray that their dreams he all of peace and bliss."

XXV

Super-Consciousness

He who crosses a chasm on a narrow plank, is liable at any moment to an abrupt accession of all his ordinary associations and sensations, with a sudden fall from his giddy height. Very like this, seem the stories, that we come across in sacred literature, of man's occasional attainment of the mind-world that lies beyond our common experience. Peter, walking on the sea, begins to sink, the moment he remembers where he is. A few weary men, sleeping on a mountainside, wake to behold their Master transfigured before them. But again they descend into the world, and already the great vision has died away, and become an echoing memory alone. Seated in the fields, watching their flocks by night, and talking in hushed voices on high themes, the shepherds become aware of the presence of angels. The moments pass, and with them the exaltation of hour and place, and lo, the angels have all faded out of the sky! Their hearers are driven to the commonplace expedient of a journey of foot into the neighbouring village, to see what great thing has come to pass.

In contrast to these, the Indian ideal is that man whose lower mind is so perfectly under his own control that he can at any moment plunge into the thought-oceans, and remain there at will, the man who can be swept along, on irresistible currents of absorption, without the least possibility of a sudden break and unexpected return to the life of the senses! Undoubtedly, this power comes nearer, with depth of education and intensity of experience. But the only thing that can make it a man's own, is a self-command so strict that he can, at will, transcend thought itself. To him who can so concentrate himself as to be able even to suppress it when he will, the mind becomes an obedient servant, a fleet steed, and the body, in its turn, the loyal subject of the mind. Short of such power, there is no perfect, no unwavering self-control. How few must be the persons born to it, in any single generation! There is a luminousness, an assuredness, about the deeds and words of such, which cannot be mistaken. 'They speak as those having authority, and not as the scribes.'

Condition of Insight

We cannot question that Sri Ramakrishna recognised such a soul, 'a *Brahmajñānī* from his birth,' in the lad Noren, when he first saw him; recognised too, like a skilled engineer measuring the force of a stream, the height to which his thought-transcendence had already mounted. "Tell me, do you see a light when you are going to sleep?" asked the old man eagerly. "Doesn't everyone?" answered the boy, in wonder. In later life, he would often mention this question, and digress, to describe to us the light he saw. Sometimes it would come as a ball, which a boy was kicking towards him. It would draw near. He would become one with it, and all would be forgotten. Sometimes it was a blaze, into which he would enter. One wonders whether sleep, thus beginning, is slumber at all, in the ordinary sense. At any rate, it is told, by the men who were young with Vivekananda, that when he would throw himself down to sleep, their Master, watching his breathing, would often tell the others that he was only apparently resting, and would explain to them what stage of meditation had now been reached. On one such occasion, while Sri Ramakrishna, lay ill in the house at Cossipore, Noren had seemed, to one who was about him, to have been sleeping for some hours, when suddenly, towards midnight, he cried out, "Where is my body?" His companion, now known as the old monk Gopal Dada, ran to his aid, and did all he could,

Samadhi

by heavy massage, to restore the consciousness that had been lost, below the head. When all was in vain, and the boy continued in great trouble and alarm, Gopal Dada ran to the Master himself, and told him of his disciple's condition. He smiled when he heard, and said, "Let him be! It will do him no harm to stay there for a while. He has teased me enough, to reach that state!" Afterwards, he told him and others, that for Noren the *Nirvikalpa Samādhi* was now over, and his part would henceforth lie in work. The Swami himself described the early stages of this experience, later, to his *gurubhāi*, Saradananda, as an awareness of light, within the brain, which was so intense that he took it for granted that someone had placed a bright lamp close to him, behind his head. Then, we may understand, the moorings of sense-consciousness were cut, and he soared into those realms of which none speaks.

Super-consciousness

In order to concentrate the mind, it will be understood, it is first of all necessary that we should be able to forget the body. It is for this purpose that asceticism is practised, and austerities undertaken. Throughout his life, a period of strict *tapasyā* was always a delight to the Swami, who was constantly returning upon this, in spite of the seeming fearlessness with which he took possession of the world. Like a practised rider, touching the reins, or a great musician, running his fingers over the keys, he loved to feel again the response of the body to the will, rejoiced to realise afresh, his own command of his instrument. "I see that I can do *anything* !" he said, when, at the end of his life, having undertaken to go through the hot season in Calcutta without swallowing water—and being allowed to rinse out the mouth—he found that the muscles of his throat closed, of their own accord, against the passage of a single drop, and he could not have drunk it, if he would. In his neighbourhood when he was keeping a fast-day, food always seemed to another unnecessary, and difficult to conceive. I have heard of an occasion when he sat, seeing as if he scarcely heard, surrounded by persons who were quarrelling and disputing. Suddenly an empty tumbler in his hand was crushed into fragments, the only sign he ever gave, of the pain this discussion had caused him!

It is not easy to realise the severity of the practices on which such a power of self-control had been developed; the number of hours spent in worship and meditation; the fixity of the gaze; the long-sustained avoidance of food and sleep. With regard to this last, indeed, there was one time when he had spent twenty-five days, allowing himself only half an hour's sleep, out of every twenty-four hours. And from this half-hour, he awoke himself! Sleep never afterwards, probably, was a very insistent or enduring guest with him. He had the 'Yogi's eyes'—as Debendra Nath Tagore had told him, in his childhood, when he climbed into his house-boat on the Ganges, to ask, "Sir, have you seen God?"—the 'Yogi's eyes,' which are said never to shut completely, and to open wide, at the first ray of light. In the West, those staying in the same house with him, would hear the chant of '*Para Brahman*,' or something of the sort, as he went, in the small hours of the morning, to take his early plunge. He never appeared to be practising austerity, but his whole life was a concentration so profound that to anyone else, it would have been the most terrible asceticism. The difficulty with which he stopped the momentum that would carry him into meditation, had been seen by his American friends, in the early days of his life, in that country of railroads and tramways and complicated engagement-lists. "When he sits down to meditate," one of his Indian hosts had said, "it is not ten minutes, before he becomes insensitive, though his body may be black with mosquitoes!" This was the habit he had to control. At first, his lapses into the depths of thought, when people were perhaps waiting for him at the other end of a journey, caused

Rule of Life

him much embarrassment. On one occasion, teaching a New York class to meditate, it was found at the end, that he could not be brought back to consciousness, and one by one, his students stole quietly away. But he was deeply mortified when he knew what had happened, and never risked its repetition. Meditating in private, with one to two, he would give a word, by which he could be recalled.

The Depths of Thoughts

Apart altogether, however, from meditation, he was constantly, always, losing himself in thought. In the midst of the chatter and fun of society, one would notice the eyes grow still, and the breath come at longer and longer intervals; the pause; and then the gradual return. His friends knew these things, and provided for them. If he walked into the house, to pay a call, and forgot to speak; or if he was found in a room, in silence, no one disturbed him; though he would sometimes rise and render assistance to the intruder, without breaking his silence. Thus his interests lay within, and not without. To the scale and range of his thought, his conversation was of course our only clue. His talk was always of the impersonal. It was not always religious, as that word goes, any more than his own Master's had been. It was very often secular. But it was always vast. There was never in it anything mean or warped or pretty. There was no limitation of sympathy anywhere. Even his criticism was felt merely as definition and analysis. It had no bitterness or resentment in it. "I can criticise even an *Avatāra*," he said of himself one day, "without the slightest diminution of my love for him! But I know quite well that most people are not so; and for them, it is safest to protect their own Bhakti!" No sentiment of dislike or contempt remained from his analysis, even in the mind of the listener.

Criticism

This largeness and sweetness of outlook was firmly based on his reverence for his own Guru. "Mine is the devotion of the dog!" he exclaimed once. "I don't want to know why! I am contented simply to follow!" And Sri Ramakrishna, in his turn, had had a similar feeling for Tota Puri—that great master, who had left his own disciples, at Kaithal, near Umballa, one day, 'to go into Lower Bengal, where I feel that a soul needs me.' He had gone back to his people again, when his work was done at Dakshineshwar, and his grave in the North-West is honoured to this day. But he whom he had initiated felt for him, ever after, a reverence so great that he would not even utter his name. '*Nangtā*, the Naked One, said unto me—' was his customary way of referring to him. Perfect love for the world and perfect faith in man are only possible, to that heart which has once seen its ideal realised.

But power to transcend the consciousness of the body is not the only condition of a development like our Master's. It is the Hindu belief that for the evolution of supreme force, it is necessary first to evoke intense energy of emotion, and then to hold this in absolute restraint. This points to a cycle of experience beyond the imagination of most of us, yet an incident in the life of the disciple Noren, gives us a glimpse of it. He was still young, when a sudden death brought about a crisis in the fortunes of his family. Day after day, as the eldest son, he was racked with anxiety on their behalf. The sufferings of those who were dear to him tore his very heart-strings, and the sudden reversal, from ease and prosperity, filled him with perplexity. He could hardly believe in the extent of their disaster.

The Great Test

At last, unable longer to bear the anguish, he fled to his Master, and overwhelmed him with reproaches. The old man listened patiently and said, with a tender smile, "Go yonder, my lad, and pray, before the image of Mother. AND WHATEVER YOU ASK HER FOR, SHE WILL ASSUREDLY BESTOW."

Looked at even from the most ordinary point of view, there was nothing wild or extravagant in the promise thus made; for Sri Ramakrishna was surrounded by wealthy disciples, of the

Marwari caste, who would have thought no cost too great, to have redeemed his word. The boy, somewhat soothed by the quietness and assurance of the direction, left his presence and went to pray before the image. It was sometime before he returned, and when he came, he had a dazed look, say those who were present, and seemed to speak with some difficulty. "Well did you pray?" asked Sri Ramakrishna. "Oh yes!" answered his disciple.

"And what did you ask Mother to give you?" said the Master.

"The highest *Bhakti* and *Jnānam*!" replied Noren.

"Go again," said Sri Ramakrishna, briefly, without further comment, and again he went.

But there was no change. Three times he was sent, to ask for what he would, and three times he came back, with the same reply. Once before the Mother, he had forgotten all else, and could not even remember the cause that had brought him there. Have any of us risen at times to the height where we lose the memory of self, in intensity of prayer for the beloved? If so, we have perhaps gained some measure of the infinitely greater remoteness of this experience, from our common world of relativity and difference.

The Swami's thought soared, as he talked. Is thought itself but one form of expression of the inner Self, the *Ādi Śakti*? And is the force spent in it to be reckoned as lost, from the point of view of the thinker's own good? First, a circle of phenomena; then a circle of thought; lastly, the Supreme! If so, surely there can be no greater unselfishness than the sharing of their mind-treasure by the great souls, the *Mahāpuruśas*. To enter into their dream, must in itself be redemption, for it is the receiving objectively, of a seed that cannot die, till it has become, subjectively the Beatific Vision!

Thought-characteristics

Ideals were the units of our Master's thought, but ideals made so intensely living that one never thought of them as abstractions. Men and nations alike, were interpreted by him through their ideals, and their ethical up-reaching. I have sometimes thought that two different grades of mind are distinguishable, according to their instinct for classification under two heads or three. The Swami's tendency was always to divide into three. Recognising the two extremes of a quality, he never failed to discriminate also that point of junction between them, where, being exactly balanced, both might be said to be non-existent. Is this a universal characteristic of genius, or is it a distinction of the Hindu mind?

One never knew what he might see in a thing, never quite knew what might appeal to him. He would often speak in answer to thought, or respond to a thought more easily and effectively than to words. It was only gradually, from a touch here, and a hint there, that one could gather the great preoccupation, that all words, and thoughts were designed to serve. It was not till the end of our summer in Kashmir, that he told us how he was always conscious of the form of the Mother, as a bodily presence, visible amongst us. Again, in the last winter of his life, he told his disciple Swarupananda that for some months continuously, he had been conscious of two hands, holding his own in their grasp. Going on a pilgrimage, one would catch him telling his beads. Seated with one's back to him in a carriage one would hear him repeating an invocation over and over. One knew the meaning of his early morning chant, when, before sending a worker out to the battle, he said, "Ramakrishna Paramahamsa used to begin every day by walking about in his room for a couple of hours, saying '*Satchidananda!*' or '*Śivoham!*' or some other holy word," This hint, publicly given, was all.

Constant Devotion

Constant devotion, then, was the means by which he maintained his unbroken concentration. Concentration was the secret of those incessant flashes of revelation, which he was always giving. Like one who had plunged his cup into a deep well, and brought up from it water of a sparkling coldness, was his entrance into a conversation. It was the quality of his thought, quite as much as its beauty or its intensity, that told of the mountain-snows of spiritual vision, whence it was drawn.

An Unexpected Answer

Some measure of this concentration was afforded by the stories he would tell of his lecturing experiences. At night, in his own room, a voice, he said, would begin to shout at him the words he was to say on the morrow, and the next day he would find himself repeating, on the platform, the things he had heard it tell. Sometimes there would be two voices, arguing with each other. Again the voice would seem to come from a long distance, speaking to him down a great avenue. Then it might draw nearer and nearer, till it would become a shout. "Depend upon it," he would say, "whatever in the past has been meant by inspiration, it must have been something like this!"

In all this, however, he saw no miracle. It was merely the automatic working of the mind, when that had become so saturated with certain principles of thought, as to require no guidance in their application. It was probably an extreme form of the experience to which Hindus refer, as the 'mind becoming the Guru.' It also suggests that almost perfectly balanced as the two highest senses were in him, the aural may have had a slight preponderance over the visual. He was, as one of his disciples once said of him, 'a most faithful reporter of his own states of mind,' and he was never in the slightest danger of attributing these voices to any but a subjective source.

Another experience of which I heard from him, suggesting the same automatic mentality, perhaps in a less developed form, was that when any impure thought or image appeared before him, he was immediately conscious of what he called 'a blow,'—a shattering, paralysing blow—struck from within upon the mind itself, as if to say 'no! not this way!'

He was very quick to recognise in others those seemingly instinctive actions, that were really dictated by the higher wisdom of super-consciousness. The thing that was right, no one could tell why, while yet it would have seemed, judged by ordinary standards, to have been a mistake—in such things he saw a higher impulsion. Not all ignorance was, in his eyes, equally dark.

His Master's prophecy that again he would eat his mango, of the *Nirvikalpa Samādhi*, when his work was done, was never forgotten, by the brethren of his youth. None at any time knew the moment when the work might be ended, and the mounting realisation some may have suspected. During the last year of his life, a group of his early comrades were one day talking over the old days, and the prophecy that when Noren should realise who and what he had already been, he would refuse to remain in the body, was mentioned. At this, one of them turned to him, half-laughing, "Do you know yet, who you were, Swamiji?" he said, "Yes, I know now," was the unexpected answer, awing them into earnestness and silence, and no one could venture at that time to question him further.

The Mind the Guru

As the end came nearer, meditation and austerity took up more and more of life. Even those things that had interested him most, elicited now only a far-away concern. And in the last hour, when the supreme realisation was reached, some ray of its vast super-conscious energy seemed to touch many of those who loved him, near and far. One dreamt that Sri Ramakrishna had died again that night, and woke in the dawn to hear the messenger at his gate. Another, amongst the closest friends of his boyhood, had a vision of his coming in triumph and saying "Shoshi! Shoshi! I have spat out the body!" and still a third, drawn irresistibly in that evening hour, to the place of meditation, found the soul face to face with an infinite radiance, and fell prostrate before it, crying out '*Śiva Guru*!'

XXV

The Passing of the Swami

Late in the year 1900, the Swami broke off from the party of friends with whom he was travelling in Egypt, and went home suddenly, to India. "He seemed so tired!" says one of those who were with him at this time. As he looked upon the Pyramids and the Sphinx, and the rest of the great sights in the neighbourhood of Cairo, it was in truth like one who knew himself to be turning the last pages in the book of experience! Historic monuments no longer had the power to move him deeply.

He was cut to the quick, on the other hand, to hear the people of the country referred to constantly as 'natives', and to find himself associated, in his visit, rather with the foreigner than with them. In this respect, indeed, it would seem that he had enjoyed his glimpse of Constantinople vastly more than Egypt, for towards the end of his life he was never tired of talking about a certain old Turk who kept an eating house there, and had insisted on giving entertainment without price to the party of strangers, one of whom came from India. So true it was, that to the oriental, untouched by modern secularity, all travellers were pilgrims, and all pilgrims guests.

In the winter that followed, he paid a visit to the Dacca, in East Bengal, and took a large party up the Brahmaputra, to make certain pilgrimages in Assam. How rapidly his health was failing at this time, only those immediately around him knew. None of us who were away, had any suspicion. He spent the summer of 1901 at Belur, 'hoping to hear again the sound of the rains, as they fell in his boyhood!' And when the winter again set in, he was so ill as to be confined to bed.

Bodh-Gaya and Benares

Yet he made one more journey, lasting through January and February 1902, when he went, first to Bodh-Gaya and next to Benares. It was a fit end to all his wanderings. He arrived at Bodh-Gaya on the morning of his last birthday, and nothing could have exceeded the courtesy and hospitality of the Mahunt*. Here, as afterwards at Benares, the confidence and affection of the orthodox world were brought to him in such measure and freedom that he himself stood amazed at the extent of his empire

* Adhyaksha or Chief of the Ashrama

in men's hearts. Bodh-Gaya, as it was now the last, had also been the first, of the holy places he had set out to visit. And it had been in Benares, some few years later that he had said farewell to one, with the words, 'Till that day when I fall on society like a thunderbolt, I shall visit this place no more!'

Many of his disciples from distant parts of the world gathered round the Swami on his return to Calcutta. Ill as he looked, there was none, probably, who suspected how near the end had come. Yet visits were paid, and farewells exchanged, that it had needed voyages half round the world to make. Strangely enough, in his first conversation after coming home from Benares, his theme was the necessity of withdrawing himself for a time, in order to leave those that were about him a free hand.

"How often," he said, "does a man ruin his disciples, by remaining always with them! When men are once trained, it is essential that their leader leave them, for without his absence they cannot develop themselves!"

Social Ideals

It was as the result of the last of those foreign contacts that had continued without intermission throughout his mature life, that he realised suddenly the value to religion of high ideals of faithfulness in marriage. To the monk, striving above all things to be true to his own vows, not only in word and deed, but still more earnestly and arduously, in thought itself, the ideals of social life are apt to appear as so much waste material. Suddenly the Swami saw that a people to whom chastity was not precious could never hope to produce a faithful priesthood, or a great monastic order. Only where the inviolability of marriage was fully recognized, could the path that lay outside marriage be truthfully held. By the sacredness of the social ideal, was the holiness of the super-social rendered possible.

This realisation was the crown of his philosophy. It could not but mark the end of 'the play of Mother'. The whole of society was necessary, with its effort and its attainment, to create the possibility of life of *Sannyās*. The faithful house-holder was as essential to the *Sanātan Dharma* as the faithful monk. The inviolability of marriage and the inviolability of the monastic vow, were obverse and reverse of a single medal. Without noble citizenship, there could be no mighty apostolate. Without the secular, no sacerdotal, without temporal, no spiritual. Thus all was one, yet no detail might be willfully neglected, for through each atom shone the whole. It was in fact his own old message in a new form. Integrity of character, as he and his Master before him, had insisted, was a finer offering than religious ecstasy. Without the strength to hold, there was no achievement in surrender.

For the sake of the work that constantly opened before him, the Swami made a great effort, in the spring of 1902, to recover his health, and even undertook a course of treatment under which, throughout April, May, and June, he was not allowed to swallow a drop of cold water. How far this benefited him physically, one does not know; but he was overjoyed to find the unflawed strength of his own will, in going through the ordeal.

Fore-Knowledge

When June closed, however, he knew well enough that the end was near. "I am making ready for death," he said to one who was with him on the Wednesday before he died. "A great *tapasyā* and meditation had come upon me, and I am making ready for death."

And we who did not dream that he would leave us till at least some three or four years had passed, knew nevertheless that the words were true. News of the world met but a far-away rejoinder from him at this time. Even a word of anxiety as to the scarcity of the rains, seemed almost to pass him by as in a dream. It was useless to ask him now for an opinion on the questions of the day. "You may be right," he said quietly, "but I cannot enter any more into these matters. I am going down into death."

Once in Kashmir, after an attack of illness I had seen him lift a couple of pebbles, saying, "Whenever death approaches me, all weakness vanishes. I have neither fear, nor doubt, nor thought of the external, I simply busy myself making ready to die. I am as hard as *that*"—and the stones struck one another in his hand—"for I *have* touched the feet of God!"

Personal revelation was so rare with him, that these words could never be forgotten. Again, on returning from the cave of Amarnath, in that same summer of 1898, had he not said, laughingly, that he had there received the grace of Amarnath—not to die till he himself should will to do so? Now this, seeming to promise that death would never take him by surprise had corresponded so well with the prophecy of Sri Ramakrishna—that when he should know who and what he was, he would refuse to remain a moment longer in the body—that one had banished from one's mind all anxiety on this score, and even his own grave and significant words at the present time did not suffice to revive it.

Did we not remember, moreover, the story of the great *Nirvikalpa Samādhi* of his youth, and how, when it was over, his Master had said,

"This is your mango. Look! I lock it in my box. You shall taste it once more, when your work is finished."

"—And we may wait for that," said the monk who told me the tale. "We shall know when the time is near. For he will tell us that again he has tasted his mango."

How strange it seems now, looking back on that time, to realise in how many ways the expected hint was given, only to fall on ears that did not hear, to reach minds that could not understand!

It would seem, indeed, that in his withdrawal from all weakness and attachment, there was one exception. That which had ever been dearer to him than life, kept still its power to move him. It was on the last Sunday before the end that he said to one of his disciples, "You know the Work is always my weak point! When I think *that* might come to an end, I am all undone!"

The Work

On Wednesday of the same week, the day being *Ekādaśī*, and himself keeping the fast in all strictness, he insisted on serving the morning meal to the same disciple. Each dish as it was offered—boiled seeds of the jackfruit, boiled potatoes, plain rice, and ice-cold milk—formed the subject of playful chat; and finally, to end the meal, he himself poured the water over the hands, and dried them with a towel.

"It is I who should do these things for you, Swamiji! Not you, for me!" was the protest naturally offered. But his answer was startling in its solemnity—"Jesus washed the *feet* of His disciples!"

Something checked the answer "But that was the *last* time!" as it rose to the lips, and the words remained unuttered. This was well. For here also, the last time had come.

The Play of Life

There was nothing sad or grave about the Swami, during these days. In the midst of anxiety about over-fatiguing him, in spite of conversation deliberately kept as light as possible, touching only upon the animals that surrounded him, his garden, experiments, books and absent friends, over and beyond all this, one was conscious the while of a luminous presence, of which his bodily form seemed only as a shadow, or symbol. Never had one felt so strongly as now, before him, that one stood on the threshold of an infinite light. Yet none was prepared, least of all on that last happy Friday, July the 4th, on which he appeared so much stronger and better than he had been for years, to see the end so soon.

He had spent hours of that day in formal meditation. Then he had given a long Sanskrit lesson. Finally, he had taken a walk from the monastery gates to the distant high road.

On his return from this walk, the bell was ringing for evensong, and he went to his own room, and sat down, facing towards the Ganges, to mediate. It was the last time. The moment was come that had been foretold by his Master from the beginning. Half an hour went by, and then, on the wings of that meditation, his spirit soared whence there could be no return, and the body was left, like a folded vesture, on the earth.

XXVI

THE END

Towards Christmas of the year 1902, a few of the Swami Vivekananda's disciples gathered at Khandagiri near Cuttack to keep the festival. It was evening, and we sat on the grass, round a lighted log, while on one side of us rose the hills, with their caves and carven rocks, and all around us whispered the sleeping forest. We were to keep Christmas Eve, in the old-time fashion of the Order of Ramakrishna. One of the monks held a long crook, and we had with us a copy of the Gospel of St. Luke, wherewith to read and picture the coming of the angels, and the singing of the world's first Gloria.*

We lost ourselves in the story, however, and the reading could not be stopped at Christmas Eve, but must needs drift on from point to point. The Great Life as a whole was passed in review;

---

* Glory to God in the highest, and on earth peace, good will to men! (The Song of the Angels : St. Luke, 2, 24.)

then the Death; and finally the Resurrection. We turned to the twenty-fourth chapter of the Gospel, and read incident after incident.

But the tale sounded as never before, in our ears. Instead of a legal document, dated and attested, whose credibility must stand or fall by the clearness and coherence of its various parts, it read now like the gasping, stammering witness of one who had striven to put on record the impalpable and the intangible. The narrative of the Resurrection was no longer, for us, an account of an event, to be accepted or rejected. It had taken its place forevermore as a spiritual perception, which one who experienced it had striven, not always successfully, to put into words. The whole chapter sounded fragmentary, cumulative, like some longing attempt to convince, not the reader only, but even, to some extent, the writer himself.

The Resurrection Tale

For had we not had our own glimmerings of a like back-coming to put beside it? One remembered and understood suddenly, the clear and deliberate statement of our Master himself—'Several times in my life I have seen returning spirits; and once—in the week after the death of Ramakrishna Paramahamsa—the form was luminous.'

We were face to face, not merely with the longing of the disciples to see once more the

Master who had gone from them, but with the far deeper yearning of the Incarnation, to return again to comfort and bless the disciples He had left.

'*Did not our hearts burn within us, while he talked with us by the way*?'—How many moments of such exaltation had we ourselves not known, in the first weeks after the passing of the Master, when we would fain have believed that his actual presence had been with us!'

'*He was known unto them in the breaking of bread*.'—Even so. Only a touch here, a word there, a moment of sweetness, or a flash of inner clearness and knowledge, any of these had been sufficient, at various times in those early weeks, to bring back the throbbing awareness of the beloved presence, with the mingling of doubt and assurance in its poignant longing.

We passed over, that night at Khandagiri, those features of the Resurrection that would seem to have been added later by minds that believed in the hard and fast, black and white, character of the story. It was the older record, shining through this palimpsest, on which our thoughts were fastened, that simple old record, full of the pathos of sudden sights and vanishings, with its gatherings of the Eleven, whispering amongst themselves. 'The Lord is risen indeed!' with its tale, at the last, of a parting in the midst of a benediction.

A Presence Beyond Death

It was not of any re-appearances of the body at all, as it seemed to us reading, that this older story had told, but of sudden and unforeseen meetings of the will, returns of thoughts and love, brief upliftings of prayer, from One who in the Vedic phrase, had been 'resumed into His shining Self', and moved now on subtler and more penetrative planes of action than we, entangled amidst the senses, could conceive.

Nor were they so objective that alike might be equally conscious of these fleeting gleams, half-seen, half-heard. The grosser perception they passed by altogether. Even to the finest, they were matters to be questioned, to be discussed eagerly, to be pieced together in sequence, and cherished tenderly in the heart. Amongst the closest and most authoritative of the apostles, there might well be some who doubted altogether. And yet, and yet, in the midst of the caves and forests of Khandagiri that night, we who followed the Christian story of the Resurrection, could not but feel that behind it, and through it, glistened a thread of fact, that we were tracing out the actual footsteps left by a human soul somewhere, somewhen, as it trod the glimmering pathway of this fugitive experience. So we believed, so we felt, because, in all its elusiveness, a like revelation, at like time, had made itself evident to us also.

May God grant that this living presence of our Master, of which death itself had not had the power to rob us, become never, to us his disciples, as a thing to be remembered, but remain with us always in its actuality, even unto the end!

APPENDIX

Appendix A, To Chapter I

Notes Of A Lecture Delivered In London November 16, 1895

Just as it is necessary for a man to go through symbols and ceremonies first, in order to arrive at the depths of realisation, so we say in India : 'It is good to be born in a church, but bad to die in one.' A sapling must be hedged about for protection, but when it becomes a tree, a hedge would be a danger. So there is no need to criticise and condemn the old forms. We forget that in religion there must be *growth*.

At first, we think of a Personal God, and call Him Creator, Omnipotent, Omniscient, and so forth. But when love comes, God is only love. The loving worshipper does not care what God is, because he wants nothing from Him. Says an Indian saint, "I am no beggar!" Neither does he fear. Man should not try to approach God : to come to God is all he has to do. Anthropomorphic conceptions follow. God is loved as a human being.

Here are some of the systems founded on love. (1) *Śāntah*, common, peaceful love, with such thoughts as those of fatherhood and help; (2) *Dāsyam*, the ideal of service; God as master or general or sovereign, giving punishments and rewards; (3) *Vātsalyam*, God as mother or child. In India the mother never punishes.

In each of these stages, the worshipper forms an ideal of God and follows it. Then He becomes (4) *the Friend.* There is here no fear. There is also the feeling of equality and familiarity. There are some Hindus who worship God as friend, and playmate. Next comes (5) *Madhuram*, the sweetest love, the love of husband and wife. Of this S. Teresa and the ecstatic saints have been examples. Amongst the Persians, God has been looked upon as the wife, amongst Hindus as the husband. We may recall the great queen Meera Bae, who preached that the Divine Spouse was all. Some carry this to such an extreme that to call God 'mighty' or 'father' seems to them blasphemy. The language of this worship is erotic. Some even use that of illicit passion. To this cycle belongs the story of Krishna and the Gopi-girls. All this probably seems to you to entail great degeneration on the worshipper. And so it does. Yet many great saints have been developed by it. And no human institution is beyond abuse. Would you cook nothing because there are beggars? Would you possess nothing because there are thieves? 'Oh Beloved, one kiss of Thy lips once tasted, hath made me mad!'

The fruit of this idea is that one can no longer belong to any sect, or endure ceremonial. Religion in India culminates in freedom. But even this comes to be given up, and all is love, for love's sake.

Last of all comes LOVE WITHOUT DISTINCTION, the Self. There is a Persian poem that tells how a lover came to the door of his beloved, and knocked. She asked, "Who art thou?" and he replied, "I am so and so, thy beloved!" and she answered only, "Go, I know none such!" But when she had asked for the fourth time, he said, "I am thyself, O my beloved, therefore open thou to me!" and the door was opened.

A great saint said, using the language of a girl, describing love. "Four eyes met. There were changes in two souls. And now I cannot tell whether he is a man, and I a woman, or he a woman and I a man. This only I remember, two souls were, Love came, and there was one."

Is the highest love, union is only of the spirit. All love of another kind is quickly evanescent. Only the spiritual lasts, and this grows.

Love sees the Ideal. This is the third angle of the triangle. God has been the Cause, Creator, Father. Love is the culmination. The mother regrets that her child is humpbacked, but when she has nursed him for a few days, she loves him and thinks him most beautiful. The lover sees Helen's beauty in a brow of Egypt. We do not commonly realise what happens. The brow of Egypt is merely a suggestion : the man sees Helen. His ideal is thrown upon the suggestions and covers it, as the oyster makes sand into a pearl. God is this ideal, through which man may see all.

Hence we come to love Love itself. This love cannot be expressed. No words can utter it. We are dumb about it.

The senses become very much heightened in love. Human love, we must remember, is mixed up with attributes. It is dependent, too, on the other's attitude. Indian languages have words to describe this interdependence of love. The lowest love is selfish; it consists in the pleasure of being loved. We say in India, 'One gives the cheek, the other kisses.' Above this is mutual love. But this also ceases mutually. True love is all giving. We don't even want to see the other, or to do anything to express our feelings. It is enough to give. It is almost impossible to love a human being like this, but is possible so to love God.

In India, there is no idea of blasphemy, if boys fighting in the street use the name of God. We say, 'Put your hand into the fire, and whether you feel it or not, you will be burnt. So to name the name of God can bring nothing but good.'

The notion of blasphemy comes from the Jews, who were impressed by the spectacle of Persian royalty. The ideas that God is judge and punisher are not in themselves bad, but they are low and vulgar. The three angles of the triangle are : Love begs not. Love knows no fear. Love is always of the ideal.

"Who would be able to live one second,

Who would be able to breathe one moment,

If the Loving One had not filled this universe?"

Most of us will find that we were born for service. We must leave the results to God. If failure comes, there need be no sorrow. The work was done only for God.

In women, the mother nature is much developed. They worship God as the child. They ask nothing and will do anything.

The Catholic Church teaches many of these deep things, and though it is narrow, it is religious in the highest sense. In modern society, Protestantism is broad but shallow. To judge truth by what good it does, is as bad as to question the value of a scientific discovery to a baby.

Society must be outgrown. We must crush the law and become outlaws. We follow nature, only in order to conquer her. Renunciation means that none can serve God and Mammon.

Deepen your own power of thought and love. Bring your own lotus to blossom : the bees will come of themselves. Believe first in yourself, then in God. A handful of strong men will move the world. We need a heart to feel; a brain to conceive; and a strong arm to do the work. Buddha gave himself for the animals. Make yourself a fit agent to work. But it is God who works, not you. One man contains the whole universe. One particle of matter has all the energy of the Universe at its back. In a conflict between the heart and brain follow your heart.

Yesterday, competition was the law, Today, cooperation is the law. Tomorrow, there is no law. Let sages praise thee, or let the world blame. Let fortune itself come, or let poverty and rags stare thee in the face. Eat the herbs of the forest one day, for food; and the next, share a banquet of fifty courses. Looking neither to the right hand nor to the left, follow thou on!

Appendix B, To Chapter I

Notes Of A Lecture Delivered In London November 23, 1895

The Swami began by telling, in answer to questions, the story of how Pavhari Baba snatched up his own vessels, and ran after the thief, only to fall at his feet and say—

"O Lord, I knew not that Thou wast there! Take them! They are Thine! Pardon me, They child!"

Again he told how the same saint was bitten by a cobra, and when, towards nightfall, he recovered, he said, "A messenger came to me from the Beloved."

The greatest force is derived from the power of thought. *The finer the element, the more powerful.* The silent power of thought influences people, even at a distance, because the mind is one, as well as many. The universe is a cobweb; minds are the spiders.

The universe equals the phenomena of one Universal Being. He, seen through our senses, is the Universe. Jesus or Buddha sees the Universe as God. This is *Māyā*. So the world is an illusion, that is, the imperfect vision of the Real, a semi-revelation, even as the sun in the morning is a red ball. Thus all evils and wickedness are but weakness, the *imperfect Vision of Goodness*.

A straight line projected infinitely becomes a circle. The search for God comes back to the self. I am the whole mystery, God. I am a body, the lower self; and I am the Lord of the Universe.

Why should a man be moral and pure? Because this strengthens his will. Everything that strengthens the will, by revealing the real nature, is moral. Everything that does the reverse, is immoral. The standard varies from country to country, and from individual to individual. Man must recover from his state of slavery to laws, to words, and so on. We have no freedom of the will now, but we shall have, when we are free. Renunciation is this giving up of the world. Through the senses, anger comes, and sorrow comes. As long as it is not yet there, self and the passion are different. At last, they become identified, and the man is an animal at once. The instrument within is infinite. Become possessed with the feeling of renunciation.

I once had a body, was born, struggled, and died. What awful hallucinations! To think that one was cramped in a body, weeping for salvation!

But does renunciation demand that we all become ascetics? Who then is to help the others? Renunciation is not asceticism. Are all beggars Christs? Poverty is not a synonym for holiness; often the reverse. Renunciation is of the mind. How does it come? In a desert, when I was thirsty, I saw a lake. It was in the midst of a beautiful landscape. There were trees surrounding it, and their reflections could be seen in the water, upside down. But the whole thing proved to be a mirage. Then I knew that every day for a month I had seen this, and only today, being thirsty, had learnt it to be unreal. Every day for a month I should see it again. But I should never again take it to be real. So, when we reach God, the idea of the universe, the body and so on, will vanish. It will return, afterwards. But next time we shall know it to be unreal.

The history of the world is the history of Buddha and Jesus. The passionless and unattached do most for the world. Picture Jesus in the slums. He sees beyond the misery. 'You, my brethren, are all divine.' His work is calm. He removes causes. You are only able to work for the good of the world when you know for a fact that this work is all illusion. The more unconscious this work, the better, because the more superconscious. Our search is not for good or evil, but happiness and good are nearer to truth than their opposites. A man ran a thorn into his finger, and with another thorn took it out. The first thorn is Evil. The second thorn is Good. The Self is that Peace which passeth beyond both evil and good. The universe is melting down : man draws nearer to God. For one moment, he is real—God. He is re-differentiated—a prophet. Before him, now, the world trembles. A fool sleeps, and wakes a fool. A man, unconscious and superconscious, returns with infinite power, purity and love—the God-Man. This is the use of the superconscious state.

Wisdom can be practised even on a battlefield. The Gita was preached so. There are three states of mind : the active, the passive and the serene. The passive state is characterized by slow vibrations, the active, by quick vibrations, and the serene by the most intense vibrations of all. Know that the soul is sitting in the chariot. The body is the chariot; the outer senses are the horses; and the inner senses are the charioteer. So man crosses the ocean of *Māyā*. He goes beyond. He reaches God. When a man is under the control of his senses, he is of this world. When he has controlled the senses, he has renounced.

Even forgiveness, if weak and passive, is not true; fight is better. *Forgive* when you could bring legions of angels to the victory. Krishna, the charioteer of Arjuna, hears it said, "The general will forgive," and answers, "You speak the words of wise men, but you are not a wise man, but a coward." As a lotus leaf, living in the water yet untouched by it, so should the soul be, in the world. This is a battlefield, fight your way out. This world is a poor attempt to see God. Make your life a manifestation of will strengthened by renunciation.

We must learn to control all our brain centres consciously. The first step is happiness. Asceticism is fiendish. To laugh is better than to pray. Sing, Get rid of misery. Don't for heaven's sake infect others with it. Never think God sells a little happiness and a little unhappiness. Surround yourself with flowers, pictures and incense. The saints went to the mountaintops to enjoy nature.

The Second step is Purity.

The third is full training of the mind. Reason out what is true from what is untrue. Se that God alone is true. If for a moment you think you are not God, great terror will seize you. As soon as you think *I am He*, great peace and joy will come to you. Control the senses. If a man curses, see in him God, whom through my weakness I see as curser, as tiger, as chair. The poor to whom you do good, are extending a privilege to you. He allows you, through His mercy, to worship Him thus.

The history of the world is the history of a few men who had faith in themselves. That faith calls out the divinity within. You can do anything. You fail, only when you do not strive sufficiently to manifest infinite power. As soon as man, or a nation, loses faith in himself, death comes.

There is a divine within, that cannot be overcome, either by church dogmas or by blackguardism. A handful of Greeks speak, wherever there is civilisation. Some mistakes there must always be. Do not grieve. Have great insight. Do *not* think, 'What is done is done. Oh, that 'twere done better!' If man had not been God, humanity would by this time have become insane, with its litanies and its penitence.

None will be left, none destroyed. All will in the end he made perfect. Say, day and night. 'Come up, my brothers! You are the infinite Ocean of Purity! Be God! Manifest as God!'

What is civilisation? It is the feeling of the divine within. When you find time, repeat these ideas to yourself, and desire freedom. That is all. Deny everything that is not God. Assert everything that is God. Mentally assert this, day and night. So the veil grows thinner.

I am neither man nor angel. I have no sex nor limit. I am knowledge itself. I am He. I have neither anger nor hatred. I have neither pain nor pleasure. Death or birth I never had. For I am Knowledge Absolute, and Bliss Absolute. I am He, my soul, I am He!

Find yourself bodiless. You never had a body. It was all superstition. Give back the divine consciousness to all the poor, the downtrodden, the oppressed, and the sick.

Apparently, every five hundred years or so, a wave of this thought comes over the world. Little waves arise, in many directions; but one swallows up all the others, and sweeps over society. That wave does this, which has most character at its back.

Confucius, Moses, and Pythagoras; Buddha, Christ, Mahomet; Luther, Calvin, and the Sikhs; Theosophy, Spiritualism, and the like; all these mean only the preaching of the Divine-in-Man.

Never say man is weak. Wisdom-Yoga is no better than the others. Love is the ideal, and requires no object. Love is God. So even through devotion, we reach the subjective God. I am He! How can one work, unless one loves city, country, animals, the universe? Reason leads to the finding of unity in variety. Let the atheist and the agnostic work for the social good. So God comes.

But this you must guard. Do not disturb the faith of any. For you must know that religion is not in doctrines. Religion lies in being and becoming in realisation. All men are born idolaters. The lowest man is an animal. The highest man is perfect. And between these two, all have to think in sound and colour, in doctrine and ritual.

The test of having ceased to be an idolater is, When you say '*I*', does the body come into your thought, or not? If it does, then you are still a worshipper of idols. Religion is not intellectual jargon at all, but realisation. If you *think* about God, you are only a fool. The ignorant man, by prayer and devotion, can reach beyond the philosopher. To know God, no philosophy is necessary. Our duty is not to disturb the faith of others. Religion is experience. Above all and in all, be sincere. Identification brings misery, because it brings desire. Thus the poor man sees gold, and identifies himself with the need of gold. Be the witness. Learn never to react.

In answer to a question : The artist is the witness who testifies of the beautiful. Art is the most unselfish form of happiness in the world.

Appendix C, To Chapter XVI

Notes Of Lectures Delivered At The Vedanta Society, New York; Sunday Afternoons, June, 1900

The Unity

The different sectarian systems of India all radiate from one central idea of Unity or Dualism.

They are all under Vedanta, all interpreted by it. Their final essence is the teaching of Unity. This, which we see as many, is God. We perceive matter, the world, manifold sensation. Yet is there but one existence.

These various names mark only differences of degree in the expression of that One. The worm of today is the God of tomorrow. These distinctions which we so love are all parts of one infinite fact, and only differ in the degree of expression. That one infinite fact is the attainment of Freedom.

However mistaken we may be, as to the method, all our struggle is really for Freedom. We seek neither misery nor happiness, but Freedom.

This one aim is the secret of the insatiable thirst of man. Man's thirst, says the Hindu, man's thirst, says the Buddhist, is a burning, unquenchable thirst, for more and more. You Americans are always looking for more pleasure, more enjoyment. You cannot be satisfied. True, but at bottom what you seek is Freedom.

This vastness of his desire is really the sign of man's own infinitude. It is because he is infinite, that he can only be satisfied, when his desire is infinite, and its fulfilment infinite.

What then can satisfy man? Not gold. Not joy. Not beauty. One Infinite alone can satisfy him, and that infinite is Himself. When he realises this, then alone comes Freedom.

"This flute, with the sense organs as its key-holes,

With all its sensations, perceptions, and song,

Is singing only one thing. It longs to go back to the wood whence it was cut!"

"Deliver thou thyself by thyself!
Ah, do not let thyself sink!
For thou art thyself thy greatest friend.
And thou thyself thy greatest enemy."

Who can help the infinite? Even the hand that comes to you through the darkness will have to be your own.

Fear and desire are the two causes of all this, and who creates them? We ourselves. Our lives are but a passing from dream to dream. Man the infinite dreamer, dreaming finite dreams!

Oh, the blessedness of it, that nothing external can be eternal! They little know what they mean, whose hearts quake when they hear that nothing in this relative world can be eternal.

I am the infinite blue sky. Over me pass these clouds of various colours, remain a moment, and vanish. I am the same eternal blue. I am the witness, the same eternal witness, of all. I see, therefore nature exists. I do not see, therefore she does not. Not one of us could see or speak, if this infinite unity were broken for a moment.

What is Religion?

A locomotive, with all its powers, is only a machine, and a little worm is a living being. What is it that makes us differentiate, between the living and the dead?

All over the world is worship—of ghosts, of serpents, trees, gods. The whole world expects a miracle. We are all running after the curious, the extraordinary.

We dismiss this as ignorance, but the fact remains. I believe nothing to be vain or meaningless. The Jews were not singular : the whole world asks for a sign. Then there is this universal dissatisfaction. We work for an object, or an ideal, and before we reach it, our desire has changed. Man is a born rebel against nature, and nature's laws.

The first act of our life is one of rebellion against life. The earth, moon, and stars, tremendous as they are, are but machines. Life, from its first twinkling to its highest growth, is above all these. 'Freedom, Oh Freedom!' is the cry of life. 'Freedom, Oh Freedom!' is the song of the soul. All worship, all desire for miracles, is, at bottom, this thirst for Freedom. Science on her countless watch towers signals back to the asking soul, 'No, not yet! Nature has no freedom. She is all law,' This is why the idea of God is essential to the Mind. There must be the concept of some being or beings with Freedom.

Religion thus becomes only a question of the materialisation or personification of the idea. Even a plant could not be, without this notion of Freedom. Embodied Freedom, the Master of Nature, is what we call God.

Which of you would come or go or eat, if you did not believe yourself FREE to do or not to do? This may be a false notion, yet it shows the conception, and this is as much a fact as the bondage itself. Freedom must bring the mastery of nature. Omnipotence, Omniscience and Freedom must go hand in hand, and must be beyond nature. All its dust and mire leaves Him unstained. In us, every little thing produces change, Not so in Him! So SATCHIDANANDA alone describes Him.

'He is the Ruler of this universe. Him the sun cannot illumine, nor the moon, nor the stars. The flash of the lightning cannot irradiate Him. How then speak of this mortal fire?"

He depends upon Himself alone. All movement is His Worship. No action, no movement, no throb in the universe, but goes towards Him. Not only all that we call good, but evil also, is from the Lord. "I am the Real; I am the Unreal." He who gave us life, He is pouring out of His vial, the direct death. "He whose shadow is death, whose shadow is immortality!" We may bury our heads in the sand, like the ostrich. But there is no escape that way! Once, in Benares, I was pursued by troops of monkeys, and I turned to flee, when suddenly I heard the voice of an old *Sannyāsin* behind me call out, "Stop! Always face the brute!" So, face nature. Face ignorance, Face illusion. Never fly. You remember the story of the king who saw the vision of an enchanted palace, but he spat upon the ground, and all vanished!

Your own child comes to you masked. A moment of terror, and then—It is the Lord! The world has been even preaching the God of virtue.

I preach to you a God of virtue and of sin. No more looking up and down at each other! The less differentiation, the sooner God. This is the one sin, differentiation. This is the door to hell, differentiation. Only when this is broken, when it is pulverized to atoms, can we attain the goal. Can we, or can we not, see God in all equally?

"Thou art the man, Thou are the woman!
Thou art the youth, in the pride of his youth,
And thou the old man tottering on his crutches,
Thou the sinner, thou the saint!"

Two birds of golden plumage sat on the same tree. One above, and one below. The lower bird was pecking at the berries, some sweet, some bitter, at last, he ate one most biter, and looking up, saw his fellow, calm, majestic, immersed in his own glory. Then he drew nearer and nearer, till the rays of light from the plumage of the upper bird fell on himself; drew nearer, till he found that the upper bird was all. He, the lower, had been only a reflection seen amongst the branches.

The man who is groping his way through sin and misery, the man who had chosen for himself the path that runs through hell, will also reach. But we may choose for ourselves the path that runs through heaven, the path of unselfishness, of purity, of love and virtue. Let us come consciously, by seeing all beings as identified with ourselves. We want to move consciously.

Let us be rid, then, of all these limited ideas, and see Him, the Ever-Present Self, evident, nearer to us than our own selves! This has to be felt. This has to be realised.

May it please the Lord to grant us soon this knowledge of ourselves as one with the universe. This is the highest development of humility.

"Sharp as the blade of a razor, long, and distant, and the way so hard to find!

So the sages have declared.

Yet do not despond! Awake! Arise!

Struggle on! And stop not, till the goal is reached!"

"Giving up all these paths and struggles do thou take refuge in Me! I will take thee unto the other shore. Be not afraid! Be not afraid!" Say all the scriptures of the world.

Either say: 'I am thou, O Lord! Thus killing the lower I; or, 'I am nothing. Thou art all. Thy will be done on earth!' This last is a little easier. But we slip, and we stretch out the hand to the Mother! It has all been done. Well said an Indian philosopher, "Who says, 'Thy will be done!' twice, commits a sin." Manu says, salvation is for all, save only for a traitor. We all stand condemned as traitors, traitors against our own selves, against the majesty of Mother.

"For Thine is the Kingdom and the power and the glory! For ever and ever!"

Appendix D, To Chapter XVI

The Worship Of The Divine Mother Fragmentary Notes, Taken By Miss Waldo, On A Sunday Afternoon In June, 1900

From the tribal or clan God, man arrives, in every religion, at the sum, the God of gods.

Confucious alone has expressed the one eternal idea of Ethics. 'Manu Deva' was transformed into Ahriman. In India, the mythological expression was suppressed, but the idea remained. In an old Veda is found the *Mantram*, 'I am the Empress of all that lives, the Power in everything.'

Mother-worship is a distinct philosophy in itself. Power is the first of our ideas. It impinges upon man, at every step. Power felt within, is the soul; without, nature. And the battle between the two makes human life. All that we know or feel is but the resultant of these two forces. Man saw that the sun shines on the good and the evil alike. Here was a new idea of God, as the Universal Power behind all. The Mother-idea was born.

Activity, according to Sankhya, belongs to *Prakṛti*, to nature, not to *Puruśa*, or soul. Of all feminine types, in India, the mother is preeminent. The mother stands by her child through everything. Wife and children may desert a man, but his mother, never! Mother, again, is the *impartial* energy of the Universe, because of the colourless love, that asks not, desires not, cares not for the evil in her child, but loves him the more. And today Mother-Worship is the worship of all the highest classes, amongst the Hindus.

The goal can only be described as something not yet attained. Here, there is no goal. This world is all alike the play of Mother. But we forget this. Even misery can be enjoyed, when there is no selfishness, when we have become the witness of our own lives. The thinker of this philosophy has been struck by the idea that *one* power is behind all phenomena. In our thought of God, there is human limitation, personality : With *Śakti* comes the idea of One Universal Power. "I stretch the bow of Rudra, when He desires to kill," says *Śakti*. The Upanishads did not develop this thought; for Vedanda does not care for the God-idea. But in the Gita comes the significant saying to Arjuna, "I am the Real, and I am the Unreal. I bring good, and I bring evil."

Again the idea slept. Later came the new philosophy. This universe is a composite fact, of good and evil; and Power *must* be manifesting through both. "A lame one-legged universe makes only a lame one-legged God." And this, in the end, lands us in want of sympathy, and makes us brutal. The ethic built on such a concept is an ethic of brutality. The saint hates the sinner, and the sinner struggles against the saint. Yet even this leads onward. For finally, the wicked self-sufficient mind will die, crushed under repeated blows, and then we shall awake and know the Mother.

Eternal, unquestioning self-surrender to Mother alone can give us peace. Love Her for *Herself*, without fear or favour. Lover Her because you are Her child. See Her in all, good and bad alike. Then alone will come 'Sameness', the Bliss Eternal that is Mother Herself, when we realise Her thus. Until then, misery will pursue us. Only resting in Mother are we safe.